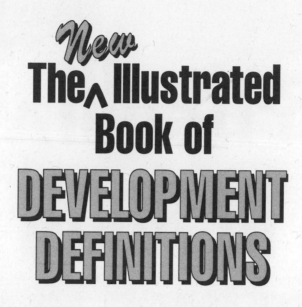

The *New* Illustrated Book of
DEVELOPMENT
DEFINITIONS

About the Authors

HARVEY S. MOSKOWITZ, P.P., A.I.C.P., is president of Moskowitz, Heyer & Gruel, PA, a planning consulting firm with offices in Florham Park, New Jersey. He is a licensed professional planner in New Jersey and is a former member and past president of the New Jersey Board of Professional Planners. Moskowitz has a Ph.D. in urban planning and policy development from Rutgers University and an M.P.A. from New York University. He was formerly on the Board of Directors of the American Planning Association.

CARL G. LINDBLOOM, P.P., A.I.C.P., is president of Carl G. Lindbloom Associates, a planning and urban design firm with offices in Princeton, New Jersey. He is a licensed professional planner in New Jersey and is a former member of the Princeton Township (New Jersey) planning board. Lindbloom has an undergraduate degree in architecture and a graduate degree in city design from Miami University, Oxford, Ohio.

The New Illustrated Book of

Book of

DEVELOPMENT DEFINITIONS

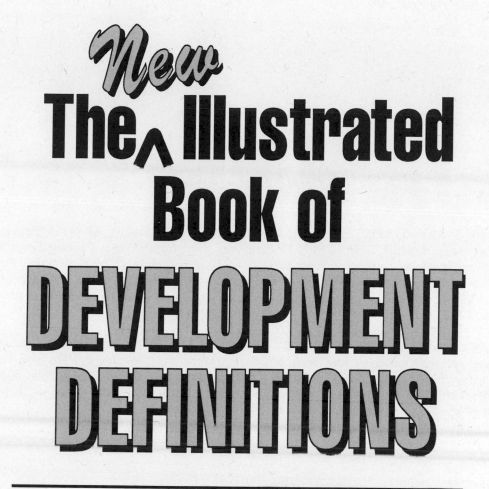

By **HARVEY S. MOSKOWITZ**
and
CARL G. LINDBLOOM

CENTER FOR URBAN POLICY RESEARCH

Third Printing 1997

Published by the Center for Urban Policy Research
New Brunswick, New Jersey   08901-1982

Printed in the United States of America

Library of Congress Cataloging-in-Publication Data

Moskowitz, Harvey S.
    The new illustrated book of development definitions / Harvey S.
Moskowitz and Carl G. Lindbloom.
        p.   cm.
    Includes bibliographical references (p.   ).
    ISBN 0-88285-144-6
    1. City planning—United States—Dictionaries.   2. Zoning—United
States—Dictionaries.   3. City planning and redevelopment law—
United States—Dictionaries.   4. Rural development—United States—
Dictionaries.   I. Lindbloom, Carl G.   II. Rutgers University.
Center for Urban Policy Research.   III. Title.
HT167.M683   1993   92-19394
307.1'216'0973—dc20   CIP

Contents

Illustrations

Preface

The New Illustrated Book of Development Definitions, like its predecessor, differs from other books and publications containing development definitions in three major respects: (1) it is illustrated; (2) most of the definitions are designed to be used directly in ordinances with little or no change; and (3) the more complex definitions are accompanied by commentaries and annotations that explain how the definition may be used in an ordinance, along with background information pertinent to the definition.

The primary purposes of including illustrations are to aid in interpreting the definitions and to suggest that they have a place in local ordinances as well. Unfortunately, illustrated definitions are rarely found in zoning and development ordinances. An occasional ordinance will show an angle-of-light or sky exposure plane diagram to establish the minimum dimension for interior courts or some similar complex and technical term, but by far, ordinances prefer the "thousand words" rather than the "single picture." Regardless of the reasons, the omission of illustrations, even if only to highlight a definition or standard, is strange because the first zoning ordinance (in New York City in 1916) was a series of three graphic overlays regulating height, use, and bulk. Even today, the heart of a zoning ordinance is the district or zone map. Subdivision and site plan regulations are primarily concerned with design or graphic representations of what eventually will be three-dimensional products. Illustrations can greatly simplify how standards should be applied, particularly where the lot or parcel is irregularly shaped or where there are a number of variables present, each of which might have an impact on how the ordinance might apply in a specific situation.

The original intent of the authors was to prepare a book of definitions that could be used directly, or with only slight modification, in any zoning, subdivision, or land development ordinance. This presented certain obvious problems, such as attempting to write a single definition that would be appropriate in various kinds of municipalities in different states. In execution, however, this objective was not as difficult to achieve as it first appeared. One of the principles that the authors used and believe should be followed in writing any definition is not to include standards in the definition. Indeed, the standard itself may vary within the municipality by zoning district. For example, the definition for HEIGHT can be constructed in such a manner that it can be applied universally while recognizing that the maximum or minimum standard will vary from municipality to municipality and even within municipalities; how the height should be measured—from what point to what point—though, is equally applicable in New York City and East Alton, Illinois.

The attempt at universality and direct application broke down when the authors discovered two or even more equally adequate definitions covering the same word or term. For instance, the definitions of RETAIL SERVICES, PERSONAL SERVICES, BUSINESS SERVICES, and SOCIAL SERVICES overlap to a great extent, but the reader may find one more appropriate than another for a particular municipality.

The use of commentaries and annotations suggests how the definition is designed to be used in development regulations and offers some discussion pertinent to the definition. While the commentaries are used primarily as a guide to the reader, the authors suggest that commentaries can be useful in local ordinances as well. Very often the background and legislative intent can be included, a device often used in state legislation but rarely, if ever, in local codes. A brief note could be inserted at the beginning of the ordinance that the commentaries are only descriptive and explanatory and are not part of the actual ordinance.

Throughout this book, the terms "zoning ordinance" and "land development ordinance" are used synonymously. Actually, a land development ordinance is much broader in scope and application, covering all aspects of development, including, in addition to zoning, subdivision and site plan regulations, stormwater management, environmental impact and similar controls, standards, and requirements. Many municipalities recognize that regardless of the type of ordinance, definitions, submission procedures, requirements for public hearings, data required for submissions, and improvements are the same. The trend is to combine the separate ordinances into a unified "land development ordinance."

HOW THIS VOLUME DIFFERS FROM ITS PREDECESSOR

The New Illustrated Book of Development Definitions differs from the original volume in a number of ways. For one thing, the number of definitions and commentaries has been significantly increased. The first edition had 1,480 definitions and 341 commentaries; this new book has 1,783 definitions and 592 commentaries. The number of illustrations has more than doubled, with 75 covering 186 definitions. In addition, many of the new illustrations provide ordinance drafters with guidance in how various standards may be applied.

Importantly, unique situations are portrayed in addition to the more conventional example. Planners know how to measure front, side, and rear yard setbacks on a regularly shaped lot, but how they are measured on a triangular or irregularly shaped lot often poses problems for many planners. The illustrations are designed to clarify such situations.

In the twelve years since the original book was published, there have been a number of excellent books, glossaries, pamphlets, and research publications defining the terms and words used in planning. The authors have researched these publications, have used and noted them where appropriate in the text, and have listed them in the reference section.

The authors also have eliminated the previous classification of definitions by type of ordinance, such as zoning, subdivision, site plan, or environmental ordinance. The national trend has been to include all of the definitions in a single section of a comprehensive land development ordinance. Even if a planning agency elects to prepare separate ordinances, the drafters can decide which definitions go where.

Finally, this expanded volume includes many words and phrases that probably will never be included in a local ordinance. They have been included here to provide local planners with a better understanding of planning and zoning terms in order to expand their knowledge and to assist them in drafting local ordinances that are comprehensive, unambiguous, direct, and focused.

A WORD OF CAUTION

The New Illustrated Book of Development Definitions expands significantly the references to legal decisions and statutes to analyze and explain how various definitions are applied, their limits, and their evolution. Neither of the authors is an attorney; consequently, while we have relied on opinions from attorneys and published legal sources, the reader is urged to consult with local counsel on specific questions of law and, in particular, on how their respective state enabling acts or court decisions affect the application of specific definitions in their jurisdiction.

Acknowledgments

Most zoning or land development ordinance definitions are "borrowed," "inherited," or "stolen" from other ordinances. Indeed, most ordinances are written in this way. If a planner is especially astute, early on he or she will start collecting definitions—adding, discarding, or modifying as the planner comes across new definitions or finds old ones not working. Many of the definitions in this book came about in this manner, but we do acknowledge other, particularly valuable contributions as follows:

1. The drafting committee of the New Jersey Municipal Land Use Law (Chapter 291, Laws of 1975), consisting of attorneys Harry Bernstein (now deceased), Fred Stickel III, Stewart Hutt, William Cox, Jim Jaeger, and planners Harry Maslow and Malcolm Kasler, who labored long and hard in developing the final version of the law. An important part of the statute was the excellent set of definitions that covered many aspects of development.

2. The *Standard Industrial Classification Manual* (1987), Executive Office of the President, Office of Management and Budget. This book contains the best single source of definitions on all types of economic activity. More planners should use this source to allow definitions of various types of use activities to become standardized.

3. Acknowledgment also is given to those anonymous technicians in New Jersey government who helped write many of the laws adopted by the state legislature. These laws provided definitions related to specific types of development. For example, the New Jersey Casino Control Act (Chapter 110, Laws of 1977) provided the definitions related to casino gambling and casino operation. Other New Jersey state sources included the proposed State Highway Access Code and the Fair Housing Act (Chapter 222, Laws of 1985), as well as the regulations of the New Jersey Council on Affordable Housing. Recent amendments to the New Jersey State Standard Barrier-Free Design Code (Chapter 220, Laws of 1975) provided excellent definitions designed to make public buildings accessible to the physically handicapped.

4. The authors acknowledge the use of several excellent publications of the Urban Land Institute for definitions relating to shopping centers, industrial parks, recreational development, and other planned developments; the New Jersey Federation of Planning Officials' (now New Jersey Planning Officials) bimonthly newsletter, *The New Jersey Planner;* the American Planning Association's (APA) *Land Use Law and Zoning Digest;* APA's Planning Advisory Service research reports on zoning and planning definitions; and APA's *Zoning News,* a monthly publication on current

planning and zoning matters. Specific citations are contained in the reference section and throughout the text in appropriate locations.

5. The definitions relating to solar energy were taken from the U.S. Department of Housing and Development's publication, *Protecting Solar Access for Residential Development, A Guidebook for Planning Officials.* That document and its companion piece, *Site Planning for Solar Access, A Guidebook for Residential Developers and Site Planners,* are recommended to all planners for practical suggestions for implementing energy conservation objectives.

6. In the predecessor volume, John Duryee, then a member of the Planning Board of the Township of Cranford, New Jersey, and chairman of the land development ordinance subcommittee, focused an unusually critical eye on many of the definitions and contributed extremely helpful suggestions to improve readability and application. In addition, the research for many of the definitions in the original volume was undertaken by Megan Seel, a professional planner (and now a practicing attorney in New Jersey) with a keen sense of organization, excellent research capabilities, and a practical knowledge of development ordinances.

7. For this volume, Mary Winder, P.P., formerly a planning consultant in New Jersey and now senior planner in the long-range planning division of the Sarasota County (Florida) Planning Department, provided comments and suggestions on all the definitions and particularly the ones related to specialized housing types. Ms. Winder recently completed a soon-to-be-published book on housing for the elderly for the New Jersey Department of Community Affairs.

8. Since the original volume was printed, the authors have continued in active planning practice, including testifying before zoning and planning boards and in the courts. In more cases than not, *The Illustrated Book of Development Definitions* (1981) is hauled out and the authors are forced to explain, clarify, or substantiate their position vis-à-vis the definitions in the book. To those many attorneys who have vigorously questioned and cross-examined us, we give our thanks at this time. Many of the changes in this new edition are the result of that process. Some of these attorneys included Jerry Baranoff, Fred Becker, Daniel Bernstein, Peter Buchsbaum, David Connolly, Clive Cummis, Michelle Donato, Richard Downes, Alfred Ferguson, Arthur Garvin, Robert Greenbaum, Henry Hill, Guliet Hirsch, Barry Hoffman, Marc Jonas, Glen Kienz, Ed McKirdy, Michael Pane, Frank Petrino, Harry Pozycki, Michael Sklaroff, Bennett Stern, Joe Stonaker, and William Sutphin. To those who we may have inadvertently omitted, our apologies. We will no doubt expect even more vigorous cross-examination in the future.

9. Many of the insights contained in the commentaries following numerous definitions came from William M. Cox's indispensable volume, *New Jersey Zoning and Land Use Administration* (1991). In addition, Cox was always available to give us his thoughts on some of the definitions and commentaries from his unique perspective.

We would be remiss for not acknowledging the contributions, directly or indirectly, of our professional colleagues, including Peter Abeles, Dean Boorman, Robert W. Burchell, Bob Catlin, Phil Caton, John Chadwick, B. Budd Chavooshian, Howard Clark, Richard Coppola, Peter Dorram, Allen Dresdner, Susan Gruel, Carl Hintz, Jim Hughes, Clifford Johnson, Mal Kasler, David Kinsey, Bob Kirkpatrick, Jerry Lenaz, Mel Levin, David Listokin, Jay Lynch,

Betsy McKenzie, John Madden, Robert O'Grady, Gene Oross, Kevin Page, Bill Queale, George Raymond, Jerry Rose, Peter Steck, Ed Taratko, and Dave Wallace.

A special thanks to George Sternlieb, who, as head of the Center for Urban Policy Research, encouraged us to submit the first volume for publication.

The authors turned over to Fred Heyer, P.P., A.I.C.P., a partner in Moskowitz, Heyer & Gruel, PA, what they thought was a final draft of the manuscript for this book. We got back a thoughtful, penetrating analysis, with hundreds of recommended changes pointing out errors, ambiguities, vagueness, and redundancies. The result, we believe, is a much more readable, current, and focused volume. We did not accept his suggestion, however, that we illustrate those sections on adult uses.

The authors particularly thank Linda Maschler, who typed up what must have felt like two hundred drafts of the original book in her usual competent and expeditious manner. Ms. Maschler and Alice Tomasulo collaborated on this volume. To all who assisted, whether directly or indirectly, we give our thanks. Naturally, the authors alone accept the responsibility for any mistakes that may appear in this book.

Introduction

How much lighter is light industry than heavy industry? Is there a difference between an advertising sign and a business sign? Are the terms flood plain, flood hazard area, and flood fringe area interchangeable?

The answers to these questions obviously depend on how we define our terms. Like it or not, all professional fields develop a language of their own. These "words of art" have meanings not anticipated by *Webster*. The purpose, therefore, of *The New Illustrated Book of Development Definitions* is to define some of the more common planning, development, and environmental terms.

PURPOSES OF DEFINITIONS

Webster defines "definition" as "a word or phrase expressing the essential nature of a person or thing or class of persons or of things, a statement of the meaning of a word or word group".[1] However, definitions do more, and when used in complex legal documents, such as zoning ordinances or other development regulations, they have a threefold purpose[2]:

1. *They simplify the text.* By defining our terms, it is possible to combine into a single word long phrases, lists of words, or similar terms that, from a zoning or control point of view, may be treated alike. For example, rather than repeat "application for site plan approval," "permission to build in a flood plain," "soil removal application," or "application for subdivision" in an ordinance regulating development, the phrase "application for development" can be defined to mean all of the preceding terms. Similarly, the term "manufacturing" is defined to mean:

> establishments engaged in the mechanical or chemical transformation of materials or substances into new products including the assembling of component parts, the creation of products, and the blending of materials such as lubricating oils, plastics, resins or liquors.

Think how long an ordinance would be if the definiens (the words used to describe the term to be defined) had to be repeated throughout the ordinance.

2. *Definitions precisely establish the meaning of a word or term that may be subject to differing interpretations.* The precise definition eliminates ambiguity and vagueness. It focuses

on the essential elements of a word or phrase and clearly marks off and limits its application or interpretation.

For example, a zone may permit light industrial uses. Everyone knows what light industry is—right? Industry is, well, work; or is it manufacturing and is warehousing included? *Webster* has five definitions of industry, and the authoritative *Standard Industrial Classification Manual* (1987) includes retailing, finance, and real estate under the broad definition of industry. So it is not quite that apparent, and even experts can impart different meanings to the word.

If we consider defining industry difficult, we must acknowledge the equally difficult problem of defining light in conjunction with industry. Does light refer to the end product, the raw material, or the machines used in the process? Or does it refer to something else completely?

By precisely defining light industry in an ordinance, we eliminate the vagueness and ambiguity that, at best, result in confusion and, at worst, end up in costly lawsuits and delays.

3. *Definitions translate technical terms into usable and understandable terminology.* Definitions enable us to convert sometimes abstract technical terms into meaningful standards to control and guide development.

For instance, going back to our favorite example, the term light as used in light industry may be defined in terms of a number of variables, such as trip generation, bulk controls, and nuisance characteristics.[3] Each of these terms requires further definition to make the original "light industry" term meaningful and enforceable.

Thus, one nuisance characteristic may be smoke emission, and the defined characteristic of light industry in terms of smoke emission is that the smoke density cannot exceed a certain level on the Ringelmann Chart, the standard for measuring smoke density. Another nuisance characteristic is noise, and light industry can be further defined in terms of the maximum noise level as measured at the lot line.

WHAT DEFINITIONS ARE NOT

Given that definitions simplify, clarify, and translate, it might be well to point out what definitions should not be. The most important limitation is that the definition should not contain the control elements or standards that regulate the defined word or phrase. For example, most ordinances attempt to define home occupations in terms of the standards under which the home occupation can be established. These standards usually include the percentage of floor area that can be occupied, limitations on nonresident employees, parking requirements, lot sizes, and sign controls.

These controls belong in the body of the ordinance and may vary depending on the zone in which the home occupation is permitted. To locate the standards in the definition precludes this flexibility.

Another case of misplaced standards is illustrated in our previously cited light industry example. The recommended definition of light industry reads as follows:

INDUSTRY, LIGHT   Industrial uses that meet the performance standards, bulk controls, and other requirements established in an ordinance.

The ordinance then spells out the performance standards and bulk controls to which light industry must conform. In fact, as illustrated below, the controls on medium and heavy industry also could be included and the definition of medium and heavy industry need not be substantially different from light industry.[4]

A typical control chart, which would be part of the zoning chapter, might read as follows:

Control Elements	Light Industry	Medium Industry	Heavy Industry
Minimum lot size	No minimum	5 acres	10 acres
Maximum lot size	5 acres	10 acres	No limit
Maximum FAR	0.5	1.0	2.0
Maximum building height	2 stories/30'	4 stories/60'	6 stories/80'
Maximum number of vehicle trips per peak hour	100	300	No limit
Maximum noise level	70 dBA	75 dBA	82 dBA
Maximum smoke density on Ringelmann Chart	#1	#1	#2
Vibration	None permitted beyond building wall	None permitted beyond lot line	None permitted beyond zone line
Air quality	50% of maximum allowed by state law	75% of maximum allowed by state law	As permitted by state law
Buffers	25' around property line	40' around property line	50' around property line

Note: The list of control elements noted above is not complete and standards suggested are for illustration purposes only. The chart does illustrate the point—the definition is only a few lines and simple; the standard in the ordinance may be long and detailed. We would also point out that some states do not permit a local ordinance to impose more stringent standards than permitted in the state law. This may be true of noise or air quality standards.

Definitions also should not run counter to the generally accepted meaning of words and phrases. As pointed out, "If it quacks like a duck, walks like a duck . . . it must be a duck." Very often this problem manifests itself in a negative manner. A zoning ordinance may establish a retail commercial zone and then exclude an obvious retail use because of local pressures, fear of competition, or perceived impacts. The point is that the generally accepted meaning of words and phrases should not be radically altered in an ordinance. Cox (1991, p. 65) quotes a

New Jersey case—*Essex County Retail, etc., v. Newark, etc. Bev. Control*, 77 N.J. Super. 70, 77 (App. Div. 1962)—in which the court said:

> Ordinances are to receive a reasonable construction and application, to serve the apparent legislative purpose. We will not depart from the plain meaning of language which is free of ambiguity, for an ordinance must be construed according to the ordinary meaning of its words and phrases. These are to be taken in the ordinary or popular sense, unless it plainly appears that they are used in a different sense.

By the same token, however, common words and phrases often take on a specific meaning in a technical field that may differ substantially from the generally accepted or public definition. Some examples are affordable housing, cellar, basement, or home occupation. The courts also may restrict or expand commonly accepted definitions. The best illustration is the word "family," which recent state court decisions have expanded to include an unlimited number of nonrelated individuals living as a single housekeeping unit.

REAL VERSUS NOMINAL DEFINITIONS

The American Planning Association's Planning Advisory Service Report No. 72, *Planning Definitions* (1955, p. 8), contains an excellent discussion on real versus nominal definitions. It defines a nominal definition as ". . . one adopted more or less arbitrarily but which need not be a true description of the object denoted." A real definition attempts to describe precisely the object, use, or term.

Real definitions are preferred but are very often difficult to achieve. For instance, the term density may be defined as the number of dwelling units per acre of land. For control or regulation purposes, it requires a further clarification to determine whether it is a net figure (excluding certain classes or types of land) or a gross figure (inclusive of the entire area within the described boundaries). Thus, the real definition of density requires two (or even more) nominal definitions to be utilized effectively in the ordinance.

To avoid the problem of whether a definition is real or nominal, most zoning or development ordinances usually preface the definition section with a phrase similar to the following:

> Unless the context clearly indicates a different meaning, for the purposes of this ordinance, the following words and terms shall be defined as follows.

SOME GENERAL OBSERVATIONS ABOUT DEFINITIONS IN DEVELOPMENT ORDINANCES

1. *Do not define it if it is not used in the ordinance*. There are two schools of thought on whether to include a word or phrase that is not subsequently included in the ordinance. For example, in a rural farming municipality, should the term high-rise apartment be defined? Conversely, in a built-up urban area, should the term farm be defined?

Many drafters believe that if there is a possibility that the phrase will be used in the future, it should be included. The authors are of another opinion. If it is not used, either as a permitted use or one specifically excluded, it should not be defined. The reason is that it may confuse the intent of the framers. If high-rise apartments are not permitted, then there is no reason to include it anywhere in the ordinance.[5] In addition, where there may be a question as to the intent of whether or not a particular use is allowed in a zone, the fact that it is defined gives credence to the position that the intent was to allow the use.

2. *Use federal, state, or county definitions if available.* More and more categories of land use are no longer under local control or require federal, state, or county licenses or approvals even when the municipality exercises locational control. In order to avoid conflicts, the local definition should agree with the "higher" definition, to the extent possible. It also more clearly defines the intent of the framers in allowing a specific type of use or activity in a zone. For instance, all states license schools. If the local intent is to permit elementary schools in residential neighborhoods, then the definition can be "any school licensed by the state and that meets the state requirements for elementary education." This eliminates private business schools or vocational schools.

County requirements and definitions relating to roads and streets are especially appropriate for inclusion in local development codes.

One word of caution, however; what may be appropriate on a federal or state level, and defined as such, may be inappropriate on a local level. This is particularly true of public utilities and essential services.

3. *Use nationally accepted definitions if available.* The best single source of use definitions is the *Standard Industrial Classification Manual* (1987).[6] The SIC groups all land use activities in a series of categories, from very broad activity classes (such as residential, manufacturing, trade, services, and so forth) to very specific and detailed land use categories. The most detailed category (defined as the four-digit category) contains thousands of specific land use activities. The three-digit category contains 414 classes, the two-digit category 83 activities, and the single-letter category 11 major activities.

Thus, major group 82, Educational Services, is part of Division I, SERVICES. The three-digit group includes 821, Elementary and Secondary Schools; 822, Colleges, Universities, Professional Schools, and Junior Colleges; 823, Libraries Centers; and so on. A further breakdown into specific types of activities takes place at the four-digit level. For purposes of defining land use activities, though, the three-digit level appears adequate. Examples of each type of activity are included as well as comprehensive definitions in the two- and four-digit levels. It is important to keep in mind that the SIC manual defines uses; zoning controls are needed to regulate scale, intensity, and impacts.

4. *Words should be defined within the context of the legislative intent of the zone district and by the other examples of uses permitted in the district.* While these limitations may seem obvious, applicants may attempt to use uncommon or rare permutations of words in order to establish the legality of other uses. For example, a residential zone permitting single-family detached houses, home occupations, and studios as principal permitted uses does not contemplate professional office buildings or motion picture studios if one considers the legislative intent of the zone (residential) or the context of home occupations and studios in terms of scale and uses normally permitted in a single-family residential district.

5. *Legal and technical input is necessary in preparing definitions for development ordinances*. Legal review is needed to ensure that the definition does not run afoul of state or federal laws or run counter to court decisions. Engineering, architectural, and environmental review is needed for those definitions encompassing those fields.

SUMMARY

To summarize and using in part the Planning Advisory Service's previously quoted report:

1. The term being defined (a) must be exactly equivalent to the definition; (b) should not appear in the definition; (c) cannot be defined by a synonym; and (d) should not be defined by other indefinite or ambiguous terms.
2. Definitions phrased in positive terms are preferable to definitions in negative terms.
3. Definitions should not include the standards, measurements, or other control regulations.
4. Anything not specifically included in a definition is automatically excluded.
5. A defined term can have none other but the defined meaning throughout the entire ordinance.
6. If a group of objects is being divided into two or more groups by definitions, be sure that all members of the group are included in one or the other of the groups.
7. Use particular care in the grammatical construction of definitions.
8. Do not define terms that are not used in the ordinance.
9. Check definitions in related local ordinances and make sure they do not conflict.
10. Use county, state, or federal definitions where appropriate.
11. Use standard definitions from national organizations or agencies when available.
12. Words can be further defined in context with other examples or in terms of the legislative intent of the zone where located.
13. Legal and technical review is needed to ensure the legality of terms and their technical correctness.

Notes

1. *Webster's Third New International Dictionary of the English Language* (Springfield, MA: G. and C. Merriam, 1976).

2. The reader is referred to Planning Advisory Service Report No. 72, *Planning Definitions* (1955), American Society of Planning Officials (now American Planning Association), for a more detailed discussion on the theory of zoning definitions. The material on the objectives of definitions is adopted from that excellent publication.

3. It is not defined in terms of the end product, raw material, or the size of machines used in the process. See the comment under INDUSTRY, LIGHT in the text definitions.

4. A municipality might want to allow outdoor storage in heavy industrial districts and amend the light industry definition accordingly.

5. The one exception may be in an ordinance that lists prohibited uses. Then the definition of the prohibited use becomes important. Prohibitive use ordinances generally are being replaced by permissive ordinances because, among other reasons, no ordinance could possibly list all the excluded uses.

6. *Standard Industrial Classification Manual*. Executive Office of the President, Office of Management and Budget (Springfield, VA: National Technical Information Service, 1987).

DEVELOPMENT DEFINITIONS

A

ABANDONMENT

The relinquishment of property, or a cessation of the use of the property, by the owner or lessee without any intention of transferring rights to the property to another owner or of resuming the use of the property.

Comment: In zoning, abandonment of a nonconforming use requires (1) a discontinuance of the use and (2) an intent to abandon (*Shack v. Trumble,* 28 N.J. 40, 1958; *Marino v. Mayor and Council of Norwood,* 77 N.J. Super. 587, L.D. 1963). Since intent is often difficult to prove, many zoning ordinances sidestep the issue by stating that a nonconforming use not exercised for a continuous period of time (one year, for example) cannot be resumed. Cox (1991) points out, however, that nonuse may not be enough and that absent any significant changes or changes to suggest an intent to abandon the nonconforming use, the nonconforming rights remain. Conversion of a nonconforming use to a conforming one, though, is always indicative of an intent to abandon the use.

ABATEMENT

The method of reducing the degree and intensity of pollution.

ABATTOIR

A place where livestock is killed and prepared for distribution to butcher shops and food markets.

Comment: An abattoir is a very intensive use, often requiring a rail siding. It is usually a twenty-four-hour operation, noisy and often odorous, with special solid and septic waste considerations. Some abattoirs have small retail operations selling directly to consumers.

ABSORPTION

(1) The penetration of one substance into or through another; (2) the length of time It takes for a product or real estate to be sold or rented.

Comment: Absorption in development terms is critical in determining whether a project is economically viable. Developers often speak of absorption rates of so many dwelling units (by type) per year or the square footage of floor area rented or leased over a fixed period of time.

ABSORPTION BED or FIELD

A large pit or system of trenches containing coarse aggregate and distribution pipe through which the septic tank effluent may seep into the surrounding soil (Toenjes 1989).

ABUT

To physically touch or border upon; or to share a common property line but not overlap. *See* ADJOINING LOT or LAND; CONTIGUOUS.

ABUTMENT

(1) A structure that supports the end of a bridge or arch; (2) the side of an earth bank that supports a dam (Toenjes 1989).

ACCELERATION LANE

An added roadway lane that permits integration and merging of slower moving vehicles into the main vehicular stream. Frequently used in connection with the exit from a major traffic generator. *See Figure 1.*

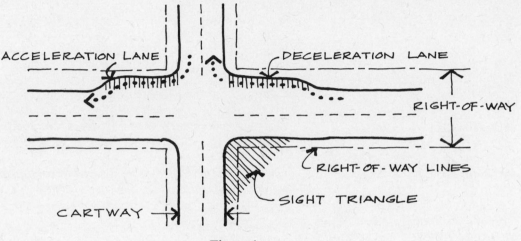

Figure 1

ACCESS

A way or means of approach to provide vehicular or pedestrian physical entrance to a property.

ACCESS CLASSIFICATION

A hierarchical rating system for streets and highways based on function, environment, and traffic characteristics, used to determine applicable access standards.

Comment: Part of a growing number of regulations governing access to state highways and, where applicable, to local and county roads.

ACCESS CODE

The highway access management code adopted pursuant to appropriate legislation. *See* ACCESS CLASSIFICATION;

4

ACCESS LEVEL; ACCESS MANAGEMENT PLAN; ACCESS PERMIT; ALTERNATE WORK ARRANGEMENT PROGRAMS; EMPLOYEE TRANSPORTATION COORDINATOR; MAJOR TRAFFIC GENERATOR; PEAK HOUR TRAFFIC; RATIONAL NEXUS; SIGNIFICANT INCREASE IN TRAFFIC; TRAFFIC GROWTH RATE; TRAFFIC IMPACT STUDY; TRANSPORTATION DEMAND MANAGEMENT PLAN; TRANSPORTATION MANAGEMENT ASSOCIATION.

Comment: Where permitted by states, municipalities and counties can adopt access codes providing for access management plans and standards of access to local and county roads.

ACCESS LEVEL

The allowable turning movements to and from access points on a highway segment based on the highway access classification.

ACCESS MANAGEMENT PLAN

A plan showing the design of access for every lot on a highway segment developed jointly by the state, the municipality in which the highway is located, and the county, if a county road intersects the segment.

Comment: In those states with highway access regulations, counties and municipalities are permitted to enact access management plans for various categories of roads under their jurisdiction.

ACCESS PERMIT

A permit issued by the appropriate governmental agency for the construction, maintenance, and use of a driveway or public street or highway connecting to a highway.

ACCESS POINT

The location of the intersection of a highway or street or driveway with the highway.

ACCESS POINT OFFSET

The distance between the centerlines of access points on opposite sides of undivided highways and the distance between the centerlines of an access point and a median opening on a divided highway.

ACCESS ROAD

See STREET, LOCAL.

ACCESSIBLE PRINCIPAL ARTERIAL

A roadway that is part of an interconnected network of continuous routes serving transportation corridors with high traffic volumes and long trips, the primary function of which is to provide safe and efficient service for major traffic movements in which access is subordinate.

ACCESSIBLE ROUTE

A continuous, unobstructed path connecting all accessible elements and spaces of a building or facility.

Comment: Accessible routes are required as part of the Americans with Disabilities Act of 1990.

ACCESSORY APARTMENT

A dwelling unit that has been added onto, or created within, a single-family house.

Comment: The accessory apartment has separate kitchen, bathing, and sleeping areas. Accessory apartments are often occupied by elderly persons, with the main structure occupied by close relatives or friends. This option provides economic, social, and security benefits since it allows older people to live independently but close to people who are concerned about their well-being.

Accessory apartments can be listed as a permitted use in residential areas. Regulations vary from municipality to municipality but usually are concerned with health and safety considerations, as well as maintaining the basic character of the neighborhood. These objectives can often be achieved by using designated minimum and maximum floor areas for the apartments, requiring off-street parking, and prohibiting any change in the basic single-family appearance of the structure.

ACCESSORY STRUCTURE

A structure detached from a principal building located on the same lot and customarily incidental and subordinate to the principal building or use. *See Figure 2.*

Comment: The accessory structure must be on the same lot as the principal structure unless the ordinance specifically permits it to be located on another lot. An example of this is a parking lot for a commercial establishment required to be located within a certain radius but not necessarily on the same lot as the establishment. In addition, it is desirable to place limits on the number and size of accessory structures, particularly in residential areas.

ACCESSORY USE

A use of land or of a building or portion thereof customarily incidental and subordinate to the principal use of the land or building and located on the same lot with the principal use.

Comment: A recent New Jersey case noted the following characteristics of an accessory use: commonly, habit-

6

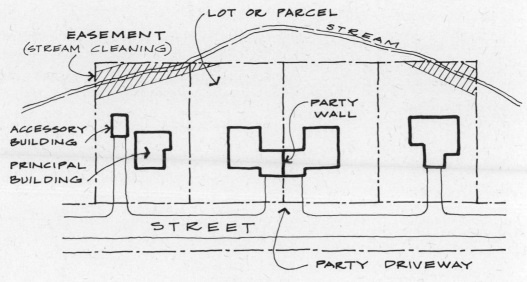

Figure 2

ually, and by long practice as being established or reasonably associated with the primary use (*Charley Brown of Chatham v. Board of Adjustment,* 202 N.J. Super. 312, App. Div. 1985). What constitutes an accessory use changes over time. For example, many ordinances now define a child-care facility as an accessory use to large-scale office or industrial buildings.

ACCLIMATIZATION

The physiological and behavioral adjustments of an organism over time to a marked change in the environment.

ACCRETION

The creation of land by the recession of a lake or stream or by the gradual deposit of solid material by water.

ACRE

A measure of land area containing 43,560 square feet.

Comment: Many ordinances use a "builder's acre" of 40,000 square feet.

ACRE-FOOT

The volume of water one-foot deep covering an acre of land.

Comment: This term is often used in defining storm or potable water storage capacity.

ACTIVATED CARBON

A highly absorbent form of carbon used to remove odors and toxic substances from gaseous emissions.

ACTIVATED SLUDGE PROCESS

The process of using biologically active sewage sludge to hasten the breakdown of organic matter in raw sewage during secondary waste treatment.

ACTIVE RECREATION

See RECREATION, ACTIVE.

ADAPTATION

A change in structure or habit of an organism that produces better adjustment to the environment.

ADAPTIVE REUSE

The development of a new use for an older building or for a building originally designed for a special or specific purpose.

Comment: Adaptive reuse is particularly useful as a technique for preserving older buildings of historic or architectural significance. It also applies to the conversion of other special use structures, such as gas stations, train stations, or school buildings, that are no longer needed for their original purpose.

ADDITION

(1) A structure added to the original structure at some time after the completion of the original; (2) an extension or increase in floor area or height of a building or structure.

Comment: ''At some time after'' is usually defined as after the certificate of occupancy has been issued for the original structure.

ADJACENT LAND

See ADJOINING LOT or LAND.

ADJOINING LOT or LAND

A lot or parcel of land that shares all or part of a common lot line with another lot or parcel of land. *See* ABUT; CONTIGUOUS.

ADMINISTRATIVE OFFICE

An establishment primarily engaged in overall management and general supervisory functions, such as executive, personnel, finance, legal, and sales activities, performed in a single location or building for other branches or divisions of the same company.

Comment: The term ''administrative office'' is obsolete given changes in the way business is conducted. Moreover, in terms of impact, there is very little difference between an administrative office or other types of business offices, with the possible exception of a corporate headquarters office. These usually have fewer employees

8

per square foot and more conference rooms than other types of offices, but here again, bottom-line considerations are eliminating these differences as well.

ADMINISTRATIVE OFFICER

The designated governmental official charged with administering land development regulations.

Comment: The administrative officer is often identified as a specific official, such as the municipal clerk, planning commission secretary, or zoning officer. Many land development ordinances will often add in the definition section, "For purposes of this ordinance, the administrative officer shall be the. . . ."

ADULT BOOKSTORE

See ADULT ENTERTAINMENT USE.

ADULT ENTERTAINMENT USE

An establishment consisting of, including, or having the characteristics of any or all of the following:

1. ADULT BOOKSTORE—An establishment having as a substantial or significant portion of its stock-in-trade books, magazines, publications, tapes, or films that are distinguished or characterized by their emphasis on matter depicting, describing, or relating to sexual activities or anatomical genital areas.
2. ADULT CABARET—(1) An establishment devoted to adult entertainment, either with or without a liquor license, presenting material distinguished or characterized by an emphasis on matter depicting, describing, or relating to sexual activities or anatomical genital areas; (2) a cabaret that features topless dancers, go-go dancers, strippers, male or female impersonators, or similar entertainers for observation by patrons.
3. ADULT MINI MOTION PICTURE THEATER—An enclosed building with a capacity for less than fifty persons used for presenting material distinguished or characterized by an emphasis on matter depicting, describing, or relating to sexual activities or anatomical genital areas.
4. ADULT MOTION PICTURE THEATER—An enclosed building with a capacity for fifty or more persons used for presenting material distinguished or characterized by an emphasis on matter depicting, describing, or relating to sexual activities or anatomical genital areas.

Comment: Regulations relating to sex businesses have generally been upheld by the courts because of the potential impact on property values and the quality of life of these uses. The regulations, however, cannot interfere with the constitutional protection against laws ". . . abridging the freedom of speech, or of the press" (First Amendment, U.S. Constitution).

Any regulations should be well documented in terms of the adverse impacts they are intended to prevent. Regulations can be enacted dispersing such uses and prohibiting them in residential neighborhoods or near schools or churches. The regulations should be based on planning studies showing the impact on property values, blighting influences, crime, and quality of life.

Supreme Court cases such as *Young v. American Mini Theatres,* 427 U.S. 50 (1976), and *City of Renton v. Playtime Theatres,* 748 F., 2d 527 (9th Cir. 1984), have upheld ". . . location restrictions on adult uses as a valid time, place and manner regulation . . . as long as the . . . ordinance leaves open reasonable alternative locations . . ." (Ziegler 1991 p. 17B–59).

ADULT RETIREMENT COMMUNITY

A planned development that emphasizes social and recreational activities but may also provide personal services, limited health facilities, and transportation. *See* RETIREMENT COMMUNITY.

Comment: Dwellings in adult retirement communities are generally for sale but occasionally rental units are available. Dwellings may be in the form of detached and attached houses, duplexes, or apartments. Activities may include a clubhouse, tennis, golf, swimming, and other recreation resources appropriate for older residents. Services, such as transportation and limited medical care, may also be provided. A manager is usually responsible for the general maintenance and upkeep of the community, and a monthly fee is generally charged for these services. Regulations usually require a certain minimum entrance age. The 1988 amendment to the Federal Fair Housing Act provides some guidance on age restrictions.

ADVANCED WASTE TREATMENT

Wastewater treatment beyond the secondary or biological stage that includes removal of nutrients, such as phosphates and nitrates, and a high percentage of suspended solids.

Comment: Advanced waste treatment, known as tertiary treatment, is the ''polishing stage'' of wastewater treatment and produces a high-quality effluent.

ADVERSE DRAINAGE CONDITION

The absence of drainage facilities, drainage easements, or drainage rights-of-way leading to, along, or through a street, road, drainage structure, or property, either within or exterior to a proposed development of such location, size, design, construction, or condition that would provide adequately for storm drainage, or that would prevent flooding, erosion, silting, or other damaging effect to a street, road, drainage structure, or property, or that would remove the threat of such damage.

ADVERSE IMPACT

A condition that creates, imposes, aggravates, or leads to inadequate, impractical, unsafe, or unhealthy conditions on a site proposed for development or on off-tract property or facilities.

Comment: Adverse impacts usually relate to circulation, drainage, erosion, potable water, sewage collection, and treatment. It may also relate to lighting and glare, aesthetics, quality of life, and impact on environment.

ADVERSE POSSESSION

The right of an occupant to acquire title to a property after having continuously and openly used and maintained a property over a statutory period of time without protest from the owner of record.

ADVERTISING DISPLAY

See SIGN.

AERATION

The process of being supplied or impregnated with air.

Comment Aeration is used in wastewater treatment to foster biological and chemical purification.

AERIAL MAP

A map created from a process involving the taking of photographs from the air with predetermined reference points marked on the ground.

AEROBIC

Life or processes that can occur only in the presence of oxygen.

AEROSOL

A suspension of liquid or solid particles in the air.

AESTHETIC

The perception of artistic elements or elements in the natural or created environment that are pleasing to the eye.

11

AESTHETIC ZONING

Regulations designed to preserve or improve building or site development so as to be more pleasing to the eye.

Comment: What constitutes "more pleasing" is difficult to define. However, planning has always had an aesthetic orientation. The origins of city planning were in the "City Beautiful" movement beginning with the World's Columbian Exposition held in Chicago in 1893. While early court decisions failed to sustain aesthetics as the sole basis for the exercise of the police power, the shift in recent cases suggests a more pragmatic approach. In *City of Lake Wales v. Lamar Advertising Association of Lakeland,* 414 So.2d 1030 (Fla. 1982), the court noted: "Zoning solely for aesthetic purposes is an ideal whose time has come; it is not outside the police power." A New Jersey case (*State v. Miller,* 83 N.J. 402, A.2d 821, 1980) upheld aesthetics as a legitimate goal of zoning and ". . . no longer a matter of luxury or indulgence." In fact, the New Jersey Municipal Land Use Law (N.J.S.A. 40:55D–1 et seq.) lists as one of the purposes of the act: "i. To promote a desirable visual environment through creative development techniques and good civic design and arrangements." Finally, the U.S. Supreme Court in *Berman v. Parker* (348 U.S. 26, 1954) recognized the right of the legislature to determine that beauty is a valid objective of police power authority.

Ordinances that purport to regulate aesthetics, however, often have problems with standards upon which to judge the "aesthetics" of an application, particularly with respect to building design. Unless an area is an official historic district, architectural design control remains difficult to achieve unless ". . . the architectural standard . . . can be objectively administered and judiciously reviewed for arbitrariness, and yet not so confining as to unlawfully inhibit expression through architectural design" (Frizell & Pozycki 1989, p. 117). Even in historic districts, specific standards are required in order to allow applicants to know in advance the standard of review.

The bulk of aesthetic regulations focus on sign control, fence regulations, landscaping and buffering requirements (including tree protection ordinances), and view protection.

AFFORDABLE

A sales price or rent within the means of a low- or moderate-income household as defined by state or federal legislation.

12

Comment: Affordable may vary by state. In New Jersey, for example, affordable housing for moderate-income households is 80 percent of the median family income for a particular area, adjusted for household size and with not more than 30 percent of the income used for rent (including utilities) or 28 percent for purchase (including principal and interest, condo fees, and insurance). The applicable figure for low-income households is 50 percent of median family income. In Florida, on the other hand, affordable housing is defined as capable of being acquired with 30 percent of gross income.

While affordable housing is most often thought of as subsidized housing, this is not necessarily so. Market housing, meeting low- and moderate-income targets, with affordability controls in place, may also qualify.

AFTERBURNER

An air pollution abatement device that removes undesirable organic gases through incineration.

AGRARIAN

Relating to land, particularly agriculture.

AGRICULTURAL MARKET

See Farm Stand.

AGRICULTURAL POLLUTION

The liquid, gaseous, and solid wastes from all types of farming, including runoff from pesticides, fertilizers, and feedlots, erosion and dust from plowing, animal manure and carcasses, and crop residue and debris.

AGRICULTURAL SERVICES

Establishments primarily engaged in supplying soil preparation services, crop services, landscaping, horticultural services, veterinary and other animal services, and farm labor and management services.

AGRICULTURE

The production, keeping, or maintenance, for sale, lease, or personal use, of plants and animals useful to man, including but not limited to: forages and sod crops; grains and seed crops; dairy animals and dairy products, poultry and poultry products; livestock, including beef cattle, sheep, swine, horses, ponies, mules, or goats or any mutations or hybrids thereof, including the breeding and grazing of any or all of such animals; bees and apiary products; fur animals; trees and forest products; fruits of all kinds, including grapes, nuts, and berries; vegetables; nursery, floral, ornamental, and greenhouse products; or lands devoted to a soil conservation or forestry management program. *See* Horticulture.

Comment: The definition is contained in the New Jersey Farmland Assessment Act (Chapter 48, Laws of 1964) and is broadly applied. It includes intensive agricultural activities, such as feedlot operations, chicken farms, and agribusiness activities, some of which may not be appropriate in all areas.

AIR PARK

A planned development that includes an airport, with its accessory and support services, as an integral part thereof.

AIR POLLUTION

The presence of contaminants in the air in concentrations beyond the normal dispensive ability of the air and that interfere directly or indirectly with health, safety, or comfort or with the full use and enjoyment of property.

AIR POLLUTION EPISODE

The occurrence of abnormally high concentrations of air pollutants usually due to low winds and temperature inversion that may be accompanied by increases in illness and death. *See* INVERSION.

AIR QUALITY CONTROL REGION

An area designated by the federal government where two or more communities, either in the same or different states, share a common air pollution problem.

AIR QUALITY CRITERIA

The levels of pollution and length of exposure at which adverse effects on health and welfare occur.

AIR QUALITY STANDARDS

The prescribed level of pollutants in the outside air that cannot be exceeded legally during a specified time in a specified geographical area.

AIR RIGHTS

The right to use space above ground level.

Comment: Many state enabling acts permit air rights to be shifted from one property to another. Air rights is actually a form of transfer of development rights. New York City's historic preservation program, for example, permits the purchase of air rights over historic structures that then can be used to increase the height and/or intensity of development on nonhistoric properties. *See* TRANSFER OF DEVELOPMENT RIGHTS.

AIR TRANSPORTATION

Establishments engaged in transportation by air, including airports and flying fields, as well as terminal services.

AIRPORT

A place where aircraft can land and take off, usually equipped with hangars, facilities for refueling and repair, and various accommodations for passengers.

Comment: The U.S. Department of Transportation, in its National Plan of Integrated Airport Systems (PL 97–248), defines five basic airport categories that reflect the type of public service provided. They are: (1) primary commercial service; (2) other commercial service; (3) reliever airport with commercial service; (4) reliever airport; and (5) general aviation airport. The five basic categories are further defined by role, which in turn affects the aircraft that can be accommodated and the roles and markets to be served. These roles are:

> BU: Basic Utility
> GU: General Utility
> BT: Basic Transport
> GT: General Transport
> TR: Transport Type
> L: Long Haul (more than 1,500 miles)
> M: Medium Haul (500 to 1,500 miles)
> S: Short Haul (less than 500 miles)
> HE: Heliport
> SP: Seaplane Base
> ST: STOLport (Short Takeoff and Landing)

BU airports accommodate most single-engine and many of the smaller twin-engine aircraft. GU airports accommodate virtually all general aviation aircraft, with maximum gross takeoff weights of 12,500 pounds or less. BT, GT, and TR airports are designed for business jets and transport-type aircraft.

From a zoning perspective, allowing airports in a zone calls for some consideration as to the type of airport, which in turn requires different types of accessory services or uses and has widely differing impacts on the municipality.

AISLE

The travelled way by which cars enter and depart parking spaces. *See Figure 59.*

ALLEY

A service roadway providing a secondary means of public access to abutting property and not intended for general traffic circulation.

15

ALLUVION

That increase of land area on a shore or bank of a stream or sea, by the force of the water, as by a current or by waves, that is so gradual that it is impossible to determine how much is added at each moment of time. *See* ACCRETION.

ALTERATION

Any change or rearrangement in the supporting members of an existing building, such as bearing walls, columns, beams, girders, or interior partitions, as well as any change in doors, windows, means of ingress or egress, or any enlargement to or diminution of a building or structure, whether horizontally or vertically, or the moving of a building or structure from one location to another.

Comment: The definition of alteration is important because most ordinances do not permit any expansion of a nonconforming structure or use. All expansions are alterations but not all alterations are expansions. This definition excludes normal repairs and maintenance, such as painting or roof replacement, but includes more substantial changes. *See* STRUCTURAL ALTERATION.

ALTERNATE LIVING ARRANGEMENT

A structure in which households maintain private rooms yet share kitchen and plumbing facilities, central heat, and common areas. *See* SINGLE-ROOM OCCUPANCY.

Comment: Alternate living arrangement includes boarding homes, residential health care facilities, group homes for the developmentally disabled and mentally ill, and congregate living arrangements.

ALTERNATE WORK ARRANGEMENT PROGRAMS

Programs that vary the traditional workday arrival and departure times for employees to avoid peak hour congestion. These programs may include flextime, a compressed workweek, staggered hours, and job sharing.

ALTERNATIVE ACCESS

The ability to enter a highway indirectly through another improved roadway instead of from a direct driveway entrance from the principal highway frontage.

AMBIANCE

The character or tone of an area, as determined by building scale and design, amount and type of activity, intensity of use, location and design of open space, and related factors that influence the perceived quality of the environment.

AMBIENT AIR

Any unconfined portion of the atmosphere; the outside air.

16

AMBIENT AIR STANDARD A maximum permissible air pollution standard.

AMBULATORY CARE *See* CLINIC
FACILITY

AMENITY A natural or created feature that enhances the aesthetic quality, visual appeal, or makes more attractive or satisfying a particular property, place, or area.

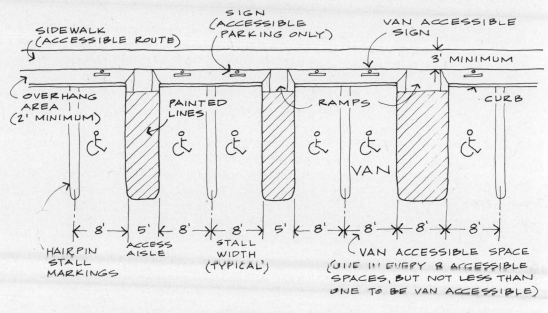

ACCESSIBLE PARKING SPACE STANDARDS

Figure 3

AMERICANS WITH DISABILITIES ACT (ADA) A 1990 federal law designed to bring disabled Americans into the economic mainstream by providing them equal access to jobs, transportation, public facilities, and services (*Zoning News,* February 1992). *See* ACCESSIBLE ROUTE; AREA OF RESCUE ASSISTANCE; CLEAR FLOOR SPACE; DISABILITY; MAJOR LIFE ACTIVITIES. *See Figure 3.*

Comment: The ADA will have a significant impact on planning and zoning activities, including public services, public accommodations, and commercial facilities. For example, every public meeting must be accessible. As the previously cited *Zoning News* states, a building or facility is accessible if it has no barriers to people with

17

disabilities. This may mean a central location with public transportation, signage, accessible rest rooms, materials and information a visually impaired person can use, and meetings in which people with hearing and speech impairments can participate and communicate. Posters announcing public hearings can be posted in senior citizen housing and meal sites, group homes, and other public centers to reach more people with disabilities.

The *Zoning News* article also made an important point about zoning ordinances. Most communities continue to produce their zoning ordinances only in written form, with limited availability to the public. Zoning administrators need to think carefully both about how zoning ordinances are published and about which citizens are excluded when the city is creating, modifying, and reviewing the ordinance. Under the ADA, other methods of communication must be adopted. Some cities have used computer data bases with a publicly accessible terminal to allow persons with disabilities to comment on proposed zoning ordinance modifications. Cities will have to apply creative alternatives so that people with disabilities can read and use important documents, such as the city's zoning ordinance.

Copies of this important law and descriptive material can be secured from the Office on the Americans with Disabilities Act, Civil Rights Division, Department of Justice, P.O. Box 66118, Washington, D.C. 20035–6118. For specific information about requirements for accessible design in new site planning, construction, and alterations, contact the U.S. Architectural and Transportation Barrier Compliance Board, 1111 Eighteenth Street NW, Suite 501, Washington, D.C. 20036. *Local Officials Guide: Complying with the Americans with Disabilities Act of 1990* is available from the National League of Cities, Education and Information Resources, 1301 Pennsylvania Avenue NW, Washington, D.C. 20004.

AMORTIZATION

A method of eliminating nonconforming uses by requiring the termination of the nonconforming use after a specified period of time.

Comment: The legality of requiring the amortization of nonconforming uses remains unclear. The most likely candidates for amortization are junkyards and signs that, in addition to not having a great deal of capital investment, are highly visible nuisances and may have significant adverse impacts on surrounding uses.

18

AMUSEMENT AND RECREATION SERVICES

Establishments engaged in providing entertainment for a fee and including such activities as dance halls; studios; theatrical productions; bands, orchestras, and other musical entertainment; bowling alleys and billiard and pool establishments; commercial facilities, such as arenas, rings, rinks, and racetracks; public golf courses; coin-operated devices; amusement parks; membership sports and health clubs; amusement and bathing beaches; swimming pools; riding academies; carnival operations; expositions; game parlors; and horse shows.

Comment: The above definition is a very broad one covering all types of amusement and recreational facilities. Many of the facilities listed are obviously not suited for all types of zones.

AMUSEMENT ARCADE

A primarily outdoor area or open structure, open to the public, that contains coin-operated games, rides, shows, and similar entertainment facilities and devices. *See* RECREATION FACILITY.

AMUSEMENT MACHINE

Any coin- or token-operated machine or device that, whether mechanical, electrical, or electronic, shall be ready for play by the insertion of a coin and may be operated by the public for use as a game, entertainment, or amusement, the object of which is to achieve either a high or low score, by comparison to the score of other players.

AMUSEMENT PARK

A facility, primarily outdoors, that may include structures and buildings, where there are various devices for entertainment, including rides, booths for the conduct of games or sale of items, buildings for shows and entertainment, and restaurants and souvenir sales.

ANCHOR STORE

See ANCHOR TENANT; MAGNET STORE.

ANCHOR TENANT

The major store or stores within a shopping center.

Comment: The anchor tenant usually is a major department store, often in excess of 100,000 square feet. It is the most important tenant in a shopping center and the one that generates the customer traffic. Superregional centers (750,000 square feet or more) may have three or more anchor stores.

ANEROBIC

Refers to life or processes that occur in the absence of oxygen.

19

ANIMAL HOSPITAL   *See* VETERINARY HOSPITAL.

ANIMAL KENNEL   Any structure or premises in which animals are boarded, groomed, bred, or trained for commercial gain. *See* KENNEL.

ANIMATED SIGN   *See* SIGN.

ANNEXATION   The incorporation of a land area into an existing community with a resulting change in the boundaries of that community.

Comment: Annexation may include newly incorporated land or land transferred from one municipality to another.

ANTENNA   A device used to transmit and/or receive radio or electromagnetic waves between terrestrially and/or orbitally based structures. *See* SATELLITE EARTH STATION ANTENNA.

ANTIDEGRADATION CLAUSE   A provision in air quality and water quality laws that prohibits deterioration of air or water quality in areas where the pollution levels are presently below those allowed.

APARTMENT, GARDEN   *See* DWELLING, GARDEN APARTMENT.

APARTMENT, HIGH-RISE   *See* DWELLING, HIGH-RISE.

APARTMENT, MID-RISE   *See* DWELLING, MID-RISE.

APARTMENT HOTEL   A facility offering transient lodging accommodation to the general public and where rooms or suites may include kitchen facilities and sitting rooms in addition to the bedroom.

Comment: The apartment hotel differs from the typical hotel in that transients are likely to rent rooms or suites for longer periods.

APARTMENT HOUSE   A structure containing three or more dwelling units. *See* DWELLING, MULTIFAMILY.

APARTMENT UNIT   One or more rooms with private bath and kitchen facilities comprising an independent, self-contained dwelling unit in a building containing three or more dwelling units.

20

APARTMENT UNIT, EFFICIENCY	*See* DWELLING UNIT, EFFICIENCY.
APPLICANT	A person submitting an application for development. *See* PERSON.
APPLICATION FOR DEVELOPMENT	The application form and all accompanying documents and exhibits required of an applicant by an approving authority for development review purposes.
APPRAISAL	An estimate or opinion of the value of real or personal property or an interest or estate in that property as determined by a qualified appraiser.
APPROVABLE SITE	(1) A site that meets all the bulk requirements of the ordinance and capable of accommodating permitted development; (2) a site that may be developed for low- and moderate-income housing in a manner consistent with the regulations of all agencies with jurisdiction over the site.
	Comment: With respect to low- and moderate-income housing, a site may be approvable although not currently zoned for low- and moderate-income housing.
APPROVED PLAN	A plan that has been granted final approval by the appropriate approving authority.
APPROVING AUTHORITY	The agency, board, group, or other legally designated individual or agency that has been charged with the review and approval of plans and applications.
APPURTENANCES	The visible, functional, or ornamental objects accessory to and part of buildings (Planning Advisory Service Report No. 379 1983).
AQUACULTURE PROJECT	(1) The commercial cultivation of aquatic life, such as fish, shellfish, and seaweed; (2) a controlled discharge of nutrients to enhance growth or propagation of harvestable freshwater, estuarine, or marine life plant or animal species (Schultz and Kasen 1984).
AQUARIUM	A building where collections of fish, live water plants, and marine animals are exhibited.
AQUATIC PLANTS	Plants that grow in water either floating on the surface,

growing up from the bottom of the body of water, or growing under the surface of the water.

AQUIFER

A geologic formation that contains a usable supply of water. *See Figure 4.*

AQUIFER RECHARGE AREA

The outcropping part of the aquifer through which water enters.

ARCADE

A continuous passageway parallel to and open to a street, open space, or building, usually covered by a canopy or permanent roofing, and accessible and open to the public. *See Figure 14.*

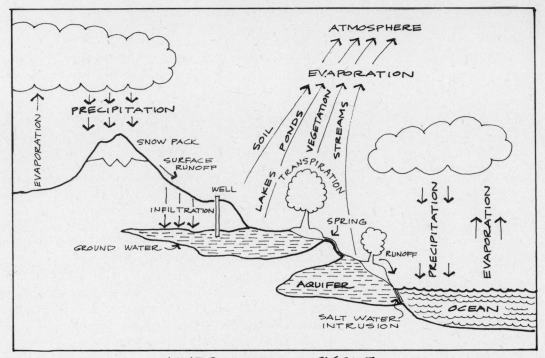

HYDROLOGIC CYCLE

Figure 4

ARCHAEOLOGICAL SITE

Land or water areas that show evidence of artifacts of human, plant, or animal activity, usually dating from periods of which only vestiges remain.

ARCHITECTURAL CONCEPT

The basic aesthetic idea of a building, or group of buildings or structures, including the site and landscape devel-

22

opment, that produces its distinctive character (Planning Advisory Service Report No. 379 1983).

ARCHITECTURAL CONTROL

Public regulation of the design of private buildings to preserve, enhance, or develop the character of a particular area.

Comment: Aesthetics is the reason architectural controls are imposed. In all ordinances calling for architectural controls, the standards upon which to judge a particular building must be precise and carefully drawn to avoid charges of vagueness and improper delegation of authority. *See* AESTHETIC ZONING.

ARCHITECTURAL FEATURE

A prominent or significant part or element of a building, structure, or site (Planning Advisory Service Report No. 379 1983).

ARCHITECTURAL STYLE

The characteristic form and detail of buildings of a particular historic period (Planning Advisory Service Report No. 379 1983). *See* HISTORIC BUILDING STYLES.

AREA OF RESCUE ASSISTANCE

An area, which has direct access to an exit, where people who are unable to use stairs may remain temporarily in safety to await further instructions or assistance during emergency evacuation.

Comment: Part of the Americans with Disabilities Act, 1990.

AREA PLAN

Part of a master plan that provides specific planning and design proposals for a defined geographic area.

Comment: Area, neighborhood, or district plans are urban design plans that are often prepared after the adoption of the local master plan. They provide the specific local planning detail, which may be adopted as amendments to the master plan.

AREA SCALE

A graphic display of the relationship between map areas and actual areas. *See* SCALE. *See Figure 5*.

AREA SOURCE

In air pollution, any small individual fuel combustion source, including any transportation source. *See* POINT SOURCE.

Comment: This is a general definition; area source is usually specifically set forth and precisely defined in appropriate federal statutes.

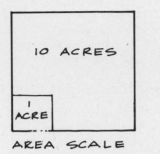

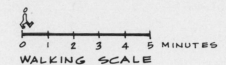

MAP SCALES

Figure 5

ARTERIAL STREET	*See* STREET, MAJOR ARTERIAL.
ARTESIAN AQUIFER	An aquifer in which water is confined under pressure between layers of impermeable (aquilude) material.
ARTIFICIAL RECHARGE	Adding water to an aquifer by artificial means, such as specially designed wells, ditches, or through other man-made methods.
ARTS CENTER	A structure or complex of structures for housing the visual and/or performing arts. *Comment:* Arts centers are often owned and/or operated by public or semipublic agencies. In any zone permitting arts centers, accessory needs, such as parking, must be considered and adverse impacts, such as noise, lighting, traffic, and hours of operation, must be carefully evaluated and mitigated.
A-SCALE SOUND LEVEL (dBA)	The measurement of sound approximating the auditory sensitivity of the human ear and used to measure the relative noisiness or annoyance of common sounds.

24

ASSEMBLAGE	The merger of separate properties into a single tract of land. *See* CONSOLIDATION.
ASSESSED VALUATION	The value at which property is appraised for tax purposes. *See* ASSESSMENT RATIO.
ASSESSMENT RATIO	The relation between the assessed value of a property and a true market value.

Comment: For a number of reasons, the assessed value of property may not reflect market value. In some states, communities are permitted to assess at a percentage of true market value. In addition, in jurisdictions that do not reassess or revalue frequently, the discrepancy between assessed valuation and true market value often increases over a period of time. In order to equalize all properties within a given taxing jurisdiction, some regional or state agency will assign an equalization ratio to a community's property. The planner must consider this equalization ratio in undertaking any cost-benefit analysis.

ASSIMILATION	The ability of a body of water to purify itself of organic pollution.
ASSISTED LIVING FACILITY	Residences for the frail elderly that provide rooms, meals, personal care, and supervision of self-administered medication. They may provide other services, such as recreational activities, financial services, and transportation. *See* RESIDENTIAL HEALTH CARE FACILITY; RETIREMENT COMMUNITY.

Comment: Assisted living facilities (or assisted care facilities) range in size from a few rooms to more than a hundred. The facilities are sometimes combined with other types of housing, such as congregate apartment housing for the elderly and residential health care facilities. In New Jersey, assisted living facilities are licensed by the state as board and care homes.

AT GRADE	*See* GRADE LEVEL.
ATMOSPHERE	The layer of air surrounding the earth. *See Figure 4.*
ATTACHED DWELLING UNIT	*See* DWELLING, ATTACHED.
ATTENTION-GETTING DEVICE	A device designed or intended to attract by noise; sudden, intermittent, or rhythmic movement; or physical

25

change or lighting change, such as banners, flags, streamers, balloons, propellers, whirligigs, searchlights, and flashing lights.

ATTIC

That part of a building that is immediately below and wholly or partly within the roof framing. *See* STORY, HALF. *See Figure 6.*

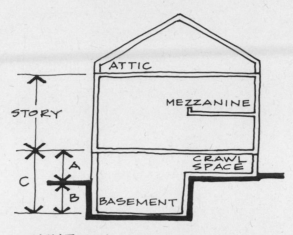

WHEN A IS LESS THAN B
- C IS A CELLAR

Figure 6

ATTRIBUTES

Physical, natural, constructed, or demographic characteristics that define and describe a building, site, or entity.

Comment: Examples of attributes include physical characteristics of a building or structure, length and width of a road, and demographic data of a municipality or census tract.

AUCTION HOUSE

A place where objects of art, furniture, and other goods are offered for sale to persons who bid on the object in competition with each other.

Comment: The above definition assumes the auction takes place within a building. Open-air auctions, such as vehicle auctions, are not included in the definition.

AUDIOMETER

An instrument for measuring hearing sensitivity.

26

AUTOMATIC CAR WASH

A structure containing facilities for washing automobiles and automatic or semiautomatic application of cleaner, brushes, rinse water, and heat for drying.

Comment: Many gas stations are incorporating on-site automatic car wash facilities. Zoning considerations include drainage and possible freezing of runoff, water use, drying areas, vehicle stacking capacity, and litter and debris.

AUTOMOBILE

A self-propelled, free-moving vehicle, with four wheels, usually used to transport not more than six passengers and licensed by the appropriate state agency as a passenger vehicle.

AUTOMOBILE REPAIR

See GARAGE, REPAIR.

AUTOMOBILE SALES

The use of any building, land area, or other premise for the display and sale of new or used automobiles generally but may include light trucks or vans, trailers, or recreation vehicles and including any vehicle preparation or repair work conducted as an accessory use.

AUTOMOBILE SERVICE STATION

Any building, land area, or other premises, or portion thereof, used for the retail dispensing or sales of vehicular fuels; servicing and repair of automobiles; and including as an accessory use the sale and installation of lubricants, tires, batteries, and similar vehicle accessories.

Comment: The name "automobile service station" is probably a misnomer as more and more stations convert to gas sales only and no longer undertake vehicle repairs. In addition, many gas-only stations are selling snack food, tobacco, drinks, newspapers, and similar convenience goods as accessory or appurtenant to the principal use. Some additional parking may be needed for shoppers other than those getting gas. At some point, the accessory use may become the principal use. Other zoning considerations include multiple use of the site, parking and circulation, signs, and landscaping.

AUTOMOBILE WASH

Any building or premises or portions thereof used for washing automobiles.

AUTOMOBILE WRECKING YARD

An establishment that cuts up, compresses, or otherwise disposes of motor vehicles. *See* JUNKYARD.

27

Comment: Wrecking yards may also store and sell salvaged auto parts, but if so, they function as junkyards.

AUTOMOTIVE REPAIR SERVICES AND GARAGES

Establishments primarily engaged in furnishing automotive repair, rental, leasing, and parking services to the general public.

Comment: This general category includes all of the major components of the automotive industry (except the dispensing of gas and oil directly into the vehicles), including parking lots and structures, all types of repairs, car washes, and rental and leasing activities.

AUXILIARY LANE

A part of the roadway striped for use but not for through traffic.

AVAILABLE SITE

A site with clear title, free of encumbrances that preclude development for low- and moderate-income housing.

AVERAGE ANNUAL DAILY TRAFFIC (AADT)

The total yearly traffic volume in both directions of travel divided by 365.

AVERAGE SETBACK

The mean setback from a street right-of-way of buildings on both sides of a lot.

Comment: In built-up neighborhoods, many ordinances establish the prevailing setback as the standard to which new houses must conform. Thus, if the houses on both sides of a vacant lot are twenty and thirty feet, respectively, the mean would be twenty-five feet. In some ordinances, all setbacks within a specific distance of the lot are averaged. The distance is often two hundred to three hundred feet. Some ordinances will specify both a minimum and maximum setback.

AVERAGE VEHICLE RIDERSHIP (AVR)

A numerical value calculated by dividing the number of employees scheduled to start work between 6:00 A.M. and 10:00 A.M. by the number of vehicles arriving to the work site between 6:00 A.M. and 10:00 A.M. *See* ACCESS CODE.

AVIATION EASEMENT

See EASEMENT, AVIATION.

AVULSION

A sudden and perceptible loss or addition to land by the action of water.

AWNING

Comment: Avulsion often occurs as the result of severe flooding or when a stream shifts course over a period of time.

A rooflike cover that is temporary or portable in nature and that projects from the wall of a building for the purpose of shielding a doorway or window from the elements and is periodically retracted into the face of the building. *See Figure 7.*

Comment: Awnings are temporary or portable devices. Once they become permanent, incapable of being retracted, then all setbacks should be measured from the end of the awning. Otherwise, most ordinances permit them to project into required yards.

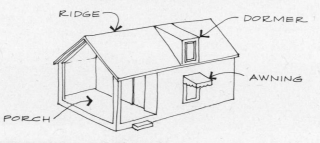

Figure 7

B

BACK-TO-BACK LOTS

Separate land parcels that have at least half of each rear lot line coterminous.

BACKFILL

Material used to refill a ditch or other excavation or the process of doing so.

BACKGROUND LEVEL

Amounts of pollutants present in the ambient air.

Comment: Background level is also referred to as the ambient level and is the base from which measurements are calculated or made.

BACKGROUND RADIATION

Normal radiation present in the lower atmosphere from cosmic rays and from earth sources.

BAFFLE

Any deflector device used to change the direction or the flow of water, sewage, products of combustion, such as fly ash or coarse particulate matter, or of sound waves.

BALING

A means of reducing the volume of solid waste by compaction.

BALLISTIC SEPARATOR

A machine that separates inorganic from organic matter in a composting process.

BAND WIDTH

The time in elapsed seconds between the passing of the first and last possible vehicle in a group of vehicles moving at the design speed of a progressive traffic signal system.

BAR

Premises used primarily for the sale or dispensing of liquor by the drink for on-site consumption and where food may be available for consumption on the premises as accessory to the principal use.

Comment: Zoning regulations should make the distinction between bars that have live entertainment or permit dancing and those that do not. Those with live entertainment and dancing may require considerably more parking and need additional setbacks because of noise. Many bars also possess licenses that permit them to sell bottled goods. This is usually accessory to the principal use of dispensing liquor by the drink for on-site consumption.

BAR SCREEN

In wastewater treatment, a device that removes large floating and suspended solids.

BARRIER

A device that prevents traffic from crossing into the path of traffic flowing in an opposite direction. *See* MEDIAN ISLAND.

BARRIER-FREE

An environment that will permit a disabled person to operate independently with comparative ease under normal circumstances and with little or no other assistance. *See* DEAF or HARD-OF-HEARING; FACILITY FOR HANDICAPPED PEOPLE; HANDICAPPED PERSON; MINIMAL ACCESSIBILITY; NONAMBULATORY HANDICAP; NONSLIP; PHYSICAL HANDICAP; PRINCIPAL ENTRANCE; PUBLIC ASSEMBLY AREA; RAMP.

BARRIER ISLAND

Land area, separated on all sides by water, usually elongated and formed by the action of the sea on land, that protects the mainland from sea action.

BASE FLOOD ELEVATION

The highest height, expressed in feet above sea level, of the level of floodwaters occurring in the regulatory base flood.

Comment: Flood elevations are calculated by engineering techniques, and observed experiences may be used to verify reliability. The base flood elevation represents the estimated height that waters will reach given a storm of certain magnitude; that is, one-year, two-year, one hundred-year, or five hundred-year. Regulations promulgated by various agencies, such as HUD (the U.S. Department of Housing and Urban Development), permit construction in certain flood-prone areas provided that the new construction is elevated or raised a given distance from the base flood elevation (usually one foot above the one hundred-year flood elevation) and that other flood damage prevention measures are taken.

BASE MAP

A map having sufficient points of reference, such as state, county, or municipal boundary lines, streets, easements, and other selected physical features, to allow the plotting of other data.

BASEMENT

A space having one-half or more of its floor-to-ceiling height above the average level of the adjoining ground and with a floor-to-ceiling height of not less than six and a half feet. *See Figure 6.*

Comment: The Building Officials and Code Administrators (BOCA) Basic/National Building Code defines basement as that portion of a building that is partly or completely below grade. If this definition is used, it eliminates the difference between basements and cellars. Ordinances should specify when the basement/cellar is counted as a story and when the floor space is used in computing the intensity of development.

Generally speaking, if a basement is used only for heating, mechanical and similar equipment, and parking, it is not counted in computing the intensity of development as measured by floor area ratio. The only exception is whether parking is also computed as part of the floor area ratio. If the basement is used for storage purposes for the principal use, for dwelling unit purposes, or for office space or a similar function, it is included in whatever standards are used to control the intensity of development.

Whether to count the basement as a story depends

31

on the vertical distance the basement ceiling is over the average adjoining grade. Some ordinances call it a story if that distance is greater than five feet.

BASIN

An area drained by the main stream and tributaries of a large river. *See* DETENTION BASIN; RETENTION BASIN.

BEACH

A nearly level stretch of pebbles and/or sand beside a body of water that may be artificially created or created by the action of the water. *See* INTERTIDAL AREA. *See Figure 8.*

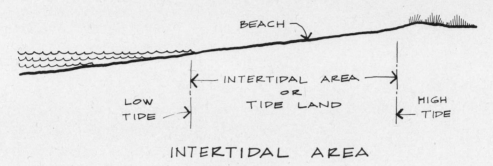

INTERTIDAL AREA

Figure 8

BED AND BREAKFAST

Overnight accommodations and a morning meal in a dwelling unit provided to transients for compensation. *See* BOARDING HOUSE.

Comment: Bed and breakfast (B&B) accommodations differ from rooming and boarding houses in that they are truly transient accommodations, with guests rarely staying more than a few days. In addition, the owner almost always lives in the facility. The impact of a B&B should not be much greater than that of a private home with frequent houseguests, with the exception of parking demand. Many B&Bs are not accessible by mass transit and, consequently, guests usually arrive by auto. Adequate parking must be provided. Other zoning regulations should address the number of rooms that can be rented out, limit breakfasts to guests only, and require the owner or renter of the house to live on the premises.

32

BEDROCK

In-place geologic formations that cannot be removed with conventional excavating equipment or that, upon excavation, include more than 60 percent formation fragments (by weight) that are retained in a one-quarter-inch mesh screen.

Comment: The above definition is from the New Jersey Department of Environmental Protection's Standards for the Construction of Individual Subsurface Sewage Disposal Systems.

BEDROOM

A private room planned and intended for sleeping, separated from other rooms by a door, and accessible to a bathroom without crossing another bedroom.

Comment: When is a den a bedroom? The distinction may be important when there are standards based on the number of bedrooms, such as parking, or requirements for a minimum or maximum number of various-sized dwelling units. A bedroom will have windows, closets, and is physically separate from other rooms.

BELTWAY

A highway, usually of limited access, around an area of high traffic congestion or urban development. *See Figure 70.*

BERM

A mound of earth or the act of pushing earth into a mound. *See Figure 9.*

Comment: Berms are usually two to six feet high and are used to shield, screen, and buffer undesirable views and to separate incompatible land uses. They also provide visual interest, decrease noise, control the direction of water flow, and act as dams. In traffic work, berm refers to the raised area between the curb line and right-of-way line.

BEST MANAGEMENT PRACTICE (BMP)

State-of-the-art technology as applied to a specific problem.

Comment: BMPs are often required as part of major land development projects. The BMP presents physical, institutional, or strategic approaches to environmental problems, particularly with respect to nonpoint source pollution control.

BIFURCATED DRIVEWAY

A roadway with two separate road openings, one for ingress to and one for egress from a street or highway.

33

BIKEWAY

A pathway, often paved and separated from streets and sidewalks, designed to be used by bikers. *See Figure 9.*

Comment: The bikeway has now become accepted as an important part of the circulation system. The U.S. Department of Transportation and various state highway departments have established specific standards for various classifications of bikeways.

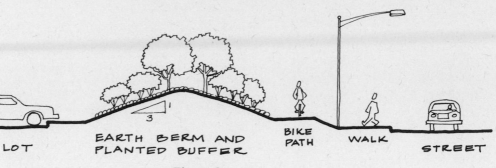

PARKING LOT · EARTH BERM AND PLANTED BUFFER · BIKE PATH · WALK · STREET

Figure 9

BILLBOARD

See SIGN, BILLBOARD.

BIOCHEMICAL BIOLOGICAL OXYGEN DEMAND (BOD)

A measure of the amount of oxygen consumed in the biological processes that break down organic matter in water.

Comment: Large amounts of organic waste use up large amounts of dissolved oxygen; thus, the greater the degree of pollution, the higher the BOD.

BIODEGRADABLE

Capable of being decomposed by the action of microorganisms.

BIOLOGICAL CONTROL

A method of controlling pests by means of introduced or naturally occurring predatory organisms, sterilization or the use of inhibiting hormones, or similar methods rather than by mechanical or chemical means.

BIOLOGICAL OXIDATION

The process by which bacterial and other microorganisms feed on complex organic materials and decompose them. Also known as biochemical oxidation.

Comment: Self-purification of waterways and activated sludge and trickling filter wastewater treatment processes depend on the principle of biological oxidation.

34

BIOMONITORING	The use of living organisms to test the suitability of effluent for discharge into receiving waters and to test the quality of such waters downstream from a discharge.
BIOSPHERE	That part of the earth and its atmosphere capable of supporting life.
BIOSTABILIZER	A machine used to convert solid waste into compost by grinding and aeration.
BIOTA	All the species of plants and animals occurring within a certain area.
BLENDING	The joining of two or more materials that combine chemically to form a new product differing chemically from either of the original materials.

Comment: The process of blending usually involves gases, liquids, or chemicals but may involve solids that are physically combined in a manner in which the individual components lose their original identities. Blending normally is classified as a manufacturing activity but is also typically part of small retail and service establishments, such as bakeries and restaurants.

BLIGHTED AREA	An area characterized by deteriorating and/or abandoned buildings; inadequate or missing public or community services; and vacant land with debris, litter, lack of sanitation facilities, trash and junk accumulation, and impacted by adverse environmental nuisances, such as noise, heavy traffic, and odors.

Comment: An alternate definition could refer to appropriate state enabling legislation. A blighted area has specific legal terminology in the application of federal and state funding. Under the Housing Act of 1949, as amended, and various state acts, an area that meets a blight definition can be acquired by public agencies by eminent domain and resold to private developers for the purpose of redevelopment and renewal. Blighted areas also may be eligible for certain favorable tax treatment and funding. An alternate and less derogatory term, "area in need of redevelopment," is used in some municipalities.

BLOCK	A unit of land bounded by streets or by a combination of streets and public land, railroad rights-of-way, water-

ways, or any other barrier to the continuity of development. *See Figure 10.*

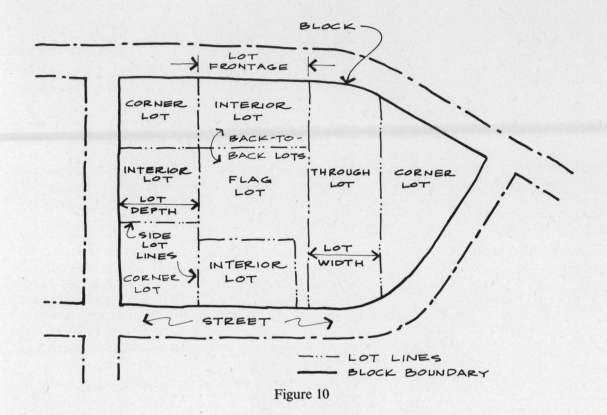

Figure 10

BLOCK STATISTICS

United States census information tabulated on a block basis.

BLOOM

A proliferation of living algae and/or other aquatic plants on the surface of lakes or ponds.

BOARD OF ADJUSTMENT

An officially constituted body whose principal duties are to hear appeals and, where appropriate, grant variances from the strict application of the zoning ordinance.

Comment: The name and work of the board of adjustment vary by state. In some states, boards of adjustment are called boards of standards and appeals or zoning hearing boards. In New Jersey, for example, appeals from decisions of the zoning officer are taken to the board of adjustment. The board of adjustment also inter-

36

prets the zoning ordinance and the zoning map, grants variances from the bulk and dimensional requirements of the ordinance, and, unlike many other states, can grant a variance for a use not specifically permitted in the zone.

BOARDER

An individual other than a member of the family occupying a dwelling unit who, for a consideration, is furnished sleeping accommodations, meals, and may be provided personal care, financial services, counseling, or other such services.

Comment: Many older zoning ordinances distinguished between roomers and boarders, the former being a person who did not receive meals. The distinction is not important from a zoning perspective. Older ordinances also made a distinction between temporary and permanent roomers or boarders, which is also not a particularly meaningful difference.

BOARDING HOME FOR SHELTERED CARE

A nonprofit or for-profit boarding home for the sheltered care of persons with special needs, which, in addition to providing food and shelter, may also provide some combination of personal care, social or counseling services, and transportation. *See* ASSISTED LIVING FACILITY; BOARDING HOUSE; COMMUNITY RESIDENCES FOR THE DEVELOPMENTALLY DISABLED; COMMUNITY SHELTERS FOR VICTIMS OF DOMESTIC VIOLENCE.

Comment: The sheltered care facility serves as a substitute for the residents' own homes, furnishing facilities and comforts normally found in a home but providing in addition such service, equipment, and safety features as are required for safe and adequate care of residents at all times. Such services may include: (1) supervision and assistance in dressing, bathing, and in the maintenance of good personal hygiene; (2) care in emergencies or during temporary illness; (3) supervision in the taking of medications; and (4) other services conducive to the residents' welfare. Boarding homes for sheltered care should be treated as boarding houses in zoning terms unless they qualify under state licensing requirements as houses for battered spouses and children or community residences for the developmentally disabled. In such cases, they are subject to the special provisions of the state law.

Many local zoning ordinances permit boarding homes for sheltered care in all residential zones if the

37

number of sheltered care residents is limited (usually a maximum of six). Homes with more than six residents may be conditional uses, and zoning regulations would include standards on maximum occupancy based on the square footage of the house (for example, 150 square feet of bedroom space per occupant), adequate parking, and, if in a residential zone, maintenance of the residential appearance of the facility. It also could include limits on the number of staff personnel.

Finally, many such facilities are licensed by states that impose additional restrictions and controls or restrict the manner in which municipalities can control such uses. *See* GROUP HOMES.

BOARDING HOUSE

A dwelling unit or part thereof in which, for compensation, lodging and meals are provided; personal and financial services may be offered as well. *See* PERSONAL SERVICES.

Comment: Over the years, the distinction between boarding and rooming houses has narrowed. Traditionally, rooming houses provided only rooms and boarding houses rooms and meals, but this distinction is no longer meaningful. The principal concern from a zoning impact is how many rooms should be permitted to be rented as a matter of right, above which the rooming or boarding house would be restricted to certain zones with controls or permitted only as a conditional use. Another concern is how to ensure that the rooming and boarding houses remain safe and sanitary.

Communities have addressed these problems by licensing boarding and rooming houses, requiring periodic inspections, limiting the number of guests, prohibiting cooking facilities in guest rooms, requiring adequate parking, both in terms of number and location, and establishing a minimum floor area for guest rooms. For boarding houses in residential zones, communities require the owner or operator to maintain their residence on site and personally collect rents to ensure that the structure remains principally a private dwelling unit.

Concerns over abuses of residents, especially the poor, aged, or special groups, have prompted some states to require state licenses for boarding houses. In New Jersey, accommodations for more than five boarders requires a state license, and a distinction is made between rooming houses, which provide only rooms or rooms and

38

meals, and boarding houses, which provide personal or financial services as well. However, the location and conditions of approval still remain local prerogatives.

Some boarding homes service special populations, and these homes may be referred to as assisted living facilities, boarding homes for sheltered care, community residences for the developmentally disabled, and community shelters for the victims of domestic violence.

BOARDING STABLE A structure designed for the feeding, housing, and exercising of horses not owned by the owner of the premises and for which the owner of the premises receives compensation.

BOARDWALK An elevated public pedestrian walkway constructed over a public street or along an oceanfront or beach.

BOATEL A combination of a motel and marina that is accessible to boats as well as automobiles and may include boat sales and servicing facilities, overnight accommodation for transients, and eating and drinking facilities.

BOG Wet, spongy land, usually poorly drained, highly acid and rich in plant residue.

BONUS ZONING *See* Incentive Zoning

BOROUGH One type of incorporated, self-governing municipality.

BRACKISH WATER A mixture of fresh and salt water.

BREEDING FARM An agricultural establishment where animals are impregnated either naturally or by artificial insemination and the principal purpose of which is to propagate the species.

BRIDGE A structure having a clear span of more than twenty feet designed to convey vehicles and/or pedestrians over a watercourse, railroad, public or private right-of-way, or any depression.

Comment: Structures having a clear span of less than twenty feet are usually designated as culverts.

BRITISH THERMAL UNIT (BTU) A unit of heat equal to 252 calories, which is the quantity of heat required to raise the temperature of one pound of water one degree Fahrenheit.

BROADCAST APPLICATION　　　The application of a chemical or seeds over an entire field, lawn, or other area.

BROOK　　　A small stream or creek.

BUFFER STRIP　　　Open spaces, landscaped areas, fences, walls, berms, or any combination thereof used to physically separate or screen one use or property from another so as to visually shield or block noise, lights, or other nuisances. *See Figure 59.*

Comment: The two basic criteria for buffers are the width of the buffer and the type of material to be planted or installed. In designing buffers, the ordinance should allow flexibility and provide for fences and berms to be used in conjunction with landscaping (*Zoning News,* February 1990).

BUFFER ZONE　　　*See* TRANSITION ZONE.

BUILDABLE AREA　　　The area of a lot remaining after the minimum yard and open space requirements of the zoning ordinance have been met. *See Figure 11.*

Comment: The buildable area should actually be buildable. If a lot is largely wetlands, very steep slopes, or easements, it may be difficult to locate a building or improvements on the land. The zoning regulations should specify that a minimum building area must be available to accommodate a building, driveway, and, where required, a well and septic system.

BUILDING　　　Any structure having a roof supported by columns or walls and intended for the shelter, housing, or enclosure of any individual, animal, process, equipment, goods, or materials of any kind.

BUILDING, ACCESSORY　　　A subordinate structure on the same lot as the principal or main building or use. *See* ACCESSORY STRUCTURE.

BUILDING, PRINCIPAL　　　A building in which is conducted the principal use of the lot on which it is located. *See Figure 2.*

BUILDING COVERAGE　　　The ratio of the horizontal area measured from the exterior surface of the exterior walls of the ground floor of all principal and accessory buildings on a lot to the total lot area. *See Figure 11.*

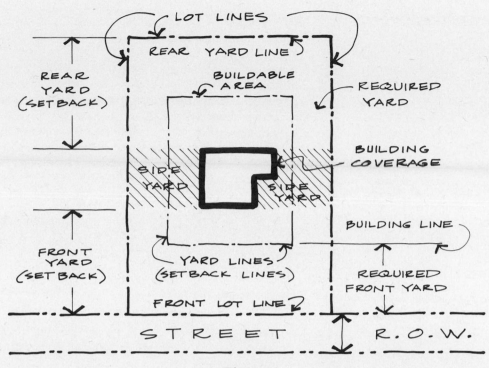

Figure 11

Comment: In single-family residential structures, porches and decks usually are excluded. For multifamily and nonresidential structures, more meaningful controls over the intensity and environmental impact of development are limits on impervious surfaces and floor area ratio, coupled with open space requirements.

BUILDING ENVELOPE

See ZONING ENVELOPE.

BUILDING HEIGHT

The vertical distance from finished grade to the top of the highest roof beams on a flat or shed roof, the deck level on a mansard roof, and the average distance between the eaves and the ridge level for gable, hip, and gambrel roofs. (BOCA National Building Code, slightly modified.) *See Figure 12.*

Comment: Mechanical equipment, chimneys, air conditioners, elevator penthouses, church spires and steeples, water towers, and similar appurtenances are usually exempted from height restrictions. However, the exclusion should apply only to those elements that are usually

41

appurtenant to a building. For example, antennas are often excluded from height restrictions. This might result in radio broadcasting antennas, often two hundred feet or higher, to be placed on the roof of a building in a zone with a maximum height of thirty-five feet. One way to preclude this is to specify that the excluded elements cannot exceed the maximum height by more than twenty-five feet. (To further complicate matters, local control of amateur radio antennas and satellite antennas is severely restricted by FCC [the U.S. Federal Communications Commission] regulations. Both types of antennas may be exempt from both height and location controls if necessary to function.)

Measuring height on sloping ground can be a problem; consequently, some limit on the number of stories is needed, at least in residential zones. Height measurements are usually taken from the front elevation of a building. Without a story limitation, a building on sloping land could result in the situation shown in *Figure 12A*. With a typical limit of thirty-five feet or two and a half stories, whichever is less, the result would be as shown in *Figure 12B*.

BUILDING INSPECTOR

The individual designated by the appointing authority to enforce the provisions of the building code. Also referred to as the construction official.

BUILDING LINE

A line parallel to the street line touching that part of a building closest to the street. *See* SETBACK LINE. *See Figure 11*.

Comment: The building line is important because many ordinances prohibit parking or other uses between the street and the building line.

BUILDING MASS

The height, width, and depth of a structure.

BUILDING PERMIT

Written permission issued by the proper municipal authority for the construction, repair, alteration, or addition to a structure.

BUILDING SCALE

The relationship of a particular building, in terms of building mass, to other nearby and adjacent buildings.

BUILT ENVIRONMENT

Artificially created fixed elements, such as buildings, structures, devices, and surfaces, that together create the physical character of an area. *See* URBAN AREA.

42

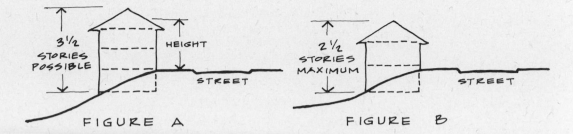

FIGURE A   FIGURE B

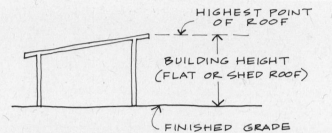

HIGHEST POINT
OF ROOF

BUILDING HEIGHT
(FLAT OR SHED ROOF)

FINISHED GRADE

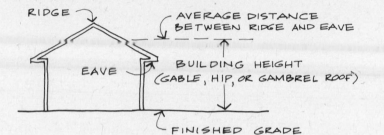

RIDGE

AVERAGE DISTANCE
BETWEEN RIDGE AND EAVE

EAVE

BUILDING HEIGHT
(GABLE, HIP, OR GAMBREL ROOF)

FINISHED GRADE

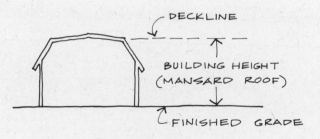

DECKLINE

BUILDING HEIGHT
(MANSARD ROOF)

FINISHED GRADE

BUILDING HEIGHT

Figure 12

43

BUILT-UP AREA

An area where less than 25 percent of the land is vacant.

Comment: While the figure of 25 percent is somewhat arbitrary, it is at this figure (75 percent developed) that an area gives the observer the impression of being totally developed.

BULK ENVELOPE

See ZONING ENVELOPE.

BULK PLANE

See SKY EXPOSURE PLANE.

BULK REGULATIONS

Standards and controls that establish the maximum size of buildings and structures on a lot and the buildable area within which the building can be located, including coverage, setbacks, height, floor area ratio, and yard requirements.

BULK STORAGE

The storage of chemicals, petroleum products, grains, and other materials in structures for subsequent resale to distributors or retail dealers or outlets.

Comment: Bulk storage is essentially a warehousing and wholesaling operation. The products are primarily sold for eventual resale and not directly to the consuming public.

BULKHEAD

A retaining wall created along a body of water behind which fill is placed. *See Figure 13.*

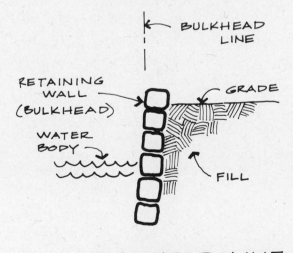

BULKHEAD LINE

Figure 13

44

BULKHEAD LINE

A line along a navigable water offshore from which no fill or structure is permitted. *See Figure 13.*

Comment: The bulkhead line defines the permanent shoreline of navigable waterways or lakes. The top is usually stated in feet above sea level. *See* PIERHEAD LINE.

BULLETIN BOARD SIGN

See SIGN, BULLETIN BOARD.

BUMPERS

Permanent devices in each parking stall that block the front wheels of a vehicle. *See Figure 59.*

Comment: Typical precast concrete stops can be a problem in that they crack easily, make it difficult to clear parking areas of snow, and are a hazard to pedestrians. They also trap debris and paper. A better arrangement is to widen the walkways or parking lot islands, install curbing, and permit the cars to overhang the curbing.

BUS POOL

A bus service, usually administered by an employer, with limited pickup and destination stops, guaranteed seats, and advance ticket purchase.

BUS SHELTER

A small, roofed structure, usually having three walls, located near a street and designed primarily for the protection and convenience of bus passengers. *See Figure 14.*

Comment: Shelters are often constructed of see-through materials for safety reasons. They are often designed to accommodate the disabled.

BUS TERMINAL or STATION

Any premises for the storage or parking of motor-driven buses and the loading and unloading of passengers.

Comment: Bus terminals may include ticket purchase facilities, restaurants, and stores.

BUS TURNOUT

A paved indentation at the side of a roadway designed to allow buses to pick up and discharge passengers. *See Figure 14.*

BUSINESS SERVICES

Establishments primarily engaged in rendering services to business establishments on a fee or contract basis, such as advertising and mailing; building maintenance; employment services; management and consulting services; protective services; equipment rental and leasing;

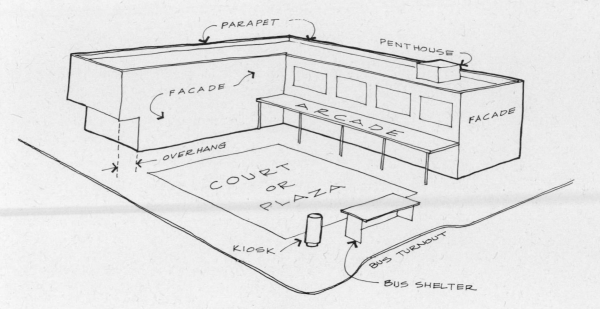

Figure 14

commercial research; development and testing; photo finishing; and personal supply services.

BUSINESS SIGN

See Sign, Business.

BUSWAY

A vehicular right-of-way or portion thereof that is reserved exclusively for the use of buses.

Comment: The exclusive reservation may be limited to peak traffic hours.

C

CALIPER

The diameter of a tree trunk. *See Figure 15*.

Comment: The measurement distance from ground level should be specified. The usual distance is six inches for trees up to four inches in diameter and twelve inches for larger diameter trees. The diameter standard, which may be used to require certain mature trees to remain on a site or require planting of minimum-age trees, will vary with the species. Certain trees, such as birches or dogwoods, are normally thinner; consequently, the standard would be different than for other species.

46

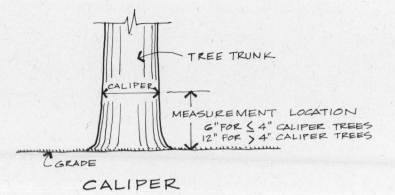

CALIPER

Figure 15

CAMPER

Any individual who occupies a campsite or otherwise assumes charge of, or is placed in charge of, a campsite.

CAMPGROUND

A plot of ground upon which two or more campsites are located, established, or maintained for occupancy by camping units as temporary living quarters for recreation, education, or vacation purposes.

Comment: Most states regulate campgrounds under a state campground code or sanitary code. Any state definition should be used in the local ordinance. The state code also may prescribe minimum standards, including the amount of space required for each campsite, provision of sanitary facilities, and so on. Local ordinance provisions usually are required to be as strict as the state's, but in some states, they may be stricter. Many state or local ordinances also prohibit occupancy for longer than a specified period of time, often ninety continuous days, in order to prevent these temporary accommodations from becoming permanent.

CAMPING UNIT

Any tent, trailer, cabin, lean-to, recreation vehicle, or similar structure established or maintained and operated in a campground as temporary living quarters for recreation, education, or vacation purposes.

CAMPING VEHICLE

See RECREATIONAL VEHICLE.

CAMPSITE

Any plot of ground within a campground intended for exclusive occupancy by a camping unit or units under the control of a camper.

47

CAMPUS

The grounds and buildings of a public or private college, university, school, or institution.

CANAL

An artificial waterway for transportation or irrigation.

CANDLEPOWER

Luminous intensity expressed in candelas.

Comment: Candlepower is a measure of illuminating power that has generally been replaced by the footcandle. For those technically inclined, the luminous intensity is the luminous flux per unit solid angle in a given direction. *See* FOOTCANDLE.

CANOPY

See AWNING.

CAPACITY, ROADWAY

The maximum hourly rate at which vehicles can reasonably be expected to traverse a point or uniform section of a lane or roadway during a given time period under the prevailing roadway, traffic, and control conditions. (*Highway Capacity Manual* 1985). *See* LEVEL OF SERVICE.

Comment: Roadway capacity is defined in terms of levels of service. Six levels of service are described, designated from A through F, with A representing the best operating conditions and level F the worst. Level C is usually designated as the minimal noncongested level. Briefly, the level of service A represents free flow; B stable flow; and C also stable but starting to be affected by other drivers. Level of service D starts to experience some congestion, with speed and freedom to maneuver restricted. Level of service E is a level in which the road is operating at or near capacity; speed is low; and comfort and convenience are poor. Level F is forced or breakdown flow, with severe congestion.

CAPITAL IMPROVEMENT

When pertaining to government, an acquisition of real property, major construction projects, or acquisition of expensive equipment expected to last a long time. *See* IMPROVEMENT.

Comment: Capital improvements are usually large, nonrecurring items. Generally, they are often financed by the sale of bonds. Many ordinances specify a minimum expenditure to qualify as a capital improvement.

CAPITAL IMPROVEMENTS PROGRAM

A timetable or schedule of all future capital improvements to be carried out during a specific period and listed in order of priority, together with cost estimates and the anticipated means and sources of financing each project.

Comment: The capital improvements program is usually a six-year program, with the first year being the capital improvements budget.

CAR WASH

See AUTOMATIC CAR WASH; AUTOMOBILE WASH.

CARBON DIOXIDE (CO₂)

A colorless, odorless, nonpoisonous gas that is a normal part of the ambient air and that is a product of fossil fuel combustion.

CARBON MONOXIDE (CO)

A colorless, odorless, highly toxic gas that is a normal by-product of incomplete fossil fuel combustion.

CAR POOL, CAR POOLING

Two or more people commuting on a regular basis to and from work by means of a privately owned vehicle, either using one car and sharing expenses or alternating vehicles so that no money changes hands.

Comment: Car pooling is similar to van pooling but differs in that under car pooling, the driver is usually the car owner. In van pooling, the vehicle is usually owned by the employer and the driver rides free in return for maintaining the van and serving as driver. From a zoning perspective, car pooling reduces the number of parking spaces needed for any use that employs the system. Zoning regulations might permit an applicant with a viable car pooling program to request relief from installing all of the required off-street parking. The site plan would show the required parking for which relief is requested, but it would not have to be installed unless a new occupant without a car pooling plan moved into the premises.

CARPORT

A roofed structure providing space for the parking of motor vehicles and enclosed on not more than three sides.

CARRYOUT RESTAURANT

An establishment that by design of the physical facilities, service, or packaging sells prepared ready-to-eat foods intended primarily to be consumed off the premises. *See* RESTAURANT, TAKE-OUT.

49

Comment: One problem with respect to carryout restaurants is whether consumption of food is permitted in motor vehicles on the premises, which, at the very least, would require additional parking. Other zoning considerations include drive-up facilities, circulation, queuing space for stacking, and parking requirements. Many primary carryout restaurants also have tables, further blurring the distinction. If space for parking is limited, then the number of tables should be restricted.

CARTWAY

The paved area of a street between the curbs, including travel lanes and parking areas but not including shoulders, curbs, sidewalks, or swales. *See Figure 1.*

Comment: If curbs are lacking and parking is restricted to the shoulders, the cartway is defined as the travelway.

CASINO

A room or rooms in which legal gaming is conducted.

CATALYTIC CONVERTER

An air pollution abatement device that removes organic contaminants by oxidizing them into carbon dioxide and water through chemical reaction and is used to reduce nitrogen oxide emissions from motor vehicles.

CATCH BASIN

An inlet designed to intercept and redirect surface waters.

CELLAR

A space with less than one-half of its floor-to-ceiling height above the average finished grade of the adjoining ground or with a floor-to-ceiling height of less than six and a half feet. *See Figure 6.*

Comment: Cellars should be used only for mechanical equipment accessory to the principal structure or for nonhabitable space. As such, they are not counted as a story or in the computation of the intensity of land use, such as floor area ratio. In residences, they can be used for recreation or storage areas.

CELLS

With respect to solid waste disposal, earthen compartments in which solid wastes are dumped, compacted, and covered over daily with layers of earth.

CEMETERY

Property used for the interring of the dead.

Comment: Most development ordinances do not include provisions for cemeteries. They are so unusual a use that they are generally handled by variance. When cemeteries are regulated in the development ordinance, height and setback standards should be established for crematories and mausoleums, where the bodies are interred above ground in stacked vaults. (In areas with high water tables, this is a fairly common type of burial.)

CENSUS

An official periodic enumeration of a designated geographic area's population, housing, and other characteristics.

CENSUS TRACT

Small areas into which large cities and adjacent areas have been divided for statistical purposes.

CENTRAL BUSINESS DISTRICT (CBD)

The largest, most intensively developed, mixed-use area within a city, usually containing, in addition to major retail uses, governmental offices; service uses; professional, cultural, recreational, and entertainment establishments and uses; residences, hotels, and motels; appropriate industrial activities; and transportation facilities.

Comment: There is no hard and fast rule as to what the CBD may include. In fact, all uses are appropriate providing they do not adversely infringe on other uses or diminish the traditional retail, office, cultural, and entertainment functions. Controls on industry in the CBD, for example, might restrict them from prime, first-floor locations, which should be used for retail activities. Even open space and passive recreational facilities have a place in the CBD.

CERTIFICATE OF APPROPRIATENESS

A certificate issued by the approving authority upon approval of the exterior architectural features of any new building construction or alterations to an existing building located within a historic zone district.

Comment: Certificates of appropriateness are typically required in historic or other special design districts prior to the issuance of a building or zoning permit. In some historic district ordinance procedures, the application review is carried out by a special design review committee of local experts and their nonbinding recommendations are forwarded to the planning board (the approving authority) for consideration and action.

In a historic district, the review is usually limited to architectural features that are visible from a public street;

51

for special design districts (a central business district, for example), the conformance of development proposals to an adopted area design plan may be the basis for review. *See* CERTIFICATE OF COMPLIANCE.

CERTIFICATE OF COMPLIANCE

A document issued by the proper authority that the plans for a proposed use meet all applicable codes and regulations.

CERTIFICATE OF NEED

A required document that must be obtained before certain facilities can be constructed or expanded.

Comment: Certificates of need are usually required before a health facility can be constructed and/or an existing one expanded. Certificates of need may also be required for subsidized housing facilities and may be a condition for certain other public uses. In many states, when a certificate of need is required, it provides the critical proof for the grant of a variance or approval of a conditional use.

CERTIFICATE OF OCCUPANCY (CO)

A document issued by a governmental authority allowing the occupancy or use of a building and certifying that the structure or use has been constructed and will be used in compliance with all the applicable municipal codes and ordinances.

Comment: One of the questions with respect to COs is whether a temporary CO is a viable regulatory device. In theory, if an applicant does not meet certain conditions of approval by certain dates, the CO is lifted. In practice, once issued, COs are difficult to revoke. A better arrangement is to require the posting of bonds to meet incomplete requirements.

CERTIFICATION

A written statement by the appropriate officer that required constructions, inspections, tests, or notices have been performed and comply with applicable requirements.

CESSION DEED

The conveyance to a local governmental body of private property street rights.

CESSPOOL

A covered pit with open jointed lining where untreated sewage is discharged, the liquid portion of which is disposed of by seepage or leeching into the surrounding porous soil, the solids or sludge being retained in the pit.

CFS

Cubic feet per second.

Comment: The measure of the amount of liquid or gas passing a given point.

CHAIN

A lineal measure equal to sixty-six feet.

Comment: This surveyor's measure is no longer in use. Many street right-of-way widths were laid out as thirty-three feet, or half a chain.

CHAIN STORE

Retail outlets with the same name, selling similar types of merchandise, operating under a common merchandising policy and usually owned or franchised by a single corporate entity.

CHANGE OF USE

Any use that substantially differs from the previous use of a building or land.

Comment: Change of use is important in that any such change usually requires site plan approval. New Jersey courts have indicated that change of occupancy or change of ownership shall not be construed as change of use. To be considered a change, a new use has to be substantially different from the previous use. Thus, a retail clothing store selling men's clothes would not be substantially different from a retail clothing store selling women's clothes. Whether a retail clothing store would be substantially different from a drugstore is debatable. One possibility is to define "substantially different" as a use that is outside the group number classification of the previous use as set forth in the *Standard Industrial Classification Manual* (1987). For example, under major group 59, Miscellaneous Retail, group 594 includes miscellaneous shopping goods stores. This three-digit group includes sporting goods establishments, bookstores, stationery stores, jewelry stores, hobby, toy, and games stores, camera and photography supplies, gift novelty, and souvenir shops. Any use within group 594 would be considered substantially the same as any other within that group. Any use in another three-digit group would be considered substantially different.

From a zoning perspective, change of use is only important if it affects any of the usual elements involved in site plan review—parking, drainage, circulation, landscaping, signage, building arrangements, and nuisance factors, such as traffic and noise. If they remain the

53

same, it is questionable as to why a new site plan is needed and a waiver of that requirement may be appropriate.

Cox (1991, p. 173) analyzes a New Jersey Supreme Court case—*Belleville v. Parrillo's, Inc.*, 83 N.J. 309 (1980)—that provides further insight as to when a change of use takes place. Cox writes:

> In that case a restaurant was changed to a "disco" and a proceeding was brought in the Municipal Court charging violation of the zoning ordinance. The defendant's conviction was reversed by the Appellate Division which held that there was not a change of use, but the Supreme Court disagreed. The Appellate Division had found that each aspect of the "new" business had been conducted previously, e.g., food had been served previously and continued to be; there had been music in the restaurant and continued to be; there was serving of alcoholic beverages previously and continued to be. The Supreme Court held that this quantitative analysis was improper and that the focus in cases of this type must be on the quality, character and intensity of the use viewed in their totality and with regard to the overall effect on the neighborhood and zoning plan. 83 N.J. at 314. As a restaurant it had been open every day, but now was only open one day and three evenings; the primary use of the dance hall had been incidental to dining but was now a primary use; the music was formerly provided by live bands and was now recorded; admission charges were now made whereas there had been none; the bulk of the prior business was food catering which now was discontinued. The Court concluded that there had indeed been a change of use and that the defendant was properly convicted. . . . The Supreme Court [also] noted that "an increase in the time period during which a conforming use is operated may justifiably be the basis for finding an unlawful extension thereof, just as changes in the functional uses of the land or increases in the area of use have been." *Belleville v. Parrillo's, Inc.* at 317–318.

CHANNEL

A watercourse with a definite bed and banks that confine and conduct the normal continuous or intermittent flow of water.

CHANNELIZATION

(1) The straightening and deepening of channels and/or the surfacing thereof to permit water to move rapidly and/or directly; (2) a traffic control device that forces vehicles into certain traffic flows or turning movements.

CHARITABLE USE

A use that provides essential goods or services, such as food, housing, clothing, counseling, aid, or assistance to those in need, for no fee or compensation or at a fee recognized as being significantly less than that charged by profit-making organizations.

CHATTEL

Personal property as contrasted with real estate.

CHEMICAL OXYGEN DEMAND (COD)

A measure of the amount of oxygen required to oxidize organic and oxidizable inorganic compounds in water.

Comment: The COD test, like the BOD (biological oxygen demand) test, is used to determine the degree of pollution in an effluent.

CHILD-CARE CENTER

An establishment providing for the care, supervision, and protection of children.

Comment: Child care emerged as one of the critical planning issues of the 1980s and will continue because of the number of women in the work force with children under the age of six years. The general definition is all-inclusive and requires further refinement for zoning use. Some of these refinements are suggested below:

Exempt Child-Care Center. Many states permit child care in private residences as permitted uses for a specified number of children, five or fewer, for example. This type of child care is the most widely used and, according to some experts, the preferred method. It is referred to as "family day-care" because it is provided in a private residence occupied by the provider of the day-care.

Family Day-Care Center/Home Occupation. New Jersey and other states use a different approach and require municipalities to treat family day-care centers as any home occupation is treated. If home occupations are allowed in residential zones, family day-care centers must also be permitted. No additional or more stringent restrictions are permitted (N.J.S.A. 40:55D–66.4). The problem in using general home occupation criteria for family day-care centers is that they often limit the amount of square footage that the home occupation can occupy. The home occupation requirements must be carefully reviewed to ensure that they are not onerous.

In New Jersey, family day-care centers are defined as: ". . . any private residence approved by the Division of Youth and Family Services or an organization with

55

which the division contracts for family day care in which child care services are regularly provided to no less than three and no more than five children for no less than 15 hours per week. A child being cared for under the following circumstances is not included in the total number of children receiving child care services: a. The child being cared for is legally related to the provider; or b. The child being cared for is part of a cooperative agreement between parents for the care of their children by one or more of the parents, where no payment of the care is being provided.''

Licensed Child-Care Center. A third category of child-care center is the licensed center that is regulated by a governmental agency (usually the state) and that by definition meets stringent licensing requirements. The requirement for state licensing is often triggered by the number of children in the center.

The planner has to decide in which zones licensed centers are appropriate. They could be permitted in residential zones, for instance, as conditional uses. In nonresidential districts, many states have followed New Jersey's lead, which makes child-care centers permitted uses in all nonresidential districts, eliminates all off-street parking requirements, and exempts the floor area from any density or floor area ratio limits (N.J.S.A. 40:55D–66.6).

Recent unpublished court cases have also recognized child-care centers in nonresidential zones as customary accessory uses.

CHIMNEY

A structure containing one or more flues for drawing off emissions from stationary sources of combustion.

CHLORINATED HYDROCARBONS

A class of generally long-lasting, broad-spectrum insecticides.

Comment: The best known of the chlorinated hydrocarbons is DDT, first used for insect control during World War II. The characteristics of persistence and effectiveness against a wide variety of insect pests were long regarded as highly desirable in agriculture, public health, and home uses. Later research has revealed that these same qualities may represent a potential hazard through accumulation in the food chain and persistence in the environment.

CHLORINATION	The application of chlorine to drinking water, sewage, or industrial waste for disinfection or oxidation of undesirable compounds.
CHLORINATOR	A device for adding a chlorine-containing gas or liquid to drinking or wastewater.
CHLOROSIS	Yellowing or whitening of normally green plant parts caused by disease organisms, lack of oxygen or nutrients in the soil, or by various air pollutants.
CHRISTMAS TREE FARM	A land area cultivated for the growing, harvesting, and marketing of evergreen trees.
CHURCH	A building or structure, or groups of buildings or structures, that by design and construction are primarily intended for conducting organized religious services and associated accessory uses.

Comment: The major problem associated with churches and other places of worship is that very often, the accessory uses may create greater impact than the primary use. Places of worship may include schools, meeting halls, recreational facilities, day-care, counseling, homeless shelters, and kitchens capable of feeding hundreds of persons. They often are rented out for weddings and other social events. In previous years, churches drew primarily from the neighborhood in which they were located. Today, the area they serve may be considerably larger. Care should be given in drafting any ordinance regulating places of worship to ensure that the accessory uses do not become nuisances. Adequate setbacks are required and parking should be provided for all the uses contemplated.

Some places of worship enjoy greater popularity during certain holidays. While it is not necessary to plan for peak use, there should be some consideration given to the several holidays or holy days within the year when occupancy will be two to three times that of normal worship services.

CIRCULATION	Systems, structures, and physical improvements for the movement of people, goods, water, air, sewage, or power by such means as streets, highways, railways, waterways, towers, airways, pipes, and conduits and the handling of people and goods by such means as terminals,

stations, warehouses, and other storage buildings or transshipment points.

CISTERN A tank or reservoir used for storing rainwater.

CITIZEN PARTICIPATION Public involvement in governmental policy formation and implementation.

CITY PLANNING The decision-making process in which goals and objectives are established, existing resources and conditions analyzed, strategies developed, and legislation and policies enacted and adopted to achieve the goals and objectives as they relate to cities and communities.

CIVIC CENTER A building or complex of buildings that house municipal offices and services and that may include cultural, recreational, athletic, convention, and entertainment facilities.

Comment: Broadly speaking, ownership and operation by a governmental agency is no longer a critical element in the definition of a civic center. Governmental participation and sanction of a private endeavor would still meet the definition.

CLARIFICATION In wastewater treatment, the removal of turbidity and suspended solids by settling, often aided by centrifugal action and chemically induced coagulation.

CLARIFIER In wastewater treatment, a settling tank that mechanically removes settled solids from water.

CLEAN AIR ACT A federal act establishing national air quality standards.

CLEAR-CUTTING The large-scale, indiscriminate removal of trees, shrubs, and undergrowth with the intention of preparing real property for nonagricultural development purposes (Planning Advisory Service Report No. 421 1989).

Comment: In a tree preservation ordinance, the removal of dead trees and selective cutting in accordance with a forest management plan (often required to be prepared by a certified forester) is usually permitted. The approving agency, in considering any development plan for a heavily wooded tract, should require submission of a tree retention plan. In addition to the removal of trees and vegetation, changes in grades and other significant cut-

58

ting and filling can have deleterious impacts on the remaining trees. Many agencies require trees to be retained to be marked and protected by placing snow-type fences around them at the drip line. This protects them, at least in theory, from bulldozer damage.

CLEAR FLOOR SPACE

The minimum unobstructed floor or ground space required to accommodate a single, stationary wheelchair and occupant.

CLINIC

An establishment where patients are admitted for examination and treatment on an outpatient basis by one or more physicians, dentists, other medical personnel, psychologists, or social workers and where patients are not usually lodged overnight.

Comment: The clinic, often associated with a hospital, is now more accurately described as an ambulatory health care facility in which outpatient treatment for patients is provided.

CLOVERLEAF

A grade-separated, multiple highway intersection that, by means of curving ramps from one level to another, permits traffic to move or turn in any of four directions without interference. *See Figure 70.*

Comment: Partial cloverleafs would permit traffic movements in fewer than four directions.

CLUB

A group of people organized for a common purpose to pursue common goals, interests, or activities and usually characterized by certain membership qualifications, payment of fees and dues, regular meetings, and a constitution and bylaws.

Comment: Older zoning ordinances usually permitted clubs in residential neighborhoods under the phrase "clubs, lodges, and social buildings." Such clubs were assumed to draw their membership from the neighborhood. Today, clubs have become much more regionally oriented; consequently, there is little reason to permit them in residential areas. A distinction also should be made between nonprofit clubs organized for religious, social, cultural, or educational purposes and those that usually are commercial in nature and primarily recreational, such as tennis and racquetball clubs. *See* FRATERNAL ORGANIZATION.

CLUBHOUSE   A building, or portion thereof, used by a club.

CLUSTER   A development design technique that concentrates build-
                             ings on a part of the site to allow the remaining land to
                             be used for recreation, common open space, and preser-
                             vation of environmentally sensitive features.

CLUSTER SUBDIVISION   A form of development that permits a reduction in lot
                             area and bulk requirements, provided there is no increase
                             in the number of lots permitted under a conventional
                             subdivision or increase in the overall density of develop-
                             ment, and the remaining land area is devoted to open
                             space, active recreation, preservation of environmentally
                             sensitive areas, or agriculture. *See Figure 16.*

                             Comment: The cluster subdivision is an excellent plan-
                             ning concept that has been used successfully in many
                             communities. Using this concept, the number of lots
                             (density) remains the same as in a conventional develop-
                             ment but open space is retained and maintenance costs
                             reduced by having shorter streets and utility lines. Devel-
                             opment costs are also reduced, which may result in less
                             costly housing. Many communities require the developer
                             to submit a conventional subdivision plat to establish the
                             number of developable lots possible and a cluster subdi-
                             vision plat to determine the appropriateness of cluster
                             design for the site. Cluster should not be used to subsi-
                             dize a developer who buys a piece of bad land and
                             expects the yield to be the same as if the land were
                             completely developable. *See* Critical Area.
                                 The cluster subdivision technique can be used in
                             conjunction with an areawide plan for a system of path-
                             ways and bikeways or the conservation of wildlife corri-
                             dors or riverside areas. This approach means that imple-
                             mentation of a circulation system, recreation program,
                             or the conservation of environmentally sensitive areas
                             can be achieved through the development process. Clus-
                             ter subdivisions can also be used to preserve lands in
                             agricultural use, thus serving as an alternative to the
                             purchase of development rights. *See* Conservation
                             Area.

COHABITATION   Households that contain two unrelated adults.

COLIFORM INDEX   An index of the purity of water based on a count of its
                             coliform bacteria.

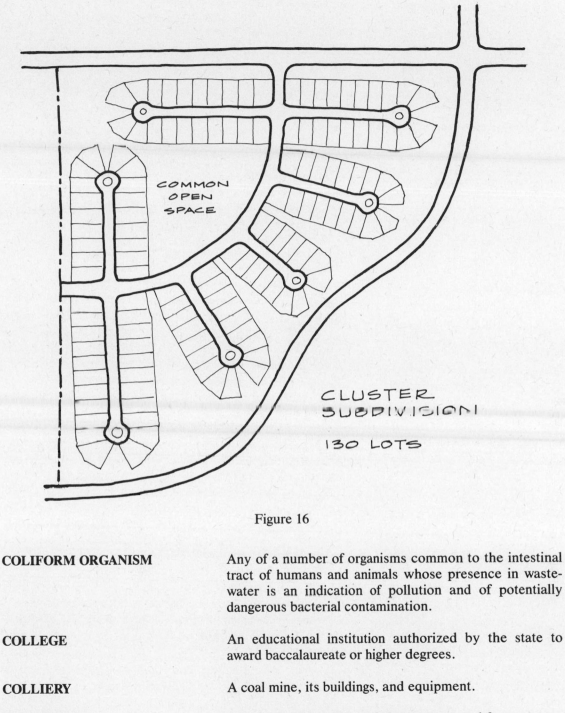

COMMON
OPEN
SPACE

CLUSTER
SUBDIVISION

130 LOTS

Figure 16

COLIFORM ORGANISM	Any of a number of organisms common to the intestinal tract of humans and animals whose presence in wastewater is an indication of pollution and of potentially dangerous bacterial contamination.
COLLEGE	An educational institution authorized by the state to award baccalaureate or higher degrees.
COLLIERY	A coal mine, its buildings, and equipment.
COLOSSEUM	A large enclosed and roofed structure used for spectator sports, exhibitions, and cultural events.

61

COMBINED SEWERS A sewerage system that carries both sanitary sewage and stormwater runoff.

COMBUSTION Burning.

Comment: Technically, combustion is a rapid oxidation accompanied by the release of energy in the form of heat and light.

COMMERCIAL CONDOMINIUM *See* CONDOMINIUM.

COMMERCIAL GARAGE *See* GARAGE, PUBLIC.

COMMERCIAL GREENHOUSE A structure in which plants, vegetables, flowers, and similar materials are grown for sale.

COMMERCIAL USE Activity involving the sale of goods or services carried out for profit.

COMMERCIAL VEHICLE Any motor vehicle licensed by the state as a commercial vehicle.

Comment: The parking or storage of commercial vehicles is usually restricted in residential zones. Current practice is to permit exceptions for certain kinds of commercial vehicles in these zones. For example, a passenger vehicle licensed as a commercial vehicle could be permitted, as could a van of up to a certain carrying capacity or gross vehicle weight limitation.

COMMINUTION Mechanical shredding or pulverizing of waste, converting it into a homogenous and more manageable material.

Comment: Used in solid waste management and in the primary stage of wastewater treatment.

COMMINUTOR A device that grinds solids to make them easier to treat.

COMMON ELEMENTS Land amenities, certain areas of buildings, such as lobbies, corridors, and hallways, central services and utilities, and any other elements and facilities owned and used by all condominium unit owners and designated in the master deed as common elements.

COMMON OPEN SPACE *See* OPEN SPACE, COMMON.

COMMON OWNERSHIP

Ownership by one or more individuals in any form of ownership of two or more contiguous lots.

COMMON PASSAGEWAY

A commonly shared or used pedestrian or vehicular way that connects or serves two or more properties. *See* PARTY DRIVEWAY.

COMMUNICATION USE

Establishments furnishing point-to-point communication services, whether by wire or radio, either aurally or visually, including radio and television broadcasting stations and the exchange or recording of messages.

Comment: Some care must be exercised in permitting all communication uses since the term covers a wide range of uses and impacts. For example, radio broadcast stations often include high, multitower antennas covering large areas. Point-to-point communication services using cable, on the other hand, may be indistinguishable from a typical office use.

COMMUNITY ASSOCIATION

A homeowners association organized to own, maintain, and operate common facilities and to enhance and protect their common interests.

COMMUNITY CENTER

A building used for recreational, social, educational, and cultural activities, open to the public or a designated part of the public, usually owned and operated by a public or nonprofit group or agency.

COMMUNITY CHARACTER

The image of a community or area as defined by such factors as its built environment, natural features and open space elements, type of housing, architectural style, infrastructure, and the type and quality of public facilities and services.

COMMUNITY FACILITY

A building or structure owned and operated by a governmental agency to provide a governmental service to the public.

COMMUNITY IMPACT STUDY

See IMPACT ANALYSIS.

COMMUNITY RESIDENCES FOR THE DEVELOPMENTALLY DISABLED (CRDD)

A residential facility, licensed by the state, providing food, shelter, and personal guidance, with supervision, to developmentally disabled or mentally ill persons who require assistance, temporarily or permanently, in order

63

to live in the community and shall include group homes, halfway houses, intermediate care facilities, supervised apartment living arrangements, and hostels (adopted from the New Jersey Municipal Land Use Law, Chapter 291, Laws of 1975).

Comment: Most regulations establish a maximum number of residents who can reside in a CRDD. In New Jersey, that number is fifteen and is tied to another regulation (N.J.S.A. 40:55D–66.1) that establishes such uses as permitted uses in all residential zones for up to six residents. Homes for more than six but less than fifteen residents, exclusive of staff, may be classified as conditional uses. The conditions can include a requirement that such uses be located not closer than 1,500 feet from a similar use and that an application can be denied if the community has fifty residents or 0.5 percent of the population, whichever is larger, already in such homes.

COMMUNITY RESIDENTIAL HOME

A dwelling unit licensed to serve clients of the appropriate governmental department that provides a living environment for unrelated residents who operate as the functional equivalent of a family, including such supervision and care by supportive staff as may be necessary to meet the physical, emotional, and social needs of an aged person, a physically disabled or handicapped person, a developmentally disabled person, a nondangerous mentally ill person, and a child as defined in the appropriate statute. *See* CONGREGATE RESIDENCES.

Comment: A community residential home is similar to congregate residences. In both cases, the residents served may be defined under a specific state statute. It would be important to cite the statute to provide a more specific definition of who the home is designed to serve.

COMMUNITY SHELTERS FOR VICTIMS OF DOMESTIC VIOLENCE

A residence providing food, shelter, medical care, legal assistance, personal guidance, and other services to persons who have been victims of domestic violence, including any children of such victims, who temporarily require shelter and assistance in order to protect their physical or psychological welfare (adopted from the New Jersey Municipal Land Use Law, Chapter 291, Laws of 1975).

Comment: The comments under COMMUNITY RESIDENCES FOR THE DEVELOPMENTALLY DISABLED also apply to COMMUNITY SHELTERS FOR VICTIMS OF DOMESTIC VIOLENCE.

COMPACT CAR

Any motor vehicle that does not exceed fifteen feet in length, bumper to bumper, and five feet, nine inches in width.

COMPACTION

Reducing the bulk of solid waste by rolling, tamping, and compression.

COMPLETE APPLICATION

An application form completed as specified by ordinance and the rules and regulations of the governmental agency and all accompanying documents required by ordinance for approval of the application.

Comment: Most states require that a determination of completeness be made within a specific period of time and upon the meeting of all requirements specified in the ordinance and in the rules and regulations of the governmental agency. On the day it is so certified by the administrative officer, the time period for action by the municipal agency begins. Problems occasionally occur when a required document upon initial review does not appear to substantially meet the ordinance requirements. For example, a landscaping plan showing only foundation plants surrounding a building on a ten-acre site may be rejected outright as incomplete. However, a better way to handle questionable submissions is to certify them as complete but, after detailed review, to reject the questionable or unacceptable element as not in conformance with the technical or design standards set forth in the ordinance.

COMPONENT FACTORS

The various parts of a road, including right-of-way, grading, surface and subsurface drainage provisions, curbs, gutters, catch basins, foundations, shoulders and slopes, wearing surfaces, bridges, culverts, retaining walls, intersections, private entrances, guide rails, trees, illumination, guideposts and signs, ornamentation, and monuments.

COMPOST

Relatively stable decomposed organic material.

COMPOSTING

A controlled process of degrading organic matter by microorganisms.

Comment: Composting may be achieved by several methods: (1) mechanical—a method in which the compost is continuously and mechanically mixed and aerated; (2) ventilated cell—compost is mixed and aerated

65

by being dropped through a vertical series of ventilated cells; and (3) windrow—an open-air method in which compostable material is placed in windrows, piles, or ventilated bins or pits and occasionally turned or mixed. The process may be anerobic or aerobic.

COMPREHENSIVE PLAN

See MASTER PLAN.

COMPRESSED WORKWEEK PROGRAM

A program that allocates the working hours into fewer than five days per week or fewer than ten days per two-week period, such as a four-day workweek or a nine-day, eighty-hour schedule.

CONCEPT PLAN

Informal review of a plan for development that carries no vesting rights or obligations on any party. *See* PLAT, SKETCH.

Comment: Many agencies use the concept plan to alert applicants to problems and requirements prior to an official submission. Use of the concept plan can save time and money for all parties.

CONDEMNATION

The exercise by a governmental agency of the right of eminent domain. *See* EMINENT DOMAIN.

CONDITIONAL USE

A use permitted in a particular zoning district upon showing that such use in a specified location will comply with all the conditions and standards for the location or operation of the use as specified in the zoning ordinance and authorized by the approving agency.

Comment: Conditional uses are permitted uses and are appropriate in the zoning district only when all conditions are met. For example, a house of worship may be desirable in a residential area but controls over parking, circulation, setbacks, and landscaping may be needed to prevent them from adversely affecting surrounding residences. By classifying them as conditional uses, separate regulations can be imposed to mitigate the adverse impacts. In some states, conditional uses are classified as special exception uses. In all cases, the conditions must be specific.

CONDITIONAL USE PERMIT

A permit issued by the approving agency stating that the conditional use meets all conditions set forth in local ordinances.

66

CONDOMINIUM

A building, or group of buildings, in which dwelling units, offices, or floor area are owned individually, and the structure, common areas, and facilities are owned by all the owners on a proportional, undivided basis.

Comment: By definition, a condominium has common areas and facilities and there is an association of owners organized for the purpose of maintaining, administering, and operating the common areas and facilities. It is a legal form of ownership of real estate and not a specific building style. The purchaser has title to his or her interior space in the building and an undivided interest in parts of the interior, the exterior, and other common elements. The property is identified in a master deed and recorded on a plat with the local jurisdiction. The common elements usually include the land underneath and surrounding the building, certain improvements on the land, and such items as plumbing, wiring, and major utility systems, the interior areas between walls, public interior spaces, exterior walls, parking areas, private roads, and recreational facilities.

Most states do not permit zoning ordinances to differentiate between various forms of ownership. Thus, an ordinance could not limit the principal use as a condominium or cooperative as opposed to rental housing or leased space.

CONDOMINIUM ASSOCIATION

The community association that administers and maintains the common property and common elements of a condominium.

Comment: Condominium associations differ from other forms of community associations in that the condominium association does not have title to the common property and facilities. These are owned by the condominium owner on a proportional, undivided basis.

CONDOMINIUM HOTEL

A building constructed, maintained, and operated and managed as a hotel in which each room is individually owned and in which some or all of the rooms are available to transients for rent and where the structure, common areas, and facilities are owned by all the owners on a proportional, individual basis.

CONFERENCE CENTER

A facility used for conferences and seminars, with accommodations for sleeping, food preparation and eating, recreation, entertainment, resource facilities, and meeting rooms.

67

Comment: The definition could also include a minimum and maximum number of rooms and a minimum floor area for seminar and conference facilities related to the number of rooms. An informal study of conference centers found approximately ninety square feet of meeting and seminar room space per sleeping room. A one hundred-room conference inn would have about nine thousand square feet of meeting rooms.

Communities also must decide whether or not to allow conference centers to rent rooms and facilities to transients. Very often a specific percentage of rooms must be reserved for conference participants and only a small percentage can be made available for transients.

CONGREGATE RESIDENCES

Apartments and dwellings with communal dining facilities and services, such as housekeeping, organized social and recreational activities, transportation services, and other support services appropriate for the residents. *See* COMMUNITY RESIDENTIAL HOME.

Comment: Congregate apartment residences are almost always rental and are often developed in conjunction with assisted living facilities. Long-term care is sometimes added as well, so that a range of accommodations and a continuum of care can be provided.

Congregate residences may also function as boarding homes for sheltered care, community residences for the developmentally disabled, and community shelters for the victims of domestic violence. For these groups, specialized on-site support services may also be provided. *See* ASSISTED LIVING FACILITY; BOARDING HOME FOR SHELTERED CARE; COMMUNITY RESIDENCES FOR THE DEVELOPMENTALLY DISABLED; COMMUNITY SHELTERS FOR VICTIMS OF DOMESTIC VIOLENCE; CONTINUING CARE RETIREMENT COMMUNITY; LONG-TERM CARE FACILITY.

CONSERVATION AREA

Environmentally sensitive areas with characteristics such as steep slopes, wetlands, flood plains, high water tables, forest areas, endangered species habitat, dunes, or areas of significant biological productivity or uniqueness that have been designated for protection from any activity that would significantly alter their ecological integrity, balance, or character (Planning Advisory Service Report No. 421 1989). *See* CLUSTER SUBDIVISION; CRITICAL AREA.

68

Comment: Local ordinances could specify more specific standards, such as the percentage of slope considered steep (often 20 percent) or how high a water table (less than three feet). Environmentally sensitive areas may also have been mapped as part of the open space and conservation element of a comprehensive plan.

CONSERVATION DISTRICT

See SOIL CONSERVATION DISTRICT.

CONSERVATION EASEMENT

See EASEMENT, CONSERVATION.

CONSIDERATION

An inducement to a contract.

CONSOLIDATION

The removal of lot lines between contiguous parcels.

Comment: Consolidation of several lots into a single lot or tract is usually considered an exempt subdivision. *See* ASSEMBLAGE; SUBDIVISION.

CONSTRUCTION OFFICIAL

See BUILDING INSPECTOR.

CONSTRUCTION PERMIT

Legal authorization for the erection, alteration, or extension of a structure.

CONTIGUOUS

Next to, abutting, or touching and having a boundary, or portion thereof, that is coterminous. *See* ABUT; ADJOINING LOT OR LAND.

CONTINUING CARE RETIREMENT COMMUNITY (CCRC)

An age-restricted development that provides a continuum of accommodations and care, from independent living to long-term bed care, and enters into contracts to provide lifelong care in exchange for the payment of monthly fees and an entrance fee in excess of one year of monthly fees.

Comment: What distinguishes a CCRC from other types of mixed residential development is (1) a contract for lifelong care; (2) monthly maintenance fees; and (3) a substantial entrance fee always greater than one year of monthly fees. Because of the substantial amounts of money required to enter a CCRC and the long-term commitment, many states have established stringent controls over CCRCs, including licensing, certificates of need, and full financial disclosure.

A CCRC typically includes independent living units, congregate residences, assisted care units, and a long-term bed care section. All units are age restricted. The independent living units may be single-family detached or attached housing or apartments.

CCRCs include health care services and meals, with common dining facilities, physical therapy facilities and activities, meeting rooms, social activities, recreation facilities, on-site services and shops, and other ancillary services customarily accessory to the principal permitted use.

From a zoning perspective, CCRCs should be designated as conditional uses. Public water and sewer are necessary and the appropriate location is in a residential area or at the edge of a residential area. Densities should be consistent with the maximum density permitted in the municipality; however, since the traffic generation is significantly lower than nonage-restricted living, a higher density can be accommodated. Setbacks typical of multi-family uses are also appropriate for CCRCs. *See* ASSISTED LIVING FACILITY; CONGREGATE RESIDENCES; RETIREMENT COMMUNITY.

CONTINUING EASEMENT

See EASEMENT, CONTINUING.

CONVENIENCE STORE

Any retail establishment offering for sale prepackaged food products, household items, newspapers and magazines, and sandwiches and other freshly prepared foods, such as salads, for off-site consumption (Planning Advisory Service Report No. 421 1989).

Comment: The convenience store is the modern equivalent of the corner grocery—open long hours and containing a myriad of items. They can be intensive operations. Parking, lighting, litter, and related impacts on adjacent residences are important planning and zoning considerations. A critical control standard is store size. Most experts agree that an appropriate maximum size for such stores is 3,500 square feet. That limitation should appear in the body of the ordinance.

CONVENTION FACILITY

A building or portion thereof designed to accommodate three hundred or more people in assembly.

Comment: The definition is admittedly broad, and the figure three hundred is arbitrary. It is designed to give the municipality as much control over these very intensive uses as possible. Most municipalities restrict them to central business districts. Standards have to be established relating to parking, setbacks, signs, landscaping, and circulation.

CONVENTIONAL ENERGY SYSTEM

Any energy system, including supply elements, furnaces, burners, tanks, boilers, related controls, and energy-distribution components, that uses any source(s) of energy other than solar energy.

Comment: The sources of conventional energy systems include the usual fossil fuels, such as gas, oil, and coal, as well as nuclear fuels. They do not include windmills.

CONVERSION

A change in the use of land or a structure.

COOLING TOWER

A device to remove excess heat from water used in industrial operations, notably in electric power generation.

CORNER LOT

See LOT, CORNER.

COST-BENEFIT ANALYSIS

An analytic method whereby the primary and secondary costs of a proposed project are measured against the benefits to be received from the project.

Comment: The field of cost-benefit analysis is complex and ill defined. For instance, some cost-benefit analyses consider primary costs and benefits. Others may include secondary and tertiary costs and benefits (Burchell and Listokin 1980).

COTTAGE

A small, detached dwelling unit.

Comment: A cottage is usually an outbuilding on a larger tract of land. Originally, the cottage may have been a seasonal dwelling without heat but later converted to an all-year-round dwelling. Local ordinances should specify minimum standards for space, heating, and sanitary facilities as a condition of conversion.

COTTAGE INDUSTRY

A home occupation.

Comment: Cottage industry is a term previously used to describe manufacturing and assembly carried out in the home, often on a contract basis with the entire family working. In later years, cottage industry was accessory to the principal residential use and was often carried out in an outbuilding or accessory structure. It is now used in place of the term "home occupation," particularly for activities calling for computer use and the electronic sending and receiving of data.

71

COUNCIL OF GOVERNMENTS

A regional planning and review authority whose membership includes representation from all communities in the designated region.

COUNTRY CLUB

Land area and buildings containing golf courses, recreational facilities, a clubhouse, and customary accessory uses, open only to members and their guests.

Comment: Communities must decide whether or not to allow country clubs to lease their facilities to outsiders for banquets, weddings, golf tournaments, conferences, and so on. These outside activities, while similar in nature to what would normally be permitted to club members, do intensify the use. On the other hand, they allow the clubs to make money and very often are the difference between continuing the primary country club use or being forced to sell for development.

COUNTY MASTER PLAN

The official master plan for the physical development of a county.

COURT

Any open space, unobstructed from the ground to the sky, that is bounded on two or more sides by the walls of a building that is on the same lot. *See* PLAZA; SQUARE. *See Figure 14.*

COURT, INNER

An open area, unobstructed from the ground to the sky, that is bounded on more than three sides by the exterior walls of one or more buildings. *See Figure 17.*

COURT, OUTER

An open area, unobstructed from the ground to the sky, that is bounded on not more than three sides by the exterior walls of one or more buildings. *See Figure 17.*

COVE

A small bay or inlet or a sheltered recess in a cliff face.

COVENANT

See RESTRICTIVE COVENANT.

COVER MATERIAL

Soil that is used to cover compacted solid waste in a sanitary landfill.

COVERAGE

See BUILDING COVERAGE; LOT COVERAGE.

COVERED EMPLOYMENT

Employees covered by the state's unemployment compensation law.

Comment: In some states, covered employment and

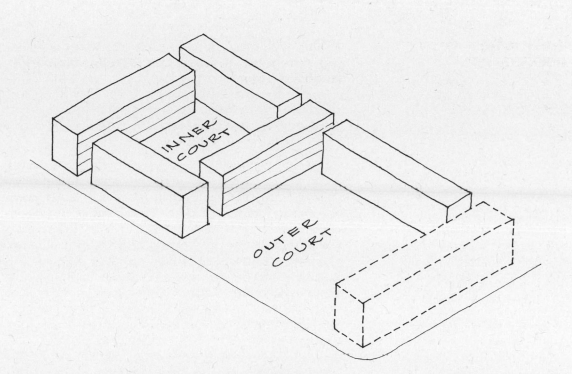

Figure 17

covered employment trends are used in formulas to determine lower income housing needs. The amount of change is measured by a linear regression equation over a time span sufficiently long—seven years, for example—to minimize the impact of short-term fluctuations.

CRAWL SPACE

A space between the ceiling of one story and floor of the next story, which usually contains pipes, ducts, wiring and lighting fixtures, and permits access but is too low for an individual to stand. *See Figure 6.*

Comment: The crawl space may be a cellar area no more than four and a half feet high or, if between a ceiling and a flat or shed roof, a cockloft.

CREEK

A small stream somewhat larger than a brook.

CRITICAL AREA

An area with one or more of the following environmental characteristics: (1) steep slopes; (2) flood plain; (3) soils classified as having high water tables; (4) soils classified as highly erodible, subject to erosion, or highly acidic; (5) land incapable of meeting percolation requirements;

73

(6) land formerly used for landfill operations or hazardous industrial use; (7) fault areas; (8) stream corridors; (9) estuaries; (10) mature stands of native vegetation; (11) aquifer recharge and discharge areas; (12) wetlands and wetland transition areas; and (13) habitats of endangered species. *See* CONSERVATION AREA.

Comment: The purpose of classifying certain lands as critical areas is to focus attention on these lands and to set standards to regulate development in these areas. Local ordinances should specify standards within these general categories, such as the percentage of slope considered steep (often 20 percent) or water table height. The additional requirements may also include the preparation and submission of an environmental impact statement or requiring the applicant to specifically address what measures will be taken with respect to the critical elements. Local development ordinances may preclude development in some types of critical areas if federal or state regulations do so or if provisions have been made to transfer development rights to another part of the site not affected by critical areas. *See* CLUSTER SUBDIVISION.

CROP

A harvestable product, planted, grown, and cultivated in the soil.

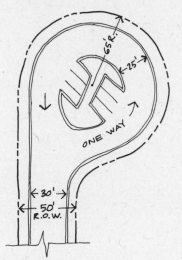

LARGE DIAMETER CUL-DE-SAC
(WITH CENTER ISLAND PARKING)

Figure 18

74

CUBIC CONTENT

The volume of space contained within the walls of a room or building found by multiplying the height, width, and length.

CUL-DE-SAC

The turnaround at the end of a dead-end street. *See Figures 18, 19, 20, 21 and 70.*

Comment: The term cul-de-sac is often used to describe the street itself, which is further defined as a street with only a single means of ingress and egress and having a turnaround at the end. *See* STREET, CUL-DE-SAC; STREET, DEAD-END.

CULTURAL EUTROPHICATION

Acceleration of the natural aging process of bodies of water.

Comment: Eutrophication often takes place because of runoff from cultivated lawns or the use of septic systems that introduce nutrients into the water, thus hastening the growth of algae and underwater plants.

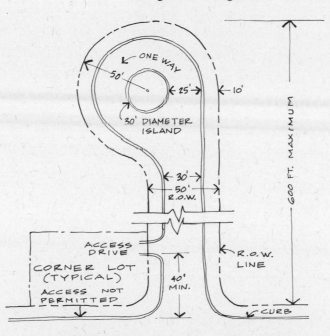

STANDARD CUL-DE-SAC
(SINGLE-FAMILY DEVELOPMENT)
MAXIMUM LENGTH - 600 FT.
MAXIMUM LOTS - 12

CENTER ISLAND STANDARDS:
- GRANITE BLOCK CURB
- 4 TREES
- MAINTENANCE BY LOT OWNERS

Figure 19

75

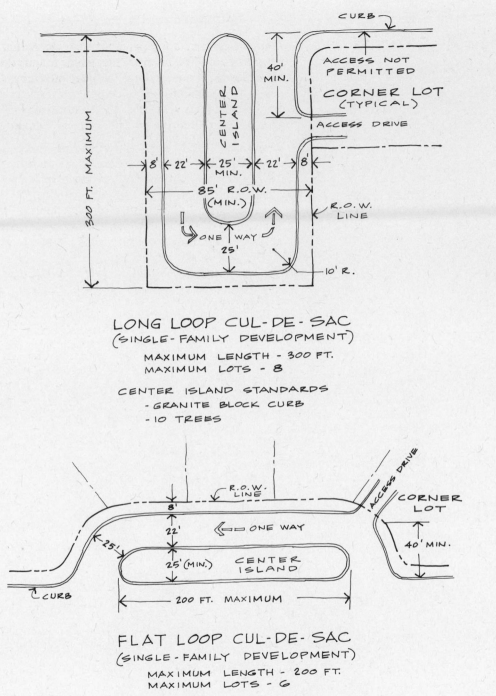

LONG LOOP CUL-DE-SAC
(SINGLE-FAMILY DEVELOPMENT)

MAXIMUM LENGTH - 300 FT.
MAXIMUM LOTS - 8

CENTER ISLAND STANDARDS
- GRANITE BLOCK CURB
- 10 TREES

FLAT LOOP CUL-DE-SAC
(SINGLE-FAMILY DEVELOPMENT)

MAXIMUM LENGTH - 200 FT.
MAXIMUM LOTS - 6

CENTER ISLAND STANDARDS
- GRANITE BLOCK CURB
- 6 TREES

Figures 20 and 21

76

CULTURAL FACILITIES

Establishments that document the social and religious structures and intellectual and artistic manifestations that characterize a society and include museums, art galleries, and botanical and zoological gardens of a natural, historic, educational, or cultural interest (*The New Lexicon Webster Dictionary of the English Language* 1989).

Comment: While these activities may charge admission fees, the bulk of their expenses are usually borne by public agencies, foundations, or donations.

CULVERT

A drain, ditch, or conduit, not incorporated in a closed system, that carries drainage water under a driveway, roadway, railroad, pedestrian walk, or public way.

CURB

A stone, concrete, or other improved boundary usually marking the edge of the roadway or paved area. *See Figures 22 and 23.*

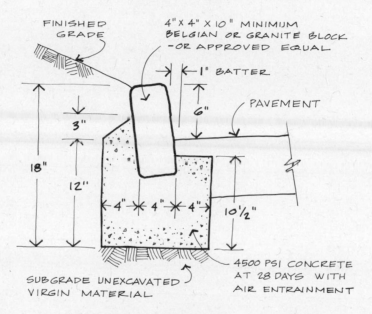

BLOCK CURB

Figure 22

CURB CUT

The opening along the curb line at which point vehicles may enter or leave the roadway. *See Figure 59.*

CURB LEVEL

The permanently established grade of the curb top in front of a lot.

77

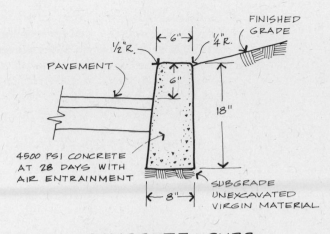

CONCRETE CURB

Figure 23

CURB RETURN

The connecting link between the street curb and the ramp or driveway curb. *See Figure 24.*

CURRENT

(1) The volume of water passing a given point measured in cubic feet per second; (2) the part of any body of water that has more or less steady flow in a definite direction for certain periods during the day.

CURRENT PLANNING CAPACITY (CPC)

A measure of the ability of a region to accommodate growth and development within the limits set by existing infrastructure and natural resource capabilities.

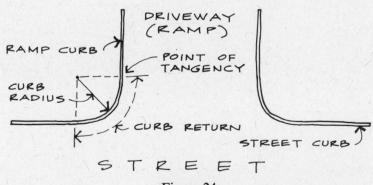

Figure 24

Comment: Generally, CPC is defined by water supply, water and air quality, sewage capability, highway capacity, and available community facilities. Some zoning ordinances award points for various infrastructure improvements and subtract them when certain environmental constraints are noted. The higher the number of points, the higher the permitted development density.

In Florida, a "CPC-like" point system, included in an Urban Area Residential checklist (part of the County Comprehensive Plan), permits applicants to request

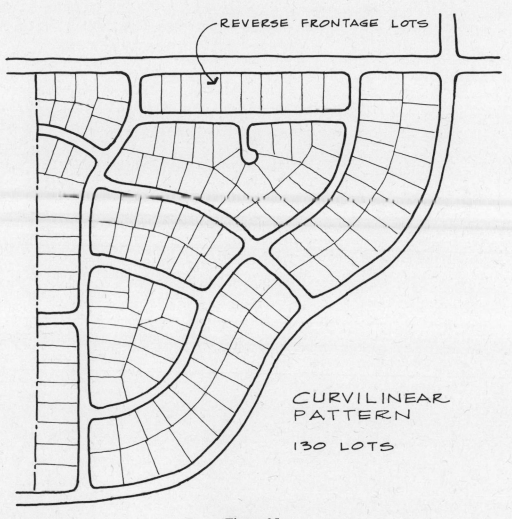

REVERSE FRONTAGE LOTS

CURVILINEAR PATTERN

130 LOTS

Figure 25

higher densities based on the following: proximity to commercial or employment centers; vehicular access to an arterial; access to mass transit; fire protection; water supply and sewers; percentage of affordable housing to be provided; access to schools; and proximity to parks and recreation.

It is important to keep in mind that CPC does not necessarily yield appropriate or desired densities or levels of development. It often represents a cap.

CURVILINEAR STREET SYSTEM

A pattern of streets that is curved. *See Figure 25.*

CUT

A portion of land surface or area from which earth has been removed or will be removed by excavation; the depth below the original ground surface or excavated surface. *See Figure 37.*

D

DATUM

A reference point, line, or plane used as a basis for measurements.

DAY-CARE CENTER/DAY NURSERY

See CHILD-CARE CENTER.

DEAD-END STREET

See STREET, DEAD-END.

DEAF or HARD-OF-HEARING

Auditory limitations that might make an individual insecure because he or she is unable to communicate or hear warning signals.

DECELERATION LANE

An added roadway lane that permits vehicles to slow down and leave the main vehicle stream. *See Figure 1.*

DECIBEL

A unit of sound pressure level.

Comment: The decibel (abbreviated dB) is used to express noise level, and a reference quantity is implied. The reference level is a sound pressure of twenty micronewtons per square meter. Zero decibels, the starting point of the scale of noise level, is about the level of the weakest sound that can be heard by someone with very good hearing in an extremely quiet location. The noise level in an average residence is about fifty decibels; twenty feet from a subway train the noise level is about ninety decibels; and two hundred feet from a jet is about one hundred and twenty decibels.

DECIDUOUS

Plants that drop their foliage annually before becoming dormant.

Comment: In specifying landscaping for buffer areas, there should be a mix of deciduous and evergreen trees, with the predominant emphasis on evergreens, which provide an all-year-round buffer.

DECK LINE

The intersection of two roof surfaces of a mansard roof forming the highest horizontal line of the steeper roof slope. *See Figure 62.*

DECOMPOSITION

Reduction of the net energy level and change in chemical composition of organic matter because of the actions of aerobic or anaerobic microorganisms.

DEDICATION

The transfer of property by the owner to another party.

Comment: Such transfer is conveyed by written instrument and is completed with an acceptance. The dedication is often for a specific use. Typically, dedication of land for roads, utilities, and open space is a requirement of subdivision or site plan approval. Where dedication is impractical because of costs or other reasons, an easement may suffice.

DEDICATION, FEE IN LIEU OF

Payments in cash as an alternative to dedication of land or construction of improvements.

Comment: In some states, mandatory construction of improvements or dedication of land for open space, recreation, services, or utilities may be a requirement for development approval. Where such construction or dedication is physically impossible or undesirable, a fee in lieu of dedication may be substituted based on a formula established by ordinance.

DEED

A legal document conveying ownership of real property.

DEED RESTRICTION

See RESTRICTIVE COVENANT.

DEFICIENT UNIT

A housing unit that is not decent, safe, or sanitary, as determined through census surrogates or on-site inspection, and that does not comply with local codes or other housing standards. *See* SURROGATE.

Comment: Surrogates for deficient housing include age of structure, overcrowding, lack of central heat, shared bathroom facilities, inadequate kitchen facilities, inadequate access, and lack of elevators in mid- and high-rise buildings.

DEMOGRAPHY   The study of population and its characteristics.

DEMOLITION PERMIT   Official authorization to remove part, or all, of a building or structure.

Comment: Demolition permits are usually authorized by the local authority. The grant of a demolition permit may be contingent on fulfilling certain requirements, such as rodent control, insurance in place, and protection against erosion.

DENSITY   The number of families, individuals, dwelling units, households, or housing structures per unit of land.

Comment: Ordinances regulating density must make it clear as to whether the standard is stated in net or gross density. Gross density includes all the area within the boundaries of the particular area, excluding nothing. Net density excludes certain areas, such as streets, easements, water areas, lands with environmental constraints, and so on. The exclusions have to be spelled out carefully. Some typical densities for various types of housing are:

	Typical Density Ranges (units per gross acre)		
Type of Unit	*Suburban Area*	*Town*	*Urban Center*
Single-family detached	1–4	4–8	8–15
Two-family	6–8	8–12	20–40
Townhouses	6–10	10–20	20–30
Flats, two- and three-story	10–18	15–30	25–40
Mid-rise	20–40	30–50	40–60
High-rise	—	50–60	70+

Allowable densities may vary depending on occupancy characteristics. For example, senior citizen apartments are typically built at higher densities than nonage-restricted units since overall impact (such as vehicle trip generation, schoolchildren, persons per acre, and so forth) is less. Mixed-type structures containing town-houses and flats, for instance, may have densities somewhere between the two types. Single-family detached variations, such as zero lot line, patio homes, or z-lots, are often built at densities of about six to ten dwelling units per net acre. *See* CRITICAL AREA; NET AREA OF LOT.

DENSITY MODIFICATION FACTOR

See CLUSTER SUBDIVISION.

DENSITY TRANSFER

The transfer of all or part of the permitted density on a parcel to another parcel.

Comment: Density transfer is also known as the transfer of development rights (TDR). TDR must be permitted by a state enabling act and then enacted in the local ordinance. Usually, density transfers are made from designated sending districts to designated receiving districts. Both types of districts must be identified in the zoning ordinance. It may be used to preserve farmland, open space, historic areas, and critical areas. *See* AIR RIGHTS; TRANSFER OF DEVELOPMENT RIGHTS.

DENSITY ZONING

Averaging residential density over an entire parcel without restriction to lot sizes (Planning Advisory Service Report No. 322 1976).

Comment: Density zoning is often confused with cluster development. Technically, it is more akin to lot averaging, in which the size of the lots may vary if the number and area of lots over the minimum lot size are equal to the number and area of lots under the minimum lot size. Density zoning may also be used to permit any housing type provided the number of units does not exceed the maximum density permitted in the ordinance.

DESALINIZATION

Salt removed from seawater or brackish water.

DESIGN CONTINUITY

A unifying or connecting theme or physical feature for a particular setting or place, provided by one or more elements of the natural or created environment.

DESIGN FIT

Consistency in scale, quality, or character between new and existing development so as to avoid abrupt and/or severe differences.

DESIGN REVIEW

The submission of a site or building design for review by a design review body constituted to comment or make recommendations on the design or to grant approval.

DESIGN STANDARDS

A set of guidelines defining parameters to be followed in site and/or building design and development.

DETENTION BASIN (POND)

A facility for the temporary storage of stormwater runoff.

Comment: Detention basins or ponds differ from retention basins in that the water storage is only temporary, often released by mechanical means at such time as downstream facilities can handle the flow. Basins are generally designed to regulate the rate of flow to predevelopment conditions. Usually, the basins are planted with grass and, if large enough, can be used for open space or recreation in periods of dry weather. Basins also serve to recharge groundwater.

DETERGENT

A synthetic washing agent that, like soap, lowers the surface tension of water, emulsifies oils, and holds dirt in suspension.

Comment: Environmentalists have criticized detergents that have large amounts of phosphorus-containing compounds that contribute to the eutrophication of waterways.

DETERIORATION

The marked diminishing of the physical condition of structures or buildings. *See* DEFICIENT UNIT; SURROGATE.

DEVELOPER

The legal or beneficial owner or owners of a lot or of any land included in a proposed development, including the holder of an option or contract to purchase or other persons having enforceable proprietary interests in such land. *See* APPLICANT.

DEVELOPMENT

The division of a parcel of land into two or more parcels; the construction, reconstruction, conversion, structural alteration, relocation, or enlargement of any structure; any mining, excavation, landfill, or land disturbance; and any use or extension of the use of land.

DEVELOPMENT, CONVENTIONAL

Development other than planned development or cluster development.

84

DEVELOPMENT, MAJOR   Any development not a minor development.

DEVELOPMENT, MINOR   Any development involving three or fewer lots and/or involving a land area of less than five acres and not requiring the extension of any new streets or other municipal or governmental facilities. *See* DEVELOPMENT.

Comment: The definition of development is sufficiently broad to cover all types of activity relating to land and building. The designation of an application as a minor development relieves the applicant of the need to meet the more stringent requirements of a major application, including advertising, notification of neighbors, a public hearing, and so on. The number of lots and land area is strictly a local determination. In many built-up communities, where the streets and major infrastructure are already installed, five lots or less may be considered a minor subdivision. In urban areas, the five-acre standard for site plans may be too large and a smaller minimum may be desirable.

There are two recurring problems with respect to minor developments. The first is the danger that the land will come in at some subsequent time for another minor—"the creeping major." This problem can be addressed by requiring any application involving land previously approved as a minor development to be submitted as a major application. The second problem is how the remaining land is proposed to be used. While applicants will often claim that they have no intention of developing the remainder, the prudent board will require at least a concept plan for the remaining land to ensure that the minor development does not pose future problems.

DEVELOPMENT, PLANNED   *See* PLANNED DEVELOPMENT.

DEVELOPMENT ANALYSIS STUDY   An analysis of potential uses and markets, whether permitted by zoning or not, for a parcel of real estate to determine the type and intensity of development.

Comment: Development analysis differs from impact analysis, which analyzes the impact of a specific development in terms of water and sewer use, traffic, and impact on community facilities, such as schools, recreation, environment, and public services. The development analysis study is often called a feasibility study.

85

DEVELOPMENT REGULATION

Any zoning, subdivision, site plan, official map, flood plain regulation, or other governmental regulation that affects the use and intensity of land development.

Comment: There is a general tendency to combine all development regulations into a single land development ordinance since procedures, informational requirements, public hearings, notices, and so forth, are the same or similar for all development applications.

DEVELOPMENT RIGHT

The right to develop property.

Comment: Fee simple ownership of property involves a bundle of rights, including but not limited to mineral rights, air rights, easements, and such. These may be sold, dedicated, or transferred in their entirety or in part. Purchase of development rights has become a method to preserve farmland, open space, or historic structures. Usually a governmental agency purchases the development rights to the property at a fair appraisal price. The owner keeps title to the property and may continue to farm the land and live on the property. Development rights can also be transferred. *See* DENSITY TRANSFER.

DEVELOPMENT TIMING

Regulating the rate and geographic sequence of development.

Comment: Large-scale developments are often phased in terms of the number of units and geographic area. The approving authority has to ensure that each phase can stand on its own in terms of circulation, utilities, and so on, in the event subsequent phases are delayed or canceled. This can be done by requiring these facilities to be built at the same time or by requiring a performance guarantee.

DILAPIDATION

A deterioration of structures or buildings to the point of being unsafe or unfit for human habitation or use.

DILUTION RATIO

The ratio of the volume of water of a stream to the volume of incoming waste.

Comment: The capacity of a stream to accept wastewater is partially dependent upon the dilution ratio.

DISABILITY

In reference to an individual, a physical or mental impairment that substantially limits one or more of the major life activities; a record of such an impairment; or being regarded as having an impairment. *See* MAJOR LIFE ACTIVITIES.

DISCOTHEQUE

A nightclub for dancing to recorded music; broadly, a nightclub often featuring psychedelic and mixed-media attractions, such as slides, movies, and special lighting effects (*The New Lexicon Webster Dictionary of the English Language* 1989).

DISCOUNT CENTER

A single store, or group of stores, offering merchandise for sale at less-than-usual retail prices.

Comment: Discount centers or stores are now emerging as a major force in retailing. They are characterized by very large structures, often converted warehouses, and merchandise offered for sale on steel industrial shelving in original shipping boxes. Many require persons to join and pay an annual fee (the club concept). From a zoning perspective, they have a market area larger than a shopping center of the same size. In addition, their major traffic impact is usually on weekends.

DISPOSAL AREA

The entire area used for underground dispersion of the liquid portion of sewage.

Comment: The disposal area usually consists of the seepage pit or a disposal field or a combination of both.

DISPOSAL BED

That part of a disposal field used for sanitary sewage.

Comment: The disposal bed is an area from which the entire earth contents have been removed and the excavation partially filled with satisfactory filtering material in which distribution lines have been laid. The entire area is then covered with topsoil and suitable vegetative cover.

DISPOSAL FIELD

An area consisting of a combination of disposal trenches and a disposal bed. *See Figure 26.*

Comment: The disposal field is used for dispersion of the liquid portion of sanitary sewage into the ground as close to the surface as possible.

DISPOSAL TRENCH

A shallow ditch with vertical sides and a flat bottom partially filled with a satisfactory filtering material in which a single distribution line has been laid and covered with topsoil and a suitable vegetative cover.

87

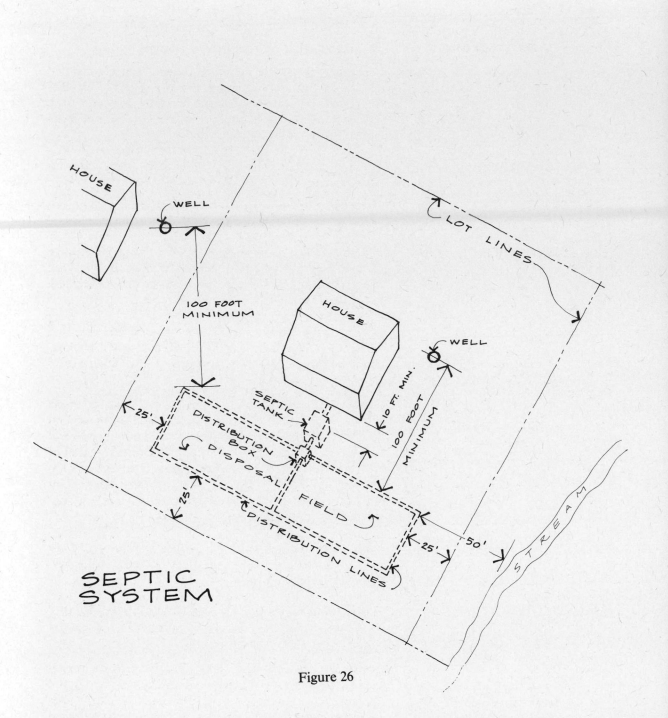

HOUSE

WELL

LOT LINES

100 FOOT
MINIMUM

HOUSE

WELL

25'

SEPTIC
TANK

10 FT. MIN.

100 FOOT MINIMUM

DISTRIBUTION
BOX

DISPOSAL FIELD

25'

50'

STREAM

DISTRIBUTION LINES

25'

SEPTIC
SYSTEM

Figure 26

DISSOLVED OXYGEN (DO)

The oxygen dissolved in water or sewage.

Comment: Adequate dissolved oxygen is necessary for the life of fish and other aquatic organisms. Low dissolved oxygen concentrations generally are due to a discharge of excessive organic solids, the result of inadequate waste treatment.

DISSOLVED SOLIDS

The total amount of dissolved material, organic and inorganic, contained in water or wastes.

Comment: Excessive dissolved solids make water unpalatable for drinking and unsuitable for industrial uses.

DISTRIBUTION BOX

A water-tight structure that receives sanitary sewage effluent from a septic tank and distributes such sewage effluent in equal portions to two or more pipelines leading to the disposal field. *See Figure 26.*

DISTRIBUTION CENTER

An establishment engaged in the receipt, storage, and distribution of goods, products, cargo, and materials, including transshipment by boat, rail, air, or motor vehicle.

Comment: Breakdown of large orders from a single source into smaller orders and consolidation of several orders into one large one for distribution to several recipients and vice versa are often part of the function of a distribution center. The functions of distribution centers and warehouses often overlap, but retail sales, manufacturing, assembly, or product processing are not considered part of the distribution process.

DISTRIBUTION LINES

A series of open, jointed, or perforated pipes used for the dispersion of sewage into disposal trenches or disposal beds. *See Figure 26.*

DISTRICT

A part, zone, or geographic area within the municipality within which certain zoning or development regulations apply.

Comment: District regulations must be uniform for all uses within the district. If a municipality wants to apply a larger lot size to service stations within a district, for example, compared to other uses, it may have to make such uses conditional or special exception uses.

DIVERSION CHANNEL

A channel constructed across or at the bottom of a slope.

DIVIDED HIGHWAY   A highway having access on only one side of the direction of travel. *See* STREET, DUAL.

DOMICILE   A residence that is a permanent home to an individual.

DONATION   A voluntary gift for which no valuable consideration is given in exchange.

DORMER   A projection from a sloping roof that contains a window. *See Figure 7.*

DORMITORY   A building used as group living quarters for a student body or religious order as an accessory use for a college, university, boarding school, convent, monastery, or other similar institutional use.

Comment: Recent court cases on the definition of family (for instance, *State of N.J. v. Dennis Baker,* A-59, Supreme Court of N.J.) make the distinction between dormitories and households of unrelated individuals less precise. Regulations based on living space or other performance standards may offer the most positive method of control. The basic difference between dormitories and dwelling units is that: (1) a dormitory is an accessory use while a dwelling unit is a principal use; and (2) a dwelling unit is designed to be occupied by one or more persons functioning as a household. Dormitories do not usually include individual kitchen facilities or private bathroom facilities as do dwelling units.

DOSE RESPONSE   A relationship between exposure to an environmental agent and physiological response in a population.

DOUBLE-WIDE UNIT   Two manufactured housing components, attached side by side, to make one complete housing unit.

DOWNZONE   To increase the intensity of use by increasing density or floor area ratio or otherwise decreasing bulk requirements.

Comment: Developers and some landowners consider this term to have the opposite meaning. *See* UPZONE.

DRAINAGE   (1) Surface water runoff; (2) the removal of surface water or groundwater from land by drains, grading, or other means, which include runoff controls to minimize erosion and sedimentation during and after construction or development.

DRAINAGE AREA	That area in which all of the surface runoff resulting from precipitation is concentrated into a particular stream.
DRAINAGE DISTRICT	A district established by a governmental unit to build and operate facilities for drainage.
DRAINAGE SYSTEM	Pipes, swales, natural features, and man-made improvements designed to carry drainage.
DRAINAGEWAY	Any natural or artificial watercourse, trench, ditch, swale, or similar depression into which surface water flows.
DREDGE AND FILL	A process that creates land by dredging material from the bottom of a body of water and depositing this material on land usually adjacent to the water.
DREDGING	A method for deepening streams, swamps, or coastal waters by removing solids from the bottom.
	Comment: Dredging and filling can disturb natural ecological cycles. For example, dredging can destroy shellfish beds and other aquatic life; filling can destroy the feeding and breeding grounds for many fish species. All dredging and filling of waterways and wetlands are regulated by the federal government.
DRIP LINE	An imaginary ground line around a tree that defines the limits of the tree canopy. *See Figure 73.*
DRIVE-IN THEATER	*See* THEATER, DRIVE-IN.
DRIVE-IN USE	An establishment that by design, physical facilities, service, or by packaging procedures encourages or permits customers to receive services, obtain goods, or be entertained while remaining in their motor vehicles.
DRIVEWAY	A private roadway providing access to a street or highway.
DRIVEWAY WIDTH	The narrowest width of driveway measured perpendicular to the driveway.
DRUGSTORE	A store where the primary business is the filling of medical prescriptions and the sale of drugs, medical devices and supplies, and nonprescription medicines but where nonmedical products may be sold as well.

Comment: A drugstore may be distinguished from a pharmacy, which deals solely with preparing and dispensing drugs and medicines. The nonmedical-related products may be cards, candy, and cosmetics. In recent years, however, the variety of nonmedical products has expanded substantially, particularly with the advent of national drugstore chains. *See* PHARMACY.

DRY WELL

A covered pit with an open jointed lining through which water is piped or directed from roofs, basement floors, other impervious surfaces, or swales or pipes to seep or leech into the surrounding soil. *See Figure 27.*

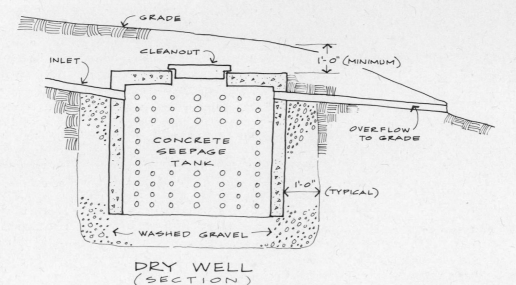

DRY WELL
(SECTION)

Figure 27

DUMP

A land site used primarily for the disposal by dumping, burial, burning, or other means and for whatever purposes, of garbage, sewage, trash, refuse, junk, discarded machinery, vehicles or parts thereof, and other waste, scrap, or discarded material of any kind.

DUPLEX

A building containing two single-family dwelling units totally separated from each other by an unpierced wall extending from ground to roof. *See* DWELLING, TWO-FAMILY.

Comment: One major advantage of a duplex is that each dwelling unit can be sold in fee simple. The two-family

92

type with one apartment over another requires condominium ownership.

DWELLING

A structure or portion thereof that is used exclusively for human habitation.

DWELLING, ATTACHED

A one-family dwelling attached to two or more one-family dwellings by common vertical walls.

DWELLING, DETACHED

A dwelling that is not attached to any other dwelling by any means.

Comment: The detached dwelling does not have any roof, wall, or floor in common with any other dwelling unit.

DWELLING, GARDEN APARTMENT

One or more two- or three-story, multifamily structures, generally built at a gross density of ten to fifteen dwelling units per acre, with each structure containing eight to twenty dwelling units and including related off-street parking, open space, and recreation. *See* Dwelling, Multifamily. *See Figure 28*.

Comment: A garden apartment is actually a multifamily development. Development controls should define the commonly accepted configuration of a garden apartment in terms of density (usually ten to fifteen dwelling units per acre in a suburban community, somewhat higher in an urban area, and lower in a rural area), height (usually

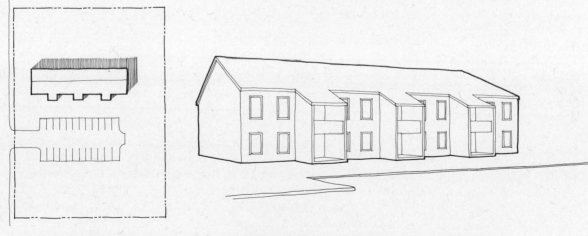

DWELLING, GARDEN APARTMENT
Figure 28

93

a maximum of three stories or thirty-five feet, with a maximum of three levels of dwelling units), and maximum length of a structure (usually between 150 to 200 feet). Access is usually from a common hall, although individual entrances can be provided. Dwelling units can be located back-to-back, adjacent, and on top of each other.

DWELLING, HIGH-RISE

A building of eight or more stories. *See Figure 29.*

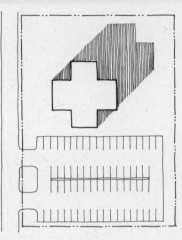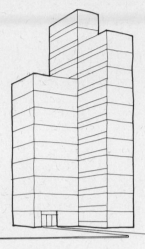

DWELLING, HIGH-RISE

Figure 29

DWELLING, MID-RISE

An apartment building containing from three to seven stories. *See Figure 30.*

DWELLING, MULTIFAMILY

A building containing three or more dwelling units, including units that are located one over the other.

Comment: Multifamily buildings include garden apartments and mid- and high-rise apartment buildings.

DWELLING, PATIO HOME

A one-family dwelling on a separate lot with open space setbacks on three sides and with a court. *See Figure 31.*

Comment: Patio homes may be attached to similar houses on adjacent lots and still meet this definition, in which case they are known as zero lot line homes.

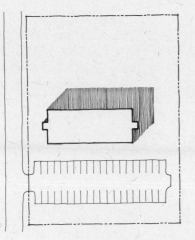
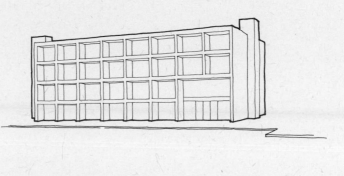

DWELLING, MID-RISE

Figure 30

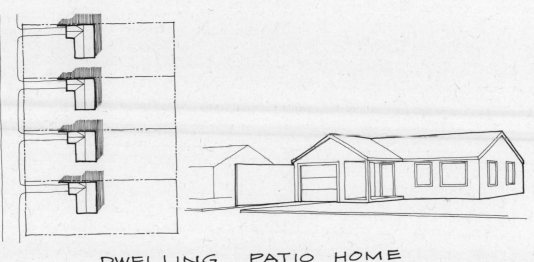

DWELLING, PATIO HOME

Figure 31

DWELLING, QUADRUPLEX

Four attached dwellings in one building in which each unit has two open space exposures and shares one or two walls with adjoining unit or units. *See Figure 32.*

DWELLING, SEASONAL

A dwelling unit not used as a principal residence that may be occupied weekends and for brief periods during the year.

95

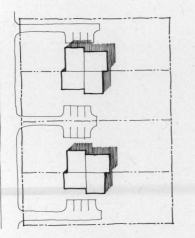
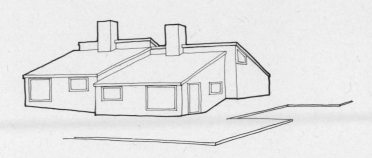

DWELLING, QUADRUPLEX

Figure 32

Comment: Brief period is difficult to define. Seasonal dwellings in oceanfront or lake areas may be occupied for three to four months. In ski areas, six months may be the norm.

At one time, seasonal units often lacked heat and insulation. Today, most municipalities do not make any distinction between seasonal and all-year-round units; both must meet the same standards.

DWELLING, SINGLE-FAMILY DETACHED

A building containing one dwelling unit and that is not attached to any other dwelling by any means and is surrounded by open space or yards. *See* DWELLING, DETACHED. *See Figure 33.*

DWELLING, SINGLE-FAMILY SEMIDETACHED

A one-family dwelling attached to one other one-family dwelling by a common vertical wall, with each dwelling located on a separate lot. *See* DUPLEX. *See Figure 34.*

Comment: The semidetached dwelling is most commonly a two-family structure with the dwelling units side by side as opposed to one on top of the other. A semidetached dwelling also could be the end unit of a townhouse row, a patio house, or a variety of zero lot line houses.

DWELLING, TOWNHOUSE

A one-family dwelling in a row of at least three such units in which each unit has its own front and rear access to

96

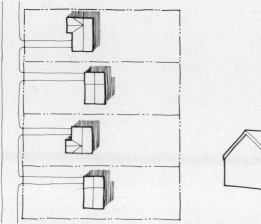

DWELLING, SINGLE-FAMILY DETACHED

Figure 33

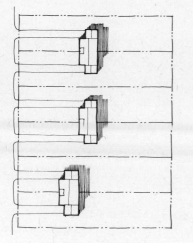

DWELLING, SEMIDETACHED

Figure 34

the outside, no unit is located over another unit, and each unit is separated from any other unit by one or more vertical common fire-resistant walls. *See Figure 35.*

Comment: Townhouses (single-family attached dwellings) usually have separate utilities, such as individual hot water and heating systems, separate electric meters, and so forth. However, in some condominium developments, the condominium association may arrange for

97

bulk purchase of certain utilities and distribute it to individual dwelling units. Consequently, the definition normally would not contain a requirement for separate utility systems. In some states—Florida, for example—one-story single-family attached dwellings are called "villas."

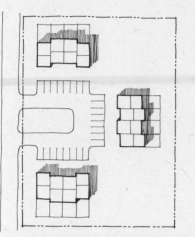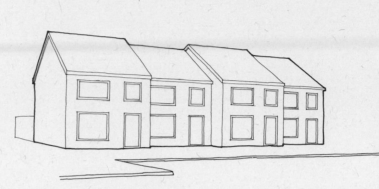

DWELLING, TOWNHOUSE

Figure 35

DWELLING, TRIPLEX

A building containing three dwelling units, each of which has direct access to the outside or to a common hall.

DWELLING, TWO-FAMILY

A building on a single lot containing two dwelling units, each of which is totally separated from the other by an unpierced wall extending from ground to roof or an unpierced ceiling and floor extending from exterior wall to exterior wall, except for a common stairwell exterior to both dwelling units.

DWELLING UNIT

One or more rooms, designed, occupied, or intended for occupancy as a separate living quarter, with cooking, sleeping, and sanitary facilities provided within the dwelling unit for the exclusive use of a single family maintaining a household. *See* HOUSING UNIT.

DWELLING UNIT, EFFICIENCY

A dwelling unit consisting of not more than one habitable room together with kitchen or kitchenette and sanitary facilities.

98

DYSTROPHIC LAKES

Lakes between eutrophic and swamp stages of aging.

Comment: Such lakes are shallow and have high humus content, low nutrient availability, and high BOD (biological oxygen demand). Such lakes are heavily stained and are commonly referred to as "brown-water lakes."

E

EASEMENT

A grant of one or more of the property rights by the property owner to and/or for use by the public, a corporation, or another person or entity. *See Figure 2.*

Comment: An easement may be a more acceptable and less expensive way to achieve certain public goals since not all of the property rights are being purchased. For instance, where property owners are reluctant to donate land for road-widening purposes, an easement may be an acceptable alternative. The property owner keeps the title but the road can be widened. This is particularly true in rural areas where land is sold by the acre. Other examples are slope rights to permit roadway grading.

EASEMENT, AFFIRMATIVE

An easement that gives the holder a right to make some limited use of land owned by another. *See* EASEMENT IN GROSS.

EASEMENT, APPURTENANT

An easement that runs with the land.

EASEMENT, AVIATION

An air rights easement that protects air lanes around airports.

EASEMENT, CONSERVATION

The grant of a property right stipulating that the described land will remain in its natural state and precluding future or additional development.

Comment: Conservation easements are usually used for the preservation of open space, environmentally sensitive areas, scenic views, or wetland buffers.

EASEMENT, CONTINUING

An easement that is self-perpetuating and runs with the land.

EASEMENT, DISCHARGE

The grant of a property right to allow runoff in excess of the previous quantity and/or rate of flow.

EASEMENT, DRAINAGE   Land required for the installation of stormwater sewers or drainage ditches and/or required for the preservation or maintenance of a natural stream or watercourse or other drainage facility.

EASEMENT, EXPRESS   An easement that is expressly created by a deed or other instrument.

EASEMENT, NEGATIVE   An easement that precludes the owner of the land from doing that which the owner would be entitled to do if the easement did not exist.

Comment: Negative easements historically have been limited to easements for light, air, views, and conservation.

EASEMENT IN GROSS   An easement created for the personal benefit of the holder.

Comment: An easement in gross allows a person, corporation, or the public to use another's land; for example, for railroad purposes or power lines. Hagman (1975) notes that the benefit of an easement in gross does not pass with the land automatically, and there is a question as to whether such easements may be assigned. The burden of an easement in gross passes with the land to all takers. *See* EASEMENT, AFFIRMATIVE.

EATING AND DRINKING PLACES   Retail establishments selling food and drink for consumption on the premises, including lunch counters and refreshment stands selling prepared foods and drinks for immediate on-site consumption.

Comment: Eating and drinking places are a specific type of food establishment. They differ from take-out places where food is ready for consumption but eaten off the premises. Restaurants, lunch counters, and drinking places operated as a subordinate service facility or accessory use in other establishments, such as the cafeteria of a large company, are not regarded as separate permitted uses but as accessory to the principal use. *See* RESTAURANT, TAKE-OUT.

EAVE   The projecting lower edges of a roof overhanging the wall of a building. *See Figure 62.*

ECHO HOUSING   A small, removable modular cottage on a concrete foundation or slab in the rear or side yard of a dwelling.

Comment: Echo housing is also known as a "granny" flat or elder cottage housing. It permits an older person to live independently but close to relatives. The cottage consists of one bedroom, a bathroom, living room, and kitchen and is connected to the utility system of the main unit.

ECOLOGICAL IMPACT

The total effect of an environmental change, either natural or man-made, on the ecology of an area.

ECOLOGY

The interrelationship of living things to one another and to their environment or the study of such relationships.

ECONOMETRICS

Statistical analysis and techniques applied to economic information and used for modeling and projection.

ECONOMIC BASE

The system of production, distribution, and consumption of goods and services within a planning area.

Comment: Economic base, as used in planning, is the sum of all activities that result in incomes for the area's inhabitants. The definition, however, is significantly broad to include all geographic and functional elements that may have an impact on the planning area, although not physically part of the area. Economic base analysis identifies and measures the components of an area's economic base and highlights strengths and weaknesses of the local economy. Do not confuse "economic base" with "base economy," a term used by economists to identify that part of a region's economy that is sold outside the region.

ECOSYSTEM

The interacting system of all living organisms and the physical environment in a geographic area.

Comment: An ecosystem can be the entire biosphere, an ocean, a parcel of land, or an aquarium, depending on the context of use.

EDGE CLEARANCE

The distance measured along the curb line from the extended property lot line to the driveway. *See Figure 36.*

EDUCATIONAL INSTITUTION

A college or university authorized by the state to award degrees.

Comment: The term as defined is applicable only to colleges and universities. Elementary, middle, and high

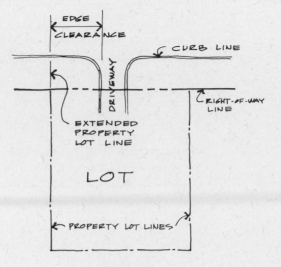

Figure 36

schools are defined under schools. The reason for purposely limiting the definition is to recognize the significant difference in impacts between the two types of facilities (schools and educational institutions). The development ordinance must consider the fact that colleges and universities are actually mini-cities with concerns relating to circulation, services, utilities, on-campus housing, and peak impacts for special events, such as athletics. The educational institution may require and support a major number of off-campus goods and service establishments. Educational institutions can also impose severe impacts on surrounding areas and generate increased competition for housing.

EFFICIENCY UNIT   *See* DWELLING UNIT, EFFICIENCY.

EFFLUENT   A discharge of liquid waste, with or without treatment, into the environment.

Comment: The term is generally used to describe discharges into water.

EGRESS   An exit.

ELECTROMAGNETIC FIELDS (EMF)   (1) A field made up of a combination of electric and magnetic fields; (2) responses to electrons moving through a conducting medium.

102

Comment: EMFs have two components, one electric, the other magnetic. The electric fields come directly from the strength of the charge. Magnetic fields result from the motion of the charge. EMFs are measured in kV/m, or kilovolts/meter. A significant amount of research is now under way on the biological effects of EMF, particularly sixty Hz (hertz) EMF, the type of electric power used in the United States. Most experts believe that prudent avoidance of sixty Hz electric and magnetic fields represents sound policy. Several states have established maximum field strength standards or transmission line rights-of-way as follows:

State Regulations That Limit Field Strengths on Transmission Line Rights-of-Way

State	Field Limit
Montana	1 kV/m at edge of ROW in residential areas
Minnesota	8 kV/m maximum in ROW
New Jersey	3 kV/m at edge of ROW
New York	1.6 kV/m at edge of ROW
North Dakota	9 kV/m maximum in ROW
Oregon	9 kV/m maximum in ROW
Florida	10 kV/m (for 500 kV), 8 kV/m (for 230 kV) maximum in ROW
	2 kV/m at edge of ROW all new lines, 200 mG (for 500 kV single circuit), 250 mG (for 500 kV double circuit), and 150 mG (for 230 kV) maximum at edge of ROW

Notes: kV = kilovolt
kV/m = kilovolts per meter
mG = milligauss
ROW = right-of-way

Source: Granger Morgan, *Electric and Magnetic Fields from 60 Hertz Electric Power: What Do We Know About Possible Health Risks?* (Pittsburgh: Department of Engineering and Public Policy, Carnegie-Mellon University, 1989).

ELEEMOSYNARY or PHILANTHROPIC INSTITUTION

A private or public organization that is organized and operated for the purpose of providing a service or carrying on a trade or business without profit.

Comment: Eleemosynary or philanthropic organizations generally provide services or goods to developmentally or physically impaired or disadvantaged persons. The nonprofit aspects are recognized by the Internal Revenue Service. A type of philanthropic institution such as a fund or foundation that distributes grants to other agencies functions more as an office use. Eleemosynary or philanthropic institutions pose problems in terms of where such uses should be located. The type of use, who it serves, what it provides, and the actual impacts on the surrounding neighborhood are key factors in locating these uses.

ELEVATION

(1) A vertical distance above or below a fixed reference level; (2) a fully dimensioned drawing of the front, rear, or side of a building showing features such as windows, doors, and relationship of grade to floor level.

EMBANKMENT

An elevated deposit of soil, rock, or other materials either constructed or natural.

EMERGENCY SHELTER

A facility providing temporary housing for one or more individuals who are otherwise temporarily or permanently homeless.

Comment: Emergency shelters are usually provided by governmental agencies and religious and eleemosynary or philanthropic institutions. In addition to housing, some shelters provide food, clothing, and other ancillary services. Emergency shelters generally serve the poor, primarily indigent, or needy; however, persons displaced by emergencies (such as fire, storm, and such) may also be temporarily housed in emergency shelters.

EMINENT DOMAIN

The authority to acquire or take, or to authorize the taking of, private property for public use or public purpose.

Comment: While eminent domain is largely the prerogative of the government, utilities and independent agencies may also have the right of eminent domain.

The Fifth Amendment of the U.S. Constitution requires just compensation for any taking. The taking must be for a public purpose, the definition of which has been significantly broadened in recent years.

EMISSION

A discharge of pollutants into the air.

EMISSION FACTOR

The average amount of a pollutant emitted from each type of polluting source in relation to a specific amount of material processed.

Comment: The emission factor is used in establishing a performance standard. Most of the factors and standards themselves are now specified and regulated by state or federal agencies.

EMISSION STANDARD

The maximum amount of a pollutant legally permitted to be discharged from a single source, either mobile or stationary.

EMPLOYEE TRANSPORTATION COORDINATOR

A person selected to develop, implement, and administer an employee transportation program.

Comment: Also referred to as a "rideshare coordinator"; their duties may include registering employees for a ride-match program, coordinating the formation of car/van/bus pools, promoting the use of public transit, and monitoring employee participation in the program.

ENABLING ACT

A legislative act authorizing a governmental agency to do something that previously could not be done.

ENCROACHMENT

Any obstruction or illegal or unauthorized intrusion in a delineated floodway, right-of-way, or on adjacent land. *See Figure 38.*

ENDANGERED SPECIES

Wildlife species whose prospects for survival are in immediate danger because of a loss or change in habitat, overexploitation, predation, competition, disease, disturbance, or contamination and designated as such by a governmental agency.

ENLARGEMENT

An increase in the size of an existing structure or use, including physical size of the property, building, parking, and other improvements.

Comment: What constitutes an enlargement is particularly critical when it comes to nonconforming uses. While a physical expansion always constitutes an enlargement, other changes, such as alterations, may or may not be considered an enlargement. Cox (1991, p. 130) notes a New Jersey Supreme Court decision—*Burbridge v. Mine Hill Twp.*, 117 N.J. 376 (1990)—in which the Court said: "Applications to expand nonconforming uses offer boards opportunities to impose conditions, frequently aesthetic, which will help integrate the use with its surroundings."

ENRICHMENT

The addition of nitrogen, phosphorus, and carbon compounds or other nutrients into a lake or other waterway.

105

Comment: Enrichment greatly increases the growth potential for algae and aquatic plants. Most frequently, enrichment results from the inflow of sewage effluent or from fertilizer runoff.

ENVIRONMENT

All external conditions and influences affecting the life, development, and, ultimately, the survival of an organism.

ENVIRONMENTAL IMPACT STATEMENT (EIS)

A statement of the effect of proposed development, and other major private or governmental actions, on the environment.

Comment: The purpose of an EIS is to provide the community with information needed to evaluate the effects of a proposed project upon the environment. The statement usually consists of an inventory of existing environmental conditions at the project site and in the surrounding area. The inventory includes air and water quality, water supply, hydrology, geology, soil type, topography, vegetation, wildlife, aquatic organisms, ecology, demography, land use, aesthetics, history, and archaeology. An EIS also includes a project description and may include a list of all licenses, permits, or other approvals required by law. The EIS assesses the probable impact of the project upon all the inventory items and includes a listing of adverse environmental impacts that cannot be avoided. The statement also includes what steps the applicant proposes to take to minimize adverse environmental impacts during construction and operation and whether there are alternatives to any part of the project.

ENVIRONMENTALLY SENSITIVE AREA

See Critical Area.

EROSION

The detachment and movement of soil or rock fragments or the wearing away of the land surface by water, wind, ice, and gravity.

ESSENTIAL SERVICES

Services and utilities needed for the health, safety, and general welfare of the community, such as underground, surface, or overhead electrical, gas, telephone, steam, water, sewerage, and other utilties and the equipment and appurtenances necessary for such systems to furnish an adequate level of service for the area in which it is located.

Comment: The definition of essential services is limited to utility-type services as opposed to other, equally important services, such as police, fire, and transportation. Essential services are either permitted or conditional uses in all zones, but some distinction is necessary for the equipment, facilities, and appurtenances associated with the service. For example, sewer lines and lift stations may be located in residential areas, but the treatment facility may not be appropriate next to dwellings. *See* PUBLIC UTILITY.

ESTABLISHMENT

An economic unit, generally at a single physical location, where business is conducted or services or industrial operations performed.

ESTUARIES

Areas where fresh water meets salt water, such as bays, mouths of rivers, salt marshes, and lagoons.

EUTROPHIC LAKES

Shallow lakes, weed-choked at the edges and very rich in nutrients.

Comment: Eutrophic lakes are characterized by large amounts of algae, low water transparency, low dissolved oxygen, and high BOD (biological oxygen demand).

EUTROPHICATION

The normally slow aging process by which a lake evolves into a bog or marsh and ultimately assumes a completely terrestrial state and disappears.

EVALUATION

A process to measure the success of an activity and how closely the results meet the anticipated outcome defined as part of the initial phase of the activity.

EVAPORATION PONDS

Shallow, artificial ponds where sewage sludge is pumped, permitted to dry, and either removed or buried by more sludge.

EVERGREEN

A plant with foliage that remains green year-round.

EXACTION

Contributions or payments required as an authorized precondition for receiving a development permit (Planning Advisory Service Report No. 322 1976).

Comment: Exactions may refer to mandatory dedications, such as for road widenings or lower income housing. In all cases, there must be some relationship between the amount of the exaction and the purpose for which it is used. Thus, an exaction fee from an office use, based on the amount of square feet, could be used for lower income housing or traffic improvements that are directly impacted by the office space.

EXCAVATION

Removal or recovery by any means whatsoever of soil, rock, minerals, mineral substances, or organic substances, other than vegetation, from water or land, on or beneath the surface thereof, or beneath the land surface, whether exposed or submerged.

EXCEPTION

Permission to depart from the design standards in the ordinance. *See* WAIVER.

Comment: The design standards are those outside the zoning ordinance or zoning chapter. Those require a variance that must be based on specific criteria such as hardship, special reasons, change of circumstances, and so forth. The exception often refers to design standards such as length of cul-de-sacs, location and type of improvements, and landscaping requirements. They are dictated by the circumstances related to the specific application that make the design requirement for which the exception is requested unnecessary or unreasonable.

As in the case of waivers, the approving agency must make findings and conclusions before granting the exception.

EXCLUSIONARY ZONING

Development regulations that result in the exclusion of low- and moderate-income and minority families from a community.

Comment: Exclusionary zoning may also serve to keep out, or limit, additional development. Exclusionary zoning provisions include allowing only large lot, single-family detached dwellings, bulk regulations in excess of that needed for health and safety, barring of multifamily development, and excessive improvement requirements that generate unnecessary costs.

EXCLUSIVE USE DISTRICT

A zoning district that allows only one use or a limited range of use types.

EXECUTIVE HEADQUARTERS

An office building occupied almost entirely by the principal office of a business or corporation.

Comment: Usually, the executive headquarters (or corporate headquarters) bears the name of the corporation and is designed to project a favorable corporate image. The buildings are often of a higher quality and cost more to build than multitenanted or speculative office buildings. Headquarters buildings have fewer employees per square foot since the executives typically have large offices and the buildings have a significant number of meeting rooms. From a planning and zoning perspective, there is no guarantee that a headquarters building will always remain so. Corporations are sold, functions change, and cost cutting requires economies. The fewer parking spaces allowed for a headquarters building may not be sufficient when the building no longer functions as originally approved.

EXISTING GRADE or ELEVATION

The vertical location above some elevation point of the ground surface prior to excavating or filling.

EXISTING USE

The use of a lot or structure at the time of the enactment of a zoning ordinance.

Comment: Some municipalities, at the time a new zoning or development ordinance is proposed, will attempt to survey existing uses in order to provide an accurate record of pre-existing nonconforming uses. The pre-existing nonconforming use, legal at the time of the passage of the ordinance but made nonconforming as a result of the ordinance, has a legal right to continue. Future problems arise because of confusion as to the extent and nature of the uses at the time of passage. Hence, an inventory is often necessary to ensure that non-conforming uses do not expand illegally.

EXIT RAMP, ENTRANCE RAMP

Access lanes leading to and from a limited access highway.

EXTENDED CARE FACILITY

A long-term facility or a distinct part of a facility licensed or approved as a nursing home, infirmary unit of a home for the aged, or a governmental medical institution. *See* Long-Term Care Facility.

EXTENDED PROPERTY LOT LINE

A line, radial or perpendicular to the street centerline, at each end of the frontage, extending from the right-of-way line to the curb line. *See Figure 36.*

EXTENSION

An increase in the amount of existing floor area beyond the exterior wall.

EXTERIOR WALL

Any wall that defines the exterior boundaries of a building or structure.

EXURBAN AREA

The fringe area between a suburbanized area and rural area, subject to development pressures with existing or planned infrastructure.

F

FABRICATION AND ASSEMBLY

The manufacturing from standardized parts of a distinct object differing from the individual components.

Comment: The term fabrication and assembly is often used to describe a general class of permitted uses. It usually involves materials with form and substance (as opposed to liquid or gas), with a physical, as opposed to chemical, mating or joining of the individual parts.

FACADE

The exterior walls of a building exposed to public view or that wall viewed by persons not within the building. *See Figure 14.*

FACILITY FOR HANDICAPPED PEOPLE

Any ramp, handrail, elevator, door, specially treated surface and similar design, convenience, or device that facilitates the health, safety, or comfort of a handicapped person.

FACTORY

A building in which raw material and semifinished or finished materials are converted to a different form or state or where goods are manufactured, assembled, treated, or processed.

FACTORY-BUILT HOUSE

See MANUFACTURED HOUSING.

FAIR MARKET VALUE

The price of a building or land that would be agreed upon voluntarily in fair negotiations between a knowledgeable owner willing, but not forced, to sell and a knowledgeable buyer willing, but not forced, to buy.

Comment: The definition describes an ideal abstract situation. In real-life situations, brokers use a variety of methods to establish the fair market value, including comparable sales, income capitalization, and replacement value.

110

FAIR SHARE PLAN
A plan or proposal—which is in a form that may readily be converted into an ordinance—by which a municipality proposes to satisfy its obligation to create a realistic opportunity to meet its fair share of the low- and moderate-income housing needs of its region and which details the affirmative measures the municipality proposes to undertake to achieve its fair share of low- and moderate-income housing.

Comment: The above definition was derived from New Jersey's Supreme Court Mt. Laurel II case—*South Burlington County NAACP v. Mt. Laurel Township*, 92 N.J. 158 (1983).

FALLOW LAND
Farmland left uncultivated.

FAMILY
A group of individuals not necessarily related by blood, marriage, adoption, or guardianship living together in a dwelling unit as a single housekeeping unit under a common housekeeping management plan based on an intentionally structured relationship providing organization and stability. *See* HOUSEHOLD.

Comment: The above definition places no limit on the number of unrelated individuals that may occupy the dwelling unit. Older definitions frequently defined family as "one or more persons related by blood, marriage, adoption, or guardianship or not more than three persons not so related."

The deletion of relationship requirements and limits on the numbers of unrelated individuals reflect the decisions by various state courts. In New Jersey, for example, in *State* v. *Baker*—81 N.J. 99, 108–109 (1979)—decided July 30, 1979, the Supreme Court invalidated a local ordinance that established a limit on the number of unrelated individuals. It suggested that by limiting unrelated individuals it prohibited many reasonable occupancies, such as unrelated widows, bachelors, or "even judges." The decision suggested that the municipality could regulate density by relating the number of occupants to the number of bedrooms, bathrooms, or a minimum number of square feet per occupant. It also suggested that traffic could be restricted by limiting the number of vehicles.

The key words in the definition are "single housekeeping unit," which is defined as common use and access to all living and eating areas, bathrooms, and food

111

preparation and serving areas. In addition to the single housekeeping unit, a family also represents an intentionally structured relationship and implies a permanent and long-term relationship as opposed to one that is short-term or transient.

FARM or FARMLAND

A parcel of land used for agricultural activities.

Comment: Many states have minimum acreage and/or agricultural income requirements for reduced tax assessment as an agricultural use. In New Jersey, the minimum requirement to qualify for a reduced tax assessment is five acres and gross revenues of $500 per year.

FARM STAND

A structure for the display and sale of farm products.

Comment: Very often, municipalities impose the additional restriction that the farm products sold at the stand must be raised on the farm or the land upon which the stand is located. In actual practice, this has proved to be impractical. A better approach is to place restrictions on: (1) where stands are permitted; (2) size of the stand; (3) size of the lot; (4) setback from the road; and (5) parking.

FARM STRUCTURE

Any building or structure used for agricultural purposes.

FAST-FOOD RESTAURANT

An establishment whose principal business is the sale of preprepared or rapidly prepared food directly to the customer in a ready-to-consume state for consumption either within the restaurant building, in cars on the premises, or off the premises.

Comment: The distinction between the fast-food restaurant and other types of restaurants is rapidly becoming blurred. The major objections to fast-food restaurants came from circulation concerns and the potential adverse impacts of high traffic generation, glare, garish design, litter, and noise. Often they became hangouts. With stringent performance standards, these problems can be controlled, and there appears to be little reason to differentiate between fast-food restaurants and other types of restaurants.

However, the "take-out" place is a distinctive use. Usually orders are called in and then picked up. Parking requirements are not as severe as eat-in restaurants. *See* RESTAURANT, DRIVE-IN; RESTAURANT, TAKE-OUT.

FEASIBILITY STUDY

An analysis of a specific project or program to determine if it can be successfully carried out.

Comment: Feasibility studies can cover a wide range of subjects. The most common is the financial feasibility study to determine whether the project will turn a profit. Other feasibility studies may cover law and various elements of planning, such as traffic, environment, building size, and so forth. The feasibility study relates capacity to demand but may also cover political and social benefits and costs. Banks may require feasibility studies to determine the estimated rate of return on investment. *See* COST-BENEFIT ANALYSIS; MARKETABILITY STUDY.

FEE SIMPLE ABSOLUTE

The most complete set of private property land rights, including mineral rights below the surface, surface rights, and air rights. *See* EASEMENT.

FEEDLOT

A confined area or structure, pen, or corral, used to fatten livestock prior to final shipment.

FENCE

An artificially constructed barrier of any material or combination of materials erected to enclose, screen, or separate areas.

Comment: Development regulations should include provisions for fences. Generally, they should be divided into categories of open, semiopen, and closed fences, and regulations should establish maximum heights and setbacks for the different categories. For example, an open fence, such as a split rail fence, might be permitted anywhere on a particular lot. Closed fences, such as brick, might be restricted to a maximum height of six feet and be required to meet all setback requirements for principal structures in the zone.

FENESTRATION

Window treatment in a building or building facade.

FESTIVAL MARKETPLACE

An anchorless retail center with a mix of small specialty shops offering one-of-a-kind merchandise, with an emphasis on gifts and crafts supplied locally and food offerings, often located in a unique architectural setting (Sawicki, 1989).

113

Comment: Sawicki notes that these shops are not primary retail centers but more like entertainment centers anchored by restaurants. Underground Atlanta is often cited as a prime example of a festival marketplace.

FILL

Sand, gravel, earth, or other materials of any composition whatsoever placed or deposited by humans. *See Figure 37.*

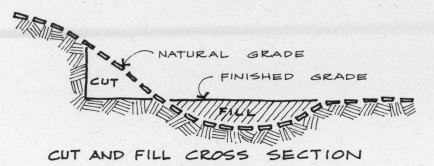

CUT AND FILL CROSS SECTION

Figure 37

FILLING

The process of depositing fill in low-lying marshy or water areas to create usable land. *See* LAND RECLAMATION; MADE LAND.

FILLING STATION

See AUTOMOBILE SERVICE STATION.

FILTRATION

In wastewater treatment, the mechanical process that removes particulate matter from water, usually by passing it through sand.

FINAL APPROVAL

The last official action of the approving agency taken on a development plan that has been given preliminary approval, after all conditions and requirements of preliminary approval have been met and the required improvements have either been installed or guarantees properly posted for their installation, or approval conditioned upon the posting of such guarantees.

Comment: Final approval permits the applicant to sell lots and build houses or buildings.

FINAL PLAN

See PLAT, FINAL.

FINANCE, INSURANCE, AND REAL ESTATE (FIRE)

Establishments such as banks and savings and loans, credit agencies, investment companies, brokers and dealers of securities and commodities, security and commodity exchanges, insurance agents, lessors, lessees, buyers, sellers, agents, and developers of real estate.

Comment: Often referred to as FIRE in use groupings.

FINGER FILL CANALS

Waterfront residential developments created by the dredging and filling of shallow bays and estuaries, built on fingerlike projections of land interspersed with deep, narrow canals.

FINISHED ELEVATION

The proposed elevation of the land surface of a site after completion of all site preparation work. *See* GRADE, FINISHED.

FINISHED PRODUCT

The end result of a manufacturing process that is ready for utilization or consumption by the ultimate consumer.

Comment: The above definition, from the *Standard Industrial Classification Manual* (1987), should be read in conjunction with the definition and comments of ''semi-finished product'' in this volume.

FIRE LANE

An unobstructed paved or improved surface area clearly defined by pavement markings and signs, at least twelve feet wide and designed to provide access for fire-fighting equipment.

Comment: Fire lanes are recommended for shopping centers and larger office buildings to assure access to the building for fire-fighting equipment. The lanes should not be used for parking but may be part of the overall circulation system.

FIRE ZONE

An area clearly delineated and marked to facilitate access to hydrants and buildings and as designated by the chief of the fire district in which the building, structure, or use is situated.

FISCAL IMPACT ANALYSIS (FIA)

An analysis of the costs and revenues associated with a specific development application.

Comment: FIAs are also known as cost-revenue analyses. They can be simple or sophisticated, depending in part on whether secondary and tertiary impacts are considered.

115

FISH FARM

An area devoted to the cultivation of fish and other seafood for commercial sale. Also known as aquaculture.

FISHING, HUNTING, TRAPPING

Establishments primarily engaged in commercial fishing, including shellfish marine products, operating fish hatcheries, and fish and game preserves, and the killing of animals by gunning or the capture in mechanical or other types of devices for commercial gain.

FLAG LOT

See LOT, FLAG.

FLEA MARKET

An occasional or periodic market held in an open area or structure where groups of individual sellers offer goods for sale to the public.

Comment: Flea markets often are regularly scheduled—such as on weekends and holidays—and while most are held outdoors or under sheds, a recent trend is to utilize large, previously vacant buildings, such as discount stores or vacant shopping centers. What differentiates flea markets from other retail stores or shopping centers is that there are no long-term leases between the sellers and owners or lessors of the site and that often the sellers use their own vehicles for display or set up temporary tables for their wares. While some flea markets are temporary in nature and are established on lands or in buildings not customarily used for such a purpose, others are more or less permanent. These long-term flea markets should be subject to site plan review to ensure appropriate circulation, safety, and off-street parking, lighting, landscaping, signage, and trash storage.

FLEXTIME

The right of an employee to determine his or her starting and finishing times.

Comment: Flextime is used to spread peak hour loads and may be required as part of traffic management systems. Employers usually determine a range of starting and finishing times, such as 6:30 A.M. to 9:30 A.M., and core hours when all employees have to be on the premises.

FLOATING ZONE

An unmapped zoning district where all the zone requirements are contained in the ordinance and the zone is fixed on the map only when an application for development, meeting the zone requirements, is approved.

Comment: Floating zones (or overlay zones) generally have declined in popularity because of charges they

116

closely resemble spot zoning and contract zoning, both illegal under current case law. The most appropriate application appears to be in rural communities where large tracts of land may be developed in accordance with planned development regulations providing the ordinance requirements are met for conversion of the land from the previous rural designation to a development zone. Some of these ordinance regulations might include direct access to major roads, availability of public water and public sewer, and proximity to other municipal facilities and services.

In recent years, floating zones have also been used to provide lower income housing in built-up municipalities. Such floating zones typically require that when previously unavailable land is proposed to be developed (such as a farm, surplus municipal land, or redevelopment areas) above a minimum area (for example, two acres) and at a higher density, then a percentage of the units must be reserved for low- and moderate-income households. An alternative to floating zones is to make the planned development or lower income housing conditional uses in those zones deemed appropriate.

FLOCCULATION

In wastewater treatment, the process of separating suspended solids by chemical creation of clumps or floes.

FLOOD

The temporary overflowing of water onto land that is usually devoid of surface water.

FLOOD, BASE FLOOD ELEVATION

See Base Flood Elevation.

FLOOD, REGULATORY BASE

Flood having a 1 percent chance of being equaled or exceeded in any given year.

Comment: This is often referred to as a one hundred-year flood.

FLOOD, REGULATORY BASE DISCHARGE

The rate of flow produced by the regulatory base flood measured in cubic feet per second (CFS).

FLOOD DAMAGE POTENTIAL

The susceptibility of a specific land use at a particular location to damage by flooding and the potential of the specific land use to increase off-site flooding or flood-related damages.

117

FLOOD FRINGE AREA   That portion of the flood hazard area outside of the floodway based on the total area inundated during the regulatory base flood plus 25 percent of the regulatory base flood discharge. *See* FLOOD; FLOODWAY; REGULATORY BASE FLOOD; REGULATORY BASE FLOOD DISCHARGE. *See Figure 38.*

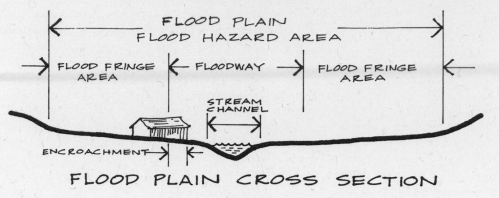

FLOOD PLAIN CROSS SECTION

Figure 38

FLOOD HAZARD AREA   The flood plain consisting of the floodway and the flood fringe area. *See* FLOOD PLAIN. *See Figure 38.*

FLOOD HAZARD DESIGN ELEVATION   The highest elevation, expressed in feet above sea level, of the level of floodwaters that delineates the flood fringe area.

FLOOD INSURANCE RATE MAP   The official map on which the Federal Insurance Administration has delineated both the areas of special flood hazards and the risk premium zones applicable to the community.

FLOOD OF RECORD   A flood that has occurred for which there are accurate local records available and that is used as the reference flood.

FLOOD PLAIN   The channel and the relatively flat area adjoining the channel of a natural stream or river that has been or may be covered by floodwater. *See Figure 38.*

FLOODPROOFING   A combination of structural provisions and changes or adjustments to properties and structures subject to flooding for the reduction or elimination of flood damage to properties, water and sanitary facilities, and other utilities, structures, and the contents of buildings.

118

FLOODWAY

The channel of a natural stream or river and portions of the flood plain adjoining the channel, which are reasonably required to carry and discharge the floodwater or flood flow of any natural stream or river. *See* FLOODWAY, REGULATORY. *See Figure 38.*

FLOODWAY, REGULATORY

The channel and the adjacent land areas that must be reserved in order to discharge the regulatory base flood without cumulatively increasing the water surface elevation more than two-tenths of one foot.

FLOOR AREA, GROSS

The sum of the gross horizontal areas of the several floors of a building or structure from the exterior face of exterior walls, or from the centerline of a wall separating two buildings, but excluding any space where the floor-to-ceiling height is less than six feet.

Comment: The above definition is all-inclusive; since it includes structures, the floor area measurement would include parking structures. If the parking structures are proposed to be excluded, then the word "structure" should be dropped.

FLOOR AREA, NET

The total of all floor areas of a building, excluding stairwells and elevator shafts, equipment rooms, interior vehicular parking or loading; and all floors below the first or ground floor, except when used or intended to be used for human habitation or service to the public.

Comment: Very often, for ease of administration, net floor area is expressed as gross floor area minus a certain percentage. Empirically, stairwells, elevator shafts, equipment rooms, and utility rooms generally average out to about 15 percent of the gross floor area. Thus, net floor area may be defined as gross floor area minus 15 percent.

FLOOR AREA RATIO (FAR)

The gross floor area of all buildings or structures on a lot divided by the total lot area. *See Figure 39.*

Comment: Some care should be exercised in applying this definition. It includes all buildings and structures and the *entire* lot area. A recent unreported court case in New Jersey set aside a FAR definition that excluded "environmentally sensitive" land from the ordinance definition of FAR. The judge said that the state enabling act defined FAR as the *total* area of the site. The judge further noted that if the site had extensive environmentally constrained areas, the FAR should be adjusted accordingly.

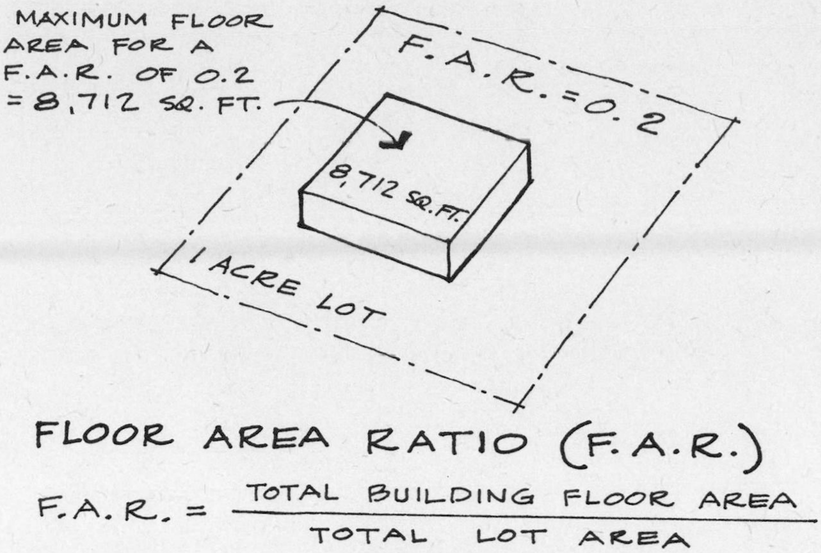

MAXIMUM FLOOR
AREA FOR A
F.A.R. OF 0.2
= 8,712 SQ. FT.

F.A.R. = 0.2

8,712 SQ. FT.

1 ACRE LOT

FLOOR AREA RATIO (F.A.R.)

$$F.A.R. = \frac{TOTAL\ BUILDING\ FLOOR\ AREA}{TOTAL\ LOT\ AREA}$$

Figure 39

FLORICULTURE	The cultivation of ornamental flowering plants.
FLOWMETER	In wastewater treatment, a meter that indicates the rate at which wastewater flows.
FLUE GAS	A mixture of gases resulting from combustion that emerges from a chimney.
FLUME	A constructed channel that carries water.
FLY ASH	All partially incinerated solids that are carried in a gas stream.
FLY-IN DEVELOPMENT	A residential development planned and integrated with airport facilities and directly accessible to recreational flyers.
FOOD PROCESSING ESTABLISHMENT	An establishment in which food is processed or otherwise prepared for eventual human consumption but not consumed on the premises.

120

Comment: A food processing establishment covers a wide range of businesses, all involved with food. It may be a caterer or a flour mill. The zoning implications are based on impacts and size of the establishment.

FOOTCANDLE   The unit of illumination when the foot is the unit of length. *See Figure 40.*

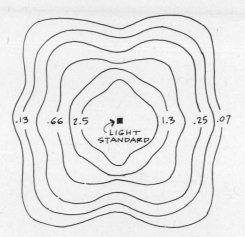

.13   .66   2.5   LIGHT STANDARD   1.3   .25   .07

250-WATT/HIGH-PRESSURE SODIUM
20-FOOT MOUNTING HEIGHT

TYPICAL LIGHTING PATTERN
(SHOWN IN FOOTCANDLES)

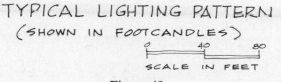

0   40   80
SCALE IN FEET

Figure 40

Comment: Zoning ordinances usually establish a minimum footcandle level required for different areas. These are shown in subdivision or site plans as isofootcandle diagrams, where all the points on the line represent the same level of illumination. The diagrams are often drawn around light standards to show the level and extent of lighting on the site.

Recommended levels of illumination for various activities are contained in the Illuminating Engineering Society of North America's *IES Lighting Handbook* (1987). Typical levels, as reprinted in Listokin and Walker (1989), are as follows:

Illumination Guidelines for Street, Parking, and Pedestrian Areas

A. Street Illumination

Area Classification

Street Hierarchy	Commercial Footcandles	Intermediate Footcandles	Residential Footcandles
"Major"	1.2	0.9	0.6
"Collector"	0.8	0.6	0.4
"Local"	0.6	0.5	0.3

B. Parking Illumination (Open Parking Facilities)

Illumination Objective

Level of Activity	Vehicular Use Area Only Footcandles	General Parking and Pedestrian Safety Footcandles
Low activity	0.5	0.2
Medium activity	1.0	0.6
High activity	2.0	0.9

C. Pedestrian Way Illumination

Walkway and Bikeway Classification	Minimum Average Horizontal Levels Footcandles	Average Levels for Special Pedestrian Security Footcandles
Sidewalks (roadside) and Type A bikeways		
Commercial areas	1.0	0.2
Intermediate areas	0.6	0.1
Residential areas	0.6	0.5
Walkways distant from roadways and Type B bikeways		
Walkways, bikeways, and stairways	0.5	0.5
Pedestrian tunnels	4.3	5.4

Type A bikeways are on-street areas reserved for bikes. Type B bikeways are separate designated bikeways.

Source: David Listokin and Carole Walker, *The Subdivision and Site Plan Handbook* (New Brunswick, NJ: Center for Urban Policy Research, Rutgers University, 1989.)

FOREST

Areas or stands of trees the majority of which are greater than twelve inches caliper, covering an area greater than one-quarter acre; or groves of mature trees without regard to minimum area consisting of substantial numbers of individual specimens.

Comment: The twelve-inch requirement does not apply to certain species, such as birches and dogwoods, and trees found in pinelands. The minimum caliper should represent a mature tree. "Substantial numbers" is difficult to define. It represents more of a visual impression as opposed to a specific number.

FORESTRY

Establishments primarily engaged in the operation of timber tracts, tree farms, forest nurseries, the gathering of forest products, or in performing forest services.

FOSSIL FUELS

Coals, oil, and animals gas; so called because they are derived from the remains of ancient plant and animal life.

FRANCHISE

The right or authority to provide specified goods or services to a defined geographic area.

Comment: The most common use of franchise in planning is with respect to utility franchises. Exclusive franchises are often granted to utility companies to provide service to a geographic area.

FRATERNAL ORGANIZATION

A group of people formally organized for a common interest, usually cultural, religious, or entertainment, with regular meetings, rituals, and formal written membership requirements.

Comment: Examples of such groups are Masons or the Knights of Columbus. The clubhouses for fraternal organizations usually were located in residential neighborhoods, but newer ordinances have properly located them in business areas or classify them as conditional uses with carefully drawn requirements for parking, buffering, lighting, and solid waste disposal because they usually draw their membership from a wide geographic area. In addition, the club facilities often are used for weddings, bingo, and weekend catering and can become nuisances to surrounding residences. *See* CLUB; MEMBERSHIP ORGANIZATION.

FRATERNITY HOUSE

A building containing sleeping rooms, bathrooms, common rooms, and a central kitchen and dining room maintained exclusively for fraternity members and their guests or visitors and affiliated with an institution of higher learning.

Comment: A fraternity house is a distinct and separate use. It is not a dwelling unit or multifamily structure. The members do not constitute a family in the zoning sense since they do not function as a single household unit.

FREEWAY

See STREET, FREEWAY.

FREIGHT FORWARDING

Establishments primarily engaged in the transshipment of goods from shippers to receivers for a charge, covering the entire transportation route and, in turn, making use of the services of other transportation establishments as instrumentalities in effecting delivery.

FREIGHT HANDLING FACILITIES

Terminals with the capability of handling a large variety of goods involving various forms of transportation and providing multimodal shipping capabilities, such as rail to truck and truck to air.

Comment: Freight handling facilities are terminals that have a variety of equipment and storage facilities and space to handle shipboard, truck, rail, and air freight containers and often liquid and raw agricultural products. They differ from warehouses in that they do not usually store the freight for any period of time, although they may have warehouses associated with them (Schultz and Kasen 1984).

FRESH WATER WETLAND

See WETLANDS, FRESHWATER.

FRINGE AREA

The area of transition between two different dominant land uses or other recognizable characteristics, including social, economic, or cultural (Schultz and Kasen 1984).

FRONT FOOT

A measure of land width, being one foot along the front lot line of a property.

Comment: Front foot measurements are usually used in assessment formulas.

FRONT LOT LINE

See LOT LINE, FRONT.

FRONT YARD

See YARD, FRONT.

124

FRONTAGE

That side of a lot abutting on a street; the front lot line. *See Figure 11.*

Comment: On corner or through lots, the frontage may be designated by the owner but it should be consistent with the orientation of the other lots and improvements on the same side of the street. On improved lots, the frontage is usually the side where the main building entrance is located and in the general direction in which the principal building faces.

FRONTAGE ROAD

A service road, usually parallel to a highway, designed to reduce the number of driveways that intersect the highway.

FUNERAL HOME

A building used for the preparation of the deceased for burial and the display of the deceased and rituals connected therewith before burial or cremation.

Comment: Funeral homes are generally very stable types of uses and are extremely well maintained. The only potential problem is the necessity for adequate off-street parking and stacking room for cars lined up for the funeral procession.

G

GAME or GAMBLING GAME

Any banking or percentage game played with cards, dice, or any mechanical device or machine for money, property, or any representative of value and located exclusively within a casino.

GAMING or GAMBLING

The dealing, operating, carrying on, conducting, maintaining, or exposing for pay of any game.

GAMING or GAMBLING ESTABLISHMENT

Any premises wherein or whereon gaming is done.

GAMING DEVICE or GAMING EQUIPMENT

Any mechanical contrivance or machine used in connection with gaming or any game.

GARAGE

A deck, building, or parking structure, or part thereof, used or intended to be used for the parking and storage of vehicles.

Comment: A distinction should be made between parking, short and long term, and storage, such as found associated with auto sales and unregistered vehicles.

GARAGE, COMMUNITY

A garage used exclusively for the parking and storage of vehicles owned or operated by residents of nearby dwelling units and their guests, which is not operated as a commercial enterprise and is not available to the general public and which is owned, leased, or cooperatively operated by such residents.

GARAGE, MUNICIPAL

A structure owned or operated by a municipality and used primarily for the parking and storing of vehicles owned by the general public.

GARAGE, PRIVATE CUSTOMER AND EMPLOYEE

A structure that is accessory to a nonretail commercial or manufacturing establishment, building, or use and is primarily for the parking and storage of vehicles operated by the customers, visitors, and employees of such building and that is not available to the general public.

GARAGE, PRIVATE RESIDENTIAL

A structure that is accessory to a residential building and that is used for the parking and storage of vehicles owned and operated by the residents thereof and that is not a separate commercial enterprise available to the general public.

GARAGE, PUBLIC

A structure, or portion thereof, other than a private customer and employee garage or private residential garage, used primarily for the parking and storage of vehicles and available to the general public.

GARAGE, REPAIR

Any building, premises, and land in which or upon which a business, service, or industry involving the maintenance, servicing, repair, or painting of vehicles is conducted or rendered. *See* AUTOMOTIVE REPAIR SERVICES AND GARAGES.

GARBAGE

Animal and vegetable waste resulting from the handling, storage, sale, preparation, cooking, and serving of foods. *See* SOLID WASTE.

GARDEN APARTMENT

See DWELLING, GARDEN APARTMENT.

GASOLINE STATION

See AUTOMOBILE SERVICE STATION.

126

GAUSS

A measure of magnetic flux density.

GENERAL DEVELOPMENT PLAN (GDP)

A plan showing general land use, circulation, open space, utilities, stormwater management, environmental factors, community facilities, housing, impacts, and phasing for parcels of land in excess of one hundred acres and proposed to be constructed as a planned development.

Comment: The GDP is a concept plan that vests for up to twenty years the right of the applicant to submit various phases for preliminary and final site plan approval. Both the vesting period and minimum acreage are usually set by local ordinances in accordance with state enabling legislation.

The GDP differs from concept plans in that the latter provides no vesting. Most GDP legislation calls for sufficient detail to allow the approving agency to determine that the plan as submitted will work. The long vesting period is needed because of the high investment in improvements. The applicant requires assurances that the zoning will not be rescinded before the project is completed.

GENERAL PUBLIC

Any and all individuals without any prior qualifications.

Comment: Facilities open to the general public may charge fees for admission or payment for services.

GLARE

The effect produced by brightness sufficient to cause annoyance, discomfort, or loss in visual performance and visibility.

Comment: The definition is subjective but can be applied in a given situation by establishing a reference line (usually the lot or zone line) and maximum footcandle reading.

GOLF COURSE

A tract of land laid out for at least nine holes for playing the game of golf and improved with tees, greens, fairways, and hazards and that may include a clubhouse and shelter. *See* COUNTRY CLUB.

GOVERNMENT AGENCY

Any department, commission, independent agency, or instrumentality of the United States, of a state, county, incorporated or unincorporated municipality, township, authority, district, or other governmental unit.

127

GRADE

(1) The average elevation of the land around a building; (2) the percent of rise or descent of a sloping surface. *See Figures 37 and 41.*

Comment: Grade is usually described as finished or natural and measured in feet above sea level. There is a distinction between percent of slope and degree of slope. For example, a forty-five-degree slope is a 100 percent grade.

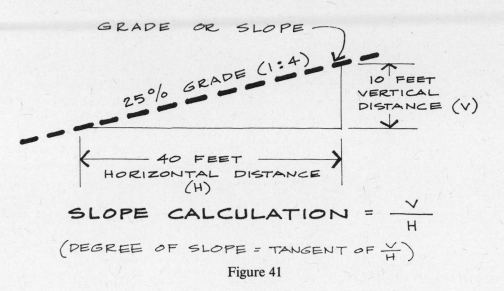

GRADE OR SLOPE

25% GRADE (1:4)

10 FEET VERTICAL DISTANCE (V)

40 FEET HORIZONTAL DISTANCE (H)

$$\text{SLOPE CALCULATION} = \frac{V}{H}$$

$$\left(\text{DEGREE OF SLOPE} = \text{TANGENT OF } \frac{V}{H}\right)$$

Figure 41

GRADE, FINISHED

The final elevation of the ground level after development. *See* FINISHED ELEVATION. *See Figure 37.*

GRADE, NATURAL

The elevation of the ground level in its natural state, before construction, filling, or excavation. *See* NATURAL GROUND SURFACE. *See Figure 37.*

GRADE LEVEL

Roads, buildings, or structures built on the ground.

Comment: Grade level (or at grade) differs from below grade or above grade. All use the existing grade, whether finished or natural, as the reference.

GRADE REQUIREMENTS

Engineering standards establishing minimum and maximum slopes, geometry of roads, such as radii, and horizontal and vertical curves, among others.

128

GRADING

Any stripping, cutting, filling, or stockpiling of earth or land, including the land in its cut or filled condition, to create new grades.

GRANT

(1) An instrument that conveys some estate or interest in the lands that it embraces; (2) financial aid.

GRAPHIC SCALE

See SCALE.

GRAVEL PIT

An open land area where sand, gravel, and rock fragment are mined or excavated for sale or off-tract use.

Comment: Gravel pits usually include sifting, crushing, and washing as part of the primary operation. To excavate the rock, blasting also may be necessary. Any ordinance that permits gravel pits should require a soil erosion plan and reuse or reclamation plan for the land as a condition of approval. *See* QUARRY; SAND PIT.

GREASE TRAP

A device in which the grease present in sewage is intercepted and congealed by cooling and from which it may be skimmed of liquid wastes for disposal.

GREEN AREA

Land shown on a development plan, master plan, or official map for conservation, preservation, recreation, landscaping, or park.

GREENBELT

An open area that may be cultivated or maintained in a natural state surrounding development or used as a buffer between land uses or to mark the edge of an urban or developed area.

GREENHOUSE

A building whose roof and sides are made largely of glass or other transparent or translucent material and in which the temperature and humidity can be regulated for the cultivation of delicate or out-of-season plants for subsequent sale or for personal enjoyment. *See* NURSERY.

GREENWAY

(1) A linear open space established along either a natural corridor, such as a riverfront, stream valley, or ridge line, or over land along a railroad right-of-way converted to recreational use, a canal, a scenic road, or other route; (2) any natural or landscaped course for pedestrian or bicycle passage; (3) an open space connector linking parks, natural reserves, cultural features, or historic sites with each other and with populated areas; and (4) locally,

certain strip or linear parks designated as a parkway or greenbelt (Little 1990).

GRID SYSTEM

A map coordinate system that allows the identification of a land area by two coordinate numbers. *See Figure 42.*

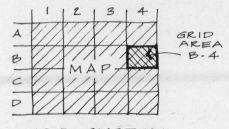

GRID SYSTEM

Figure 42

GRIDIRON PATTERN

A street and block system resulting in formal, regular rectangular blocks and resulting four-way intersections.

Comment: The gridiron pattern, characteristic of older city neighborhoods, fell into disuse because of its insensitivity to topography, excessive areas required for streets, and inflexible platting. In recent years "neotraditional" advocates are suggesting that the gridiron system deserves reexamination because of its pedestrian orientation and scale, ease of access, multipathway opportunities, and mixed-use potential.

GROSS FLOOR AREA

See FLOOR AREA, GROSS and NET.

GROSS HABITABLE FLOOR AREA

See FLOOR AREA, NET.

GROSS LEASABLE AREA (GLA)

The total floor area for which the tenant pays rent and that is designed for the tenant's occupancy and exclusive use.

Comment: GLA does not include public or common areas, such as utility rooms, stairwells, malls, and so on.

GROUND COVER

Grasses or other plants and landscaping grown to keep soil from being blown or washed away.

GROUND COVERAGE

See LOT COVERAGE.

130

GROUND FLOOR The first floor of a building other than a cellar or basement.

GROUNDWATER The supply of freshwater under the surface in an aquifer or geologic formation that forms the natural reservoir for potable water. *See Figure 4*.

GROUNDWATER RUNOFF Groundwater that is discharged into a stream channel as spring or seepage water.

GROUP CARE FACILITY *See* BOARDING HOME FOR SHELTERED CARE.

GROUP HOMES See GROUP RESIDENCES.

GROUP LIVING QUARTERS *See* GROUP RESIDENCES.

GROUP RESIDENCES *See* BOARDING HOME FOR SHELTERED CARE; BOARDING HOUSE; DORMITORY; FRATERNITY HOUSE.

GROWTH MANAGEMENT Techniques used by the government to control the rate, amount, location, timing, and type of development.

GUARANTEES Cash, letters of credit, bonds, or similar financial instruments deposited with the municipality to assure that required improvements will be constructed or installed. *See* PERFORMANCE GUARANTEE.

Comment: Guarantees are required before a development application receives final approval or before a governmental agency accepts an improvement. They are designed to assure that all streets, sidewalks, utility lines, street lighting, and similar improvements are completed and in place before certificates of occupancy are issued. Guarantees protect the municipality against a developer who may go bankrupt or is unable to complete the improvements for any reason. Performance guarantees assure that the improvement will function for a period of time (usually eighteen months to two years). If not, the developer is responsible for correcting the problem. *See* MAINTENANCE GUARANTEE; PERFORMANCE GUARANTEE.

GUIDE RAIL A safety barrier designed to protect motor vehicles from hazardous areas. *See Figure 43*.

131

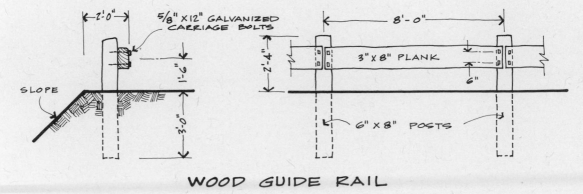

WOOD GUIDE RAIL

Figure 43

H

HABITABLE FLOOR AREA	The total floor area of all the habitable rooms in a dwelling unit.
HABITABLE ROOM	Any room in a dwelling unit other than a kitchen, bathroom, closet, pantry, hallway, cellar, storage space, garage, and basement recreation room.
HABITAT	The sum total of all the environmental factors of a specific place that is occupied by an organism, population, or a community.
HAIRPIN MARKING	A double-painted line separating parking stalls. *See Figure 44.*
HALF STORY	See STORY, HALF.
HALFWAY HOUSE	*See* BOARDING HOME FOR SHELTERED CARE.
HAMLET	A small settlement or village.
HAMMERMILL	A broad category of high-speed equipment that uses pivoted or fixed hammers or cutters to crush, grind, chip, or shred solid wastes.
HANDICAPPED PERSON	A person or persons who may be classified as having a physical impairment that manifests itself in one or more of the following ways: nonambulatory; semiambulatory;

132

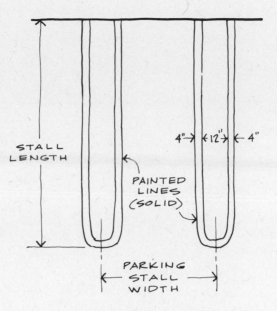

STALL LENGTH

PAINTED LINES (SOLID)

4" ← →| 12" |← → 4"

PARKING STALL WIDTH

HAIRPIN MARKING

Figure 44

visually impaired; deaf or hard-of-hearing; having faulty coordination; and having reduced mobility, flexibility, coordination, or perceptiveness due to age or physical or mental conditions. *See* AMERICANS WITH DISABILITIES ACT.

HARDSHIP VARIANCE

See VARIANCE, HARDSHIP.

HARMONIOUS RELATIONSHIP

The design, arrangement, and location of buildings or other created or natural elements of the urban environment that are sufficiently consistent in scale, character, and siting with other buildings or created or natural elements in the area, so as to avoid abrupt or severe differences.

Comment: The objective of a harmonious relationship is appropriate as part of the total quality of life. It applies equally to residential and nonresidential areas.

HAZARDOUS AIR POLLUTANT

A pollutant for which no ambient air quality standard is applicable and that may cause or contribute to an increase in mortality or serious illness.

133

Comment: Examples of hazardous air pollutants are asbestos, beryllium, and mercury.

HAZARDOUS SUBSTANCE

Any substance or material that, by reason of its toxic, caustic, corrosive, abrasive, or otherwise injurious properties, may be detrimental or deleterious to the health of any person handling or otherwise coming into contact with such material or substance.

Comment: The U.S. Environmental Protection Agency (EPA) has developed a list of hazardous wastes based upon corrosivity, reactivity, and toxicity. Hazardous substances include, but are not limited to, inorganic mineral acids of sulfur, fluorine, chlorine, nitrogen, chromium, phosphorous, selenium and arsenic and their common salts, lead, nickel, and mercury and their inorganic salts, or metallo-organic derivatives; coal, tar acids, such as phenol and cresols and their salts, and all radioactive materials.

HAZARDOUS SUBSTANCE DISPOSAL

A method for the safe disposal of hazardous substances.

HAZARDOUS USE

A building or structure or any portion thereof that is used for the storage, manufacture, or processing of highly combustible or explosive products or materials, which are likely to burn with extreme rapidity or which may produce poisonous fumes or explosions; for storage or manufacturing that involves highly corrosive, toxic, or noxious alkalies, acids, or other liquids or chemicals producing flame, fume, poisonous, irritant, or corrosive gases; and for the storage or processing of any materials producing explosive mixtures of dust or that result in the division of matter into fine particles subject to spontaneous ignition.

HEALTH CARE FACILITY

A facility or institution, whether public or private, principally engaged in providing services for health maintenance and the treatment of mental or physical conditions. *See* HEALTH SERVICES.

Comment: Health care facilities include general or special hospitals, public health centers, diagnostic centers, treatment centers, rehabilitation centers, extended care facilities, long-term care facilities, residential health care facilities, outpatient clinics, and dispensaries. They may include laundries, cafeterias, gift shops, laboratories, and medical offices as accessory uses.

134

HEALTH CLUB

An establishment that provides facilities for aerobic exercises, running and jogging, exercise equipment, game courts, swimming facilities, and saunas, showers, massage rooms, and lockers.

Comment: Health clubs may also include pro shops selling a variety of sports equipment and clothing. Instruction programs, aerobic classes, and weight control programs may be part of the club. They are usually open only to members and guests on a membership basis and not to the public at large paying a daily admission fee.

HEALTH PLANNING

The study of the provision, distribution, and financing of health facilities and services for present and probable future populations.

HEALTH SERVICES

Health care facilities as well as establishments providing support to the medical profession and patients, such as medical and dental laboratories, blood banks, oxygen, and miscellaneous types of medical supplies and services.

HEAT ISLAND EFFECT

An air circulation problem peculiar to urban areas whereby heat from buildings, structures, pavements, and concentrations of pollutants create a haze dome that prevents rising hot air from being cooled at its normal rate.

HEAVY INDUSTRY

See INDUSTRY, HEAVY.

HEIGHT

The vertical distance of a structure measured from the average elevation of the finished grade surrounding the structure to the highest point of the structure. *See* BUILDING HEIGHT. *See Figure 12.*

HELIPORT

An area, either at ground level or elevated on a structure, licensed by the federal government or an appropriate state agency and approved for the loading, landing, and takeoff of helicopters and including auxiliary facilities, such as parking, waiting room, fueling, and maintenance equipment.

HELISTOP

A heliport but without auxiliary facilities, such as parking, waiting room, fueling, and maintenance equipment.

Comment: Helistops are often constructed by major office and industrial uses and can be considered as acces-

135

sory to the principal use. Many municipalities ban them because of concerns relating to nuisance and safety. From a planning point of view, controls relating to hours of operation and the number of daily flights may be reasonable. A single helistop in an office park or industrial park may be a more viable alternative than one for each building.

HERTZ (Hz)

A unit that measures frequency in all physical systems that have a wave pattern.

HIGH-RISE

See DWELLING, HIGH-RISE.

HIGH-SPEED RURAL ROADWAY

The access classification for roadways in rural environments where the posted speed limit is fifty miles per hour (mph) or greater.

HIGH-SPEED URBAN ROADWAY

The access classification for roadways in urban environments where the posted speed limit is forty-five mph or greater.

Comment: Both the "high-speed rural" and "high-speed urban" classifications are part of highway access codes that establish standards for driveway access to roads.

HIGHEST AND BEST USE

An appraisal concept that determines the use of a particular property likely to produce the greatest net return in the foreseeable future.

Comment: The term highest and best use has little validity in planning or zoning studies. Its major application is as a comparison between several uses to determine which is more profitable.

HIGHWAY

See STREET.

HIGHWAY CAPACITY

See CAPACITY, ROADWAY.

HISTORIC AREA

A district or zone designated by a local authority or state or federal government within which the buildings, structures, appurtenances, and places are of basic and vital importance because of their association with history; or because of their unique architectural style and scale, including color, proportion, form, and architectural detail; or because of their being a part of or related to a square, park, or area the design or general arrangement

136

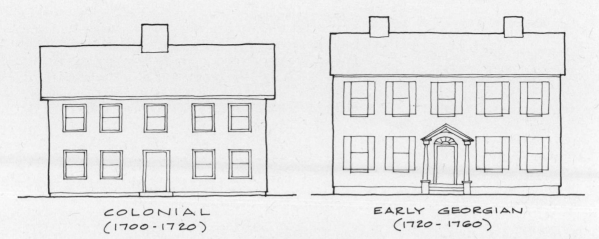

COLONIAL
(1700-1720)

EARLY GEORGIAN
(1720-1760)

Figure 45

of which should be preserved and/or developed according to a fixed plan based on cultural, historical, or architectural motives or purposes.

Comment: Historic districts or zones usually require local agency design review and approval for any exterior building changes or new construction. They generally function as overlay zones, encompassing several use districts. Some historic districts may include buildings or structures that have no special historic or architectural significance but, because of their location, require design review to assure that any exterior changes will not be detrimental to the purposes of the historic district. The

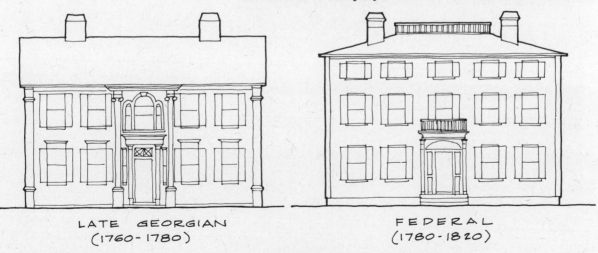

LATE GEORGIAN
(1760-1780)

FEDERAL
(1780-1820)

Figure 46

137

GREEK REVIVAL
(1820 - 1840)

VICTORIAN
(1830 - 1850)

Figure 47

delineation of historic districts or zones should be supported by appropriate studies and the local master plan.

HISTORIC BUILDING

Any building or structure that is historically or architecturally significant.

HISTORIC BUILDING STYLES

Recognized architectural styles, such as Colonial, Georgian, Federal, Greek Revival, Victorian, Gothic Revival,

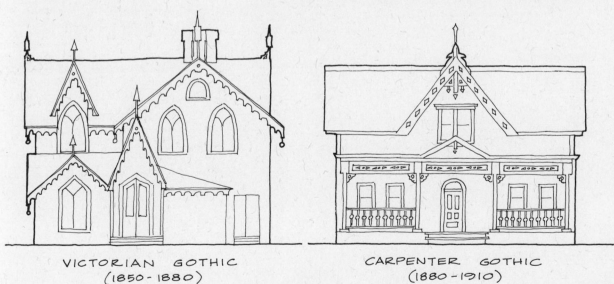

VICTORIAN GOTHIC
(1850 - 1880)

CARPENTER GOTHIC
(1880 - 1910)

Figure 48

138

Victorian Gothic, and Carpenter Gothic. *See Figures 45, 46, 47, and 48.*

Comment: The definition is actually a partial listing of major American historic building styles. For purposes of historic district zoning for a particular area, this listing might be revised as appropriate and detailed architectural definitions of each style added.

HISTORIC DISTRICT

See HISTORIC AREA.

HISTORIC PRESERVATION

The protection, rehabilitation, and restoration of districts, sites, buildings, structures, and artifacts significant in history, architecture, archaeology, or culture.

Comment: Historic preservation includes managing, stabilizing, and at times sensitive reuse of historic buildings.

HISTORIC SITE

A structure or place of outstanding historical and cultural significance and designated as such by state or federal government.

HI-VOLUME (HI-VOL) SAMPLER

A device used in the measurement and analysis of suspended particulate pollution.

HOME OCCUPATION

Any activity carried out for gain by a resident and conducted as a customary, incidental, and accessory use in the resident's dwelling unit.

Comment: The above definition is the broadest possible one covering all home occupations. It simply states that any activity that is carried out for gain by a resident in his or her dwelling unit is a home occupation. It does not mean that a municipality must permit homes occupations or that controls and limits cannot be placed on home occupations. Home occupations are best controlled through performance standards rather than listings of permitted home occupations or professions. In those zones where home occupations are permitted, the development ordinance may impose reasonable restrictions, including the number of nonresident employees, if any; controls on signs, if allowed at all; the maximum amount of square footage to be used for the home occupation; and parking requirements.

139

The home occupation must also be customary, incidental, and accessory to the principal residential use. Customary is subject to change, however, as modern technology reduces the need for face-to-face communication.

The recommended definition also avoids the necessity of attempting to spell out which home occupations would be permitted. Rather, it states that any home occupation that meets the performance standards may be permitted. To minimize any impact from home occupations in residential zones, additional restrictions might include one specifying that no goods, chattels, materials, supplies, or items of any kind can be delivered either to or from the premises in connection with the home occupation except in a passenger automobile owned by the resident. A further limitation might include limiting the number of clients, patrons, or customers or the retail sale of products on the premises. In areas or zones where appropriate, these restrictions can be altered or waived. With a broad definition and performance standards, the municipality can determine the location, extent, and intensity of home occupations.

HOME PROFESSIONAL OFFICE

A home occupation consisting of the office of a practitioner of a recognized profession. *See* HOME OCCUPATION.

Comment: The major question is defining a recognized profession. The granting of a state license in and by itself is not an indication of a recognized profession. Customary home professional offices usually include attorneys, medical practitioners, engineers, and architects. As noted in the definition of "home occupation," performance standards are preferable to distinctions between occupations and professions and/or listings of acceptable occupations.

HOMEOWNERS ASSOCIATION

A community association, other than a condominium association, that is organized in a development in which individual owners share common interests and responsibilities for costs and upkeep of common open space or facilities.

Comment: The homeowners association usually holds title to certain common property, manages and maintains the common property, and enforces certain covenants and restrictions. Condominium associations differ from homeowners associations in that the condominium associations do not have title to the common property.

HOMES FOR THE AGED

See ADULT RETIREMENT COMMUNITY; ASSISTED LIVING FACILITY; CONGREGATE RESIDENCES; CONTINUING CARE RETIREMENT COMMUNITY; HOUSING FOR THE ELDERLY; RESIDENTIAL HEALTH CARE FACILITY; RETIREMENT COMMUNITY.

Comment: An obsolete term no longer used.

HORTICULTURE

The cultivation of a garden or orchard.

HOSPITAL

An institution providing primary health services and medical or surgical care to persons, primarily inpatients, suffering from illness, disease, injury, deformity, and other abnormal physical or mental conditions and including, as an integral part of the institution, related facilities, such as laboratories, outpatient facilities, training facilities, medical offices, and staff residences.

Comment: The size, scale, type, and location of hospitals are usually regulated by state agencies. Before one can be built, a "certificate of need" or similar instrument is required. In most urban and suburban areas, new hospital construction is rare as state agencies attempt to reduce costs by limiting new facilities. However, reconstruction, rehabilitation, and new construction for older hospitals to meet new demands are increasing.

From a zoning perspective, hospitals are extremely intensive uses. They operate twenty-four-hours per day, generate significant traffic volumes, and have many employees on different shifts. A recent unpublished study by the American Hospital Association revealed that the average hospital had three employees per bed; add to this volunteers, visitors, and doctors. Site planning calls for particular attention to major entrances and exits, locations of power plants, laundries and other support uses, parking, and overall impact on surrounding neighborhoods.

Hospital care is changing rapidly, which will have an impact on the future design of hospital campuses. For instance, outpatient surgery, which accounted for less than 3 percent of all surgery ten years ago, now constitutes more than 50 percent of all surgical procedures. The result is a general downsizing of bed and long-term functions and more outpatient facilities.

141

Another change is the construction of medical office buildings (MOB) on hospital campuses. They bring doctors closer to hospitalized patients, reduce traffic and congestion, and offer some taxes from otherwise tax-exempt facilities.

HOTEL

A facility offering transient lodging accommodations to the general public and providing additional services, such as restaurants, meeting rooms, entertainment, and recreational facilities. *See* BOARDING HOUSE; INN; MOTEL; RESORT; TOURIST HOME.

Comment: Newer hotels, often referred to as all-suites hotels, offer kitchen facilities, sitting rooms, and bedrooms as added amenities to attract longer term residents. These function more as apartment hotels than as more traditional hotels. They are often located in suburban areas.

HOUSE TRAILER

See MANUFACTURED HOUSING.

HOUSEHOLD

A family living together in a single dwelling unit, with common access to and common use of all living and eating areas and all areas and facilities for the preparation and serving of food within the dwelling unit. *See* FAMILY.

HOUSING, RETIREMENT

See HOUSING FOR THE ELDERLY.

HOUSING ELEMENT

That portion of the master plan consisting of reports, statements, proposals, maps, diagrams, and text designed to meet the municipality's fair share of its region's present and prospective housing needs, particularly with regard to low- and moderate-income housing.

Comment: Housing elements usually include a good deal of other information as required by state law. In New Jersey, for example, the following information is required in a housing element:

1. An inventory of the municipality's housing stock by age, condition, purchase or rental value, occupancy characteristics, and type, including the number of units affordable to low- and moderate-income households and substandard housing capable of being rehabilitated;
2. A projection of the municipality's housing stock,

including the probable future construction of low- and moderate-income housing, for the next six years, taking into account, but not necessarily limited to, construction permits issued, approvals of applications for development, and probable residential development of lands;

3. An analysis of the municipality's demographic characteristics, including, but not limited to, household size, income level, and age;

4. An analysis of the existing and probable future employment characteristics of the municipality;

5. A determination of the municipality's present and prospective fair share for low- and moderate-income housing and its capacity to accommodate its present and prospective housing needs, including its fair share for low- and moderate-income housing; and

6. A consideration of the lands that are most appropriate for construction of low- and moderate-income housing and of the existing structures most appropriate for conversion to, or rehabilitation for, low- and moderate-income housing, including a consideration of lands of developers who have expressed a commitment to provide low- and moderate-income housing.

HOUSING FOR THE ELDERLY

Multifamily housing designed for older people. *See* ADULT RETIREMENT COMMUNITY; ASSISTED LIVING FACILITY; CONGREGATE RESIDENCES; CONTINUING CARE RETIREMENT COMMUNITY; RETIREMENT COMMUNITY.

HOUSING REGION

That geographic area, surrounding or adjacent to a municipality, from which the bulk of the employment within the municipality is drawn; or the area surrounding or adjacent to the municipality where most of the residents of the municipality are employed.

Comment: The question of housing region has assumed even greater importance in the past several years because of its application in exclusionary housing cases. In the Mt. Laurel case (*Southern Burlington County NAACP v. Township of Mt. Laurel*, 67 N.J. 151, 1975), the court determined the Mt. Laurel housing region as a twenty-mile radius from Camden but stopping at the state boundary. Norman Williams, Jr., in *After Mt. Laurel: The New Suburban Zoning* (edited by Jerome G. Rose and Robert E. Rothman, 1977), defined the housing region as "the area of continuous settlement which coincides roughly with the area within which substantial numbers of people commute to work in the old center." Williams uses the phrase, "commutershed." In *Oakwood at Madison v. Township of Madison* (72 N.J. 481), the court noted the region as "the area from which, in view of available employment and transportation, the population of the township would be drawn absent invalidly exclusionary zoning. . . ." In many other exclusionary zoning cases, the work/residents/trip destination form the basis of the housing region from which fair share allocations could then be made.

HOUSING UNIT

A room or group of rooms used by one or more individuals living separately from others in the structure, with direct access to the outside or to a public hall and containing separate bathroom and kitchen facilities. *See* DWELLING UNIT.

HUMAN SCALE

The proportional relationship of a particular building, structure, or streetscape element to the human form and function.

HUMUS

Decomposed organic material.

HYDROLOGY

The science dealing with the properties, distribution, and circulation of water and snow.

HYDROPHYTIC VEGETATION

Wetlands vegetation consisting of plant life adapted to growth and reproduction under periodically saturated root zone conditions during at least a portion of the growing season.

I

ILLUMINATED SIGN

See SIGN, ILLUMINATED.

IMPACT ANALYSIS

A study to determine the potential direct or indirect effects of a proposed development on activities, utilities, circulation, surrounding land uses, community facilities, environment, and other factors.

Comment: The impact analysis also can include fiscal, aesthetic, social, and legal impacts. The impact analysis

144

serves a variety of functions. It should point out what impact the proposed development will have on the factors considered and what steps are needed to mitigate the impact. This is particularly true for the environment, stormwater management, and utility needs. For projects that require variances, the impact analysis can be used to determine whether substantial detriment would result—an important criterion in the granting of a variance. Finally, impact analysis allows the municipality to plan. If, for example, a development of houses is expected to generate a given number of school-age children, an impact analysis can alert the local board of education to the need to accommodate the additional load.

IMPACT FEE

A fee imposed on a development to help finance the cost of improvements or services.

Comment: Developers have long been required to pay for the cost of improvements necessitated by a development. These improvements include on-site roads, utilities, and stormwater management facilities. Developers have also been required to pay for their fair share of off-tract facilities that have to be improved or installed as a result of their development. Through this method, off-tract intersections may be improved, water and sewer mains enlarged, and additional off-tract drainage basins constructed.

Impact fees are an extension of the philosophy that developments should pay their own way. Thus, where permitted by state legislation and local ordinance, an impact fee may be imposed on development for roads, schools, parks, fire stations, libraries, and other such public facilities. Where impact fees are permitted, they must be specific, be based on a reasonable formula, and be uniformly applied.

IMPERMEABLE

Not permitting the passage of water.

IMPERVIOUS SURFACE

Any material that prevents absorption of stormwater into the ground. *See Figure 49.*

Comment: Retention and detention basins and dry wells allowing water to percolate directly into the ground usually are not considered impervious surfaces. Graveled areas usually are. One method by which impervious surfaces can be defined is in terms of a percolation rate in minutes/inch. For example, the New Jersey State

145

Standards for Construction of Individual Subsurface Sewage Disposal Systems defines impervious formations as having a percolation rate slower than 120 minutes/inch.

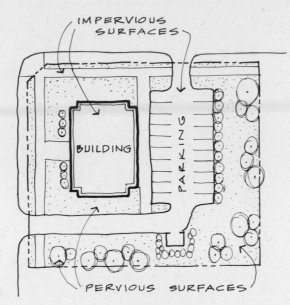

Figure 49

IMPLEMENTATION	Carrying out or fulfilling plans and proposals.
IMPOUNDMENT	A body of water, such as a pond, confined by a dam, dike, floodgate, or other barrier.
IMPROVEMENT	Any permanent structure that becomes part of, placed upon, or is affixed to real estate.
INCENTIVE ZONING	The granting by the approving authority of additional development capacity in exchange for the developer's provision of a public benefit or amenity.

Comment: In urban areas, developers are granted additional height and floor area in exchange for the development of public plazas and similar urban open spaces. In some developing suburbs and urban areas, developers are offered additional dwelling unit density if lower income housing units are created.

Incentive zoning should not be confused with off-tract improvements or impact fees. These represent at-

146

tempts to correct deficiencies in infrastructure or to assure that infrastructure needs created by a project are adequate. Incentive zoning is a quid pro quo—more development for some benefit, the need for which may not necessarily be created by the development itself. The local ordinance would have to clearly spell out the bonuses and the benefits.

INCIDENTAL

Subordinate and minor in significance and bearing a reasonable relationship with the primary use.

INCINERATION

The controlled process by which solid, liquid, or gaseous combustible wastes are burned and changed into gases and residue containing little or no combustible material.

INCINERATOR

A device used to burn waste substances and in which all the combustion factors—temperature, retention time, turbulence, and combustion air—can be controlled.

INCLUSIONARY DEVELOPMENT

A residential housing development in which a percentage of the dwelling units is affordable to low- and moderate-income households.

Comment: Depending on state law, inclusionary developments may include specific percentages of lower income dwelling units (20 percent, for example) and specify a reasonable affordable income range (low income, up to 50 percent of median family income; moderate, up to 80 percent of median family income).

INCLUSIONARY ZONING

Regulations that increase housing choice by establishing requirements and providing incentives to construct housing to meet the needs of low- and moderate-income households.

Comment: Inclusionary techniques include specific requirements for a minimum percentage of low- and moderate-income housing as part of any development and density bonuses for building low- and moderate-income units. Removal or modification of regulations to eliminate requirements unrelated or in excess of those needed for safe and sanitary housing is also another technique designed to provide more affordable housing. (For a fuller discussion of this complex subject, see Babcock and Bosselman 1973; Listokin 1976; and Mallach 1984.)

147

INDIGENOUS NEED

Existing deficient housing units within a municipality that are occupied by low- and moderate-income households. *See* SURROGATE.

Comment: Indigenous need refers to those dwelling units in a municipality that are deemed deficient (formerly dilapidated) and occupied by lower income households. In fair share programs, indigenous housing is part of the present need, as opposed to a prospective need.

INDIRECT SOURCE

An indirect pollution source that by its nature attracts large numbers of polluting sources while not actually releasing the pollutant itself.

INDIVIDUAL SEWAGE DISPOSAL SYSTEM

A system for the treatment and disposal of sanitary sewage in the ground on the lot upon which the primary use is located. *See Figure 26*.

Comment: Septic systems are designed and constructed to treat sewage in a manner that will retain most of the settleable solids in a septic tank and discharge the liquid portion to a disposal field.

INDOOR RECREATION CENTER

A permanent structure containing facilities for recreational activities, such as tennis, platform games, swimming, exercise rooms, handball, and similar activities.

Comment: The definition does not differentiate between recreational centers operated by public or semipublic agencies (Ys or a board of education, for instance) or commercial recreation centers. Recreation centers may also include facilities for lectures, arts and crafts, and special events. They may include child-care centers, snack bars, pro shops, and instruction in various games.

The zoning considerations include parking, circulation, aesthetics, hours of operation and impact on surrounding areas (Schultz and Kasen 1984).

INDOOR TENNIS FACILITY

A building or structure containing one or more roofed and enclosed tennis courts.

INDUSTRIAL PARK

A tract of land that is planned, developed, and operated as an integrated facility for a number of individual industrial uses, with consideration to transportation facilities (rail and highway), circulation, parking, utility needs, aesthetics, and compatibility.

Comment: A good reference for industrial park development standards is the 1988 *Business and Industrial*

148

Development Handbook, a part of the Urban Land Institute's Community Builders Handbook Series.

INDUSTRIAL PROPERTY

Any parcel of land containing an industrial use or any building containing such uses, as may be defined in this ordinance.

INDUSTRIAL SEPARATOR

An air pollution control device that uses the principle of inertia to remove particulate matter from a stream of air or gas.

INDUSTRIAL WASTE

Liquid, gaseous, chemical, and solid residue or by-products of an industrial process.

INDUSTRY

Those fields of economic activity including forestry, fishing, hunting, and trapping; mining; construction; manufacturing; transportation, communication, electric, gas, and sanitary services; and wholesale trade.

INDUSTRY, HEAVY

Industrial uses that meet the performance standards, bulk controls, and other requirements established in an ordinance.

Comment: See comments under INDUSTRY, LIGHT.

INDUSTRY, LIGHT

Industrial uses that meet the performance standards, bulk controls, and other requirements established in an ordinance.

Comment: Most zoning ordinances define light industry in terms of the finished product, raw materials, size of the machinery used in the process, or number of employees. A typical definition of light industry might require that the finished product shall consist of small machine parts or small electronic equipment. Another common definition would prohibit motors in excess of ten horsepower. The Institute of Transportation Engineers describes general light industrial as employing less than five hundred persons with emphasis on activities other than manufacturing (*Trip Generation* 1991).

Light industry (and heavy industry, for that matter) should be defined in terms of intensity and impact, as well as use. With the advent of stricter environmental laws regulating noise, air pollution, glare, water quality, and waste treatment, the difference between light and heavy industry essentially narrows down to traffic generation, building bulk, and intensity of site development.

149

The recommended definition states that all light industry is required to meet the performance and bulk standards established in the ordinance. Light industrial standards would restrict the intensity of development (lower FAR—floor area ratio), impervious coverage, size of the building, number of vehicles, including those for employees as well as deliveries and pickups, prohibit outdoor storage, and require that all activities are carried on within the principal building. This latter provision would rule out, for example, those facilities that require large structures outside principal buildings, such as refineries. By establishing a maximum size for the lot (possibly five acres), maximum building and impervious coverage (50 and 75 percent, respectively), a maximum height of two stories, and a maximum FAR of .5 or less, the municipality is assured that the light industry would generate a minimum amount of traffic and have limited impact on the surrounding area.

Additional requirements could be established to further define light and heavy industry. For instance, many states allow municipalities to impose higher performance standards than those required by state law. Noise standards could be established that prohibit any noise above a certain decibel rating beyond the walls of the building, with a different standard for light and heavy industrial zones. Air quality requirements could similarly be increased. Given the difficulty in enforcing the standards and determining when violations take place, the most practical approach is to establish bulk and intensity standards that limit the size and bulk of the building and consequently the impact.

Finally, specific use categories can be included to rule out certain uses that would not be permitted regardless of intensity or impact. For example, manufacturing of certain toxic gases or chemicals would not be a permitted use regardless of the size of the facility.

INFILL DEVELOPMENT *See* ODD-LOT DEVELOPMENT.

INFILTRATION The flow of a fluid into a substance through pores or small openings.

Comment: Commonly used in hydrology to describe the flow of water into soil material. Also describes stormwater inflow into a sanitary sewer system.

150

INFRASTRUCTURE	Facilities and services needed to sustain industry, residential, commercial, and all other land use activities.
	Comment: Infrastructure includes water, sewer lines, and other utilities, streets and roads, communications, and public facilities, such as firehouses, parks, schools, and such.
INGRESS	Access or entry.
INHERENTLY BENEFICIAL USES	Uses that clearly promote the public good.
	Comment: Inherently beneficial uses are those uses that are essential to society but are often grouped as NIMBYs (not in my backyard). Courts in various states have classified a variety of uses as inherently beneficial, including schools, child-care centers, medical facilities and nursing homes, public housing, lower income housing, public utility installations, sewage treatment plants, and churches and places of worship.
	Since ordinances do not often zone for many types of inherently beneficial uses, they require use variances in order to locate in the municipality. In New Jersey, the designation as an inherently beneficial use relieves the applicant of the obligation of proving special reasons for the use. The use still must meet the negative criteria that it will not be substantially detrimental to the public good and will not substantially impair the intent and purpose of the zone plan and zoning ordinance.
INN	A commercial facility for the housing and feeding of transients.
	Comment: An inn is commonly distinguished from a hotel or motel by its size and its purportedly more personal atmosphere. Inns often are contained in whole or in part in buildings that were previously private residences. *See* BED AND BREAKFAST; HOTEL; MOTEL.
INSTITUTIONAL USE	A nonprofit, religious, or public use, such as a church, library, public or private school, hospital, or government owned or operated building, structure, or land used for public purpose.
INTENSITY OF USE	The number of dwelling units per acre for residential development and floor area ratio (FAR) for nonresidential development, such as commercial, office, and industrial.

151

Comment: FAR may also be used for residential development or for mixed-use development. In residential projects, FAR may be useful in relating the size of the building to the lot area.

INTERCEPTOR DRAIN

Underground drainage system designed to catch and divert stormwater runoff away from a slope or other area sensitive to water erosion or impact.

INTERCEPTOR SEWER

Sewers used to collect the flows from main and trunk sewers and carry them to a central point for treatment and/or discharge.

INTERCHANGE

A grade-separated, bridged system of access to and from highways where vehicles may move from one roadway to another without crossing streams of traffic. *See Figure 70.*

INTERESTED PARTY

(1) In a criminal or quasi-criminal proceeding, any citizen of the state; (2) in a civil proceeding, in any court or in an administrative proceeding before a municipal agency, any individual, whether residing within or without the municipality, whose right to use, acquire, or enjoy property is or may be affected by any action taken under any law of the municipality or state or the United States.

INTERIOR LOT

See LOT, INTERIOR.

INTERMEDIATE CARE FACILITY (ICF)

A facility that provides, on a regular basis, personal care, including dressing and eating and health-related care and services, to individuals who require such assistance but who do not require the degree of care and treatment that a hospital or skilled nursing facility provides.

Comment: Most states regulate ICFs, which are often grouped under the general term nursing home or long-term care facility. Unlike nursing homes or hospitals, ICFs provide only limited medical supervision, such as the administration of medication or medical treatment by qualified personnel. *See* LONG-TERM CARE FACILITY.

INTERSECTION

The location where two or more roadways cross at grade without a bridge. *See* JUNCTION. *See Figure 70.*

INTERSTATE HIGHWAY SYSTEM

A countrywide, federally supported network of controlled and limited access highways.

152

INTERSTATE WATERS	(1) Rivers, lakes, and other waters that flow across or form a part of state or international boundaries; (2) waters of the Great Lakes; and (3) coastal waters, including ocean waters seaward to the territorial limits and waters along the coastline (including inland streams) influenced by the tide.
INTERTIDAL AREA	The land area between high and low tide, also called a beach. *See* BEACH. *See Figure 8.*
INVERSE CONDEMNATION	The taking or reduction in value of private property as a result of governmental activity without any formal direct exercise of eminent domain.

Comment: An example of an inverse condemnation is the expansion of an airport flight path that brings airplanes so low over residences as to make them uninhabitable.

INVERSION	An atmospheric condition where a layer of cool air is trapped by a layer of warm air so that it cannot rise.

Comment: Inversions spread polluted air horizontally rather than vertically so that contaminating substances cannot be dispersed widely.

ISLAND	(1) A land area totally surrounded by water; (2) in parking lot design, built-up structures, usually curbed, placed at the end or middle of parking rows as a guide to traffic and for landscaping, signing, or lighting.
ISOLATED LOT	An undeveloped substandard lot in separate ownership from surrounding property.

Comment: The isolated lot invariably becomes the subject of a variance application. A 1979 New Jersey Supreme Court decision (*Chirechello v. Zoning Board of Adjustment, Borough of Monmouth Beach*, 78 N.J. 544) offers some guidelines on how to deal with the problem. The court suggested three criteria to determine hardship:

1. Did the owner purchase the property knowing either in fact or constructively of the deficiency? For example, if the lot became nonconforming by reason of a change in the zoning regulations after the property was purchased, the owner could not know of the potential disablement.

153

2. Was an offer made to purchase the property at a fair price? If so, there is no hardship. (The court indicated that the fair market value should be based on the assumption that the variance would be granted. Otherwise, the value of the unusable lot would be zero.)
3. Conversely, can vacant land be purchased at a fair price that would make the lot conforming?

In addition to proving hardship, the applicant also must satisfy that what is being proposed will not have an adverse impact on surrounding properties or the neighborhood and that the proposed development is consistent with the intent and purpose of the zone plan and ordinance.

J

JOINT OWNERSHIP

The equal estate interest of two or more persons.

JOURNEY TO WORK

The worker's daily trip from residence to place of employment and back, by whatever mode of transportation. *See Figure 50.*

JUNCTION

A place of joining or crossing of streets or railroads. *See* INTERSECTION.

JUNK

Any scrap, waste, reclaimable material, or debris, whether or not stored, for sale or in the process of being dismantled, destroyed, processed, salvaged, stored, baled, disposed, or other use or disposition.

Comment: The definition can also include examples of what constitutes junk such as unregistered, inoperable vehicles, tires, vehicle parts, equipment, paper, rags, metal, glass, building materials, household appliances, machinery, brush, wood, and lumber. *See* GARBAGE; SOLID WASTE.

JUNKYARD

Any area, lot, land, parcel, building, or structure, or part thereof, used for the storage, collection, processing, purchase, sale, salvage, or disposal of junk.

Comment: Junkyards are intensive uses, and since they are usually operated outdoors, appropriate screening and buffering are required.

154

ILLUSTRATIVE DEFINITION
JOURNEY / TRIP / TRIP ENDS

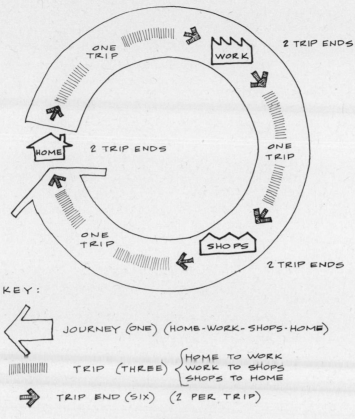

ONE TRIP

2 TRIP ENDS

WORK

ONE TRIP

HOME

2 TRIP ENDS

ONE TRIP

SHOPS

2 TRIP ENDS

KEY:

JOURNEY (ONE) (HOME - WORK - SHOPS - HOME)

TRIP (THREE) { HOME TO WORK / WORK TO SHOPS / SHOPS TO HOME }

TRIP END (SIX) (2 PER TRIP)

Figure 50

JUST COMPENSATION   Payment made to a private property owner by an agency with power of eminent domain when the private property is taken for public use.

K

KENNEL   A commercial establishment in which dogs or domesticated animals are housed, groomed, bred, boarded, trained, or sold, all for a fee or compensation.

Comment: Since kennels include animal runs, care must be taken in locating them away from residential areas and

155

providing noise buffers or barriers. Many communities license kennels, establishing a minimum number of animals after which a license is required.

KIOSK

A freestanding structure upon which temporary information and/or posters, notices, and announcements are posted. *See Figure 14.*

L

LABOR FORCE

All the population sixteen years of age or older, having the potential for active work for wages.

LAGOON

In wastewater treatment, a shallow, artificial pond where sunlight, bacterial action, and oxygen interact to restore wastewater to a reasonable state of purity.

LAKE

An inland water body fed by springs or surrounding runoff.

LAND

Ground, soil, or earth, including structures on, above, or below the surface.

LAND BANK

Government-purchased land held for future use.

LAND DISTURBANCE

Any activity involving the clearing, cutting, excavating, filling, or grading of land or any other activity that alters land topography or vegetative cover.

LANDLOCKED

A lot or parcel of land without direct access to a public road.

Comment: Local development regulations should preclude approval of any subdivision or site plan that results in any property becoming landlocked.

LAND RECLAMATION

Increasing land use capability by changing the land's character or environment through drainage and/or fill. *See* FILLING.

Comment: Land reclamation is often associated with quarried land, landfills, and quarries.

LAND SURVEYOR

One who is licensed by the state as a land surveyor and is qualified to make accurate field measurements and to mark, describe, and define land boundaries.

LAND USE	A description of how land is occupied or utilized.
LAND USE INTENSITY (LUI) STANDARDS	A system of bulk regulations, designed primarily for large-scale developments, and based on the physical relationship between specific development factors.

Comment: LUI standards attempt to correlate the land area, floor area, open space, recreation space, and car storage of a project. Details of the system were first published in the Federal Housing Administration's Land Planning Bulletin No. 7, *Land Use Intensity Rating*. It has never been fully appreciated or gained wide-scale acceptance.

LANDFILL	A disposal site in which refuse and earth, or other suitable cover material, are deposited and compacted in alternative layers of specified depth in accordance with an approved plan. *See* SANITARY LANDFILL.

Comment: Landfills are usually regulated and licensed by the state or other regional agency to accept certain types of waste. Landfills differ from dumps in that refuse is compacted and covered in the landfill.

LANDMARK	(1) Any site, building, structure, or natural feature that has visual, historic, or cultural significance; (2) a permanent marker, usually called a monument, designating property boundaries.
LANDSCAPE	(1) An expanse of natural scenery; (2) lawns, trees, plants, and other natural materials, such as rock and wood chips, and decorative features, including sculpture, patterned walks, fountains, and pools.

Comment: As noted in the definition, landscaping treatment can include some elements of street furniture. It does not include artificial trees, turf, or other artificial plants. Natural materials often are referred to as "soft" landscape, and other materials are known as "hard" landscape.

LANDSCAPE PLAN	A component of a development plan on which is shown: proposed landscape species (such as number, spacing, size at time of planting, and planting details); proposals for protection of existing vegetation during and after construction; proposed treatment of hard and soft surfaces; proposed decorative features; grade changes; buf-

157

fers and screening devices; and any other information that can reasonably be required in order that an informed decision can be made by the approving authority. *See Figures 51 and 52.*

LARGE LOT ZONING

Low-density residential development that requires a large parcel of land for each dwelling.

Comment: While there is no set definition on what constitutes a "large parcel," low density usually refers to development on lots of one acre or more.

LATERAL SEWERS

Pipes conducting sewerage from individual buildings to larger pipes called trunk or interceptor sewers that usually are located in street rights-of-way.

LAUNDROMAT

An establishment providing washing, drying, or dry-cleaning machines on the premises for rental use to the general public.

LEACHATE

Liquid that has percolated through solid waste or other mediums from which dissolved or suspended materials have been extracted.

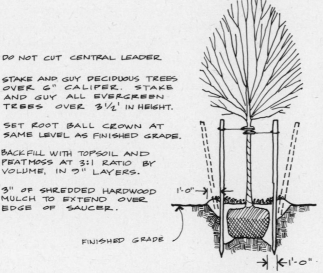

DO NOT CUT CENTRAL LEADER

STAKE AND GUY DECIDUOUS TREES OVER 6" CALIPER. STAKE AND GUY ALL EVERGREEN TREES OVER 3½' IN HEIGHT.

SET ROOT BALL CROWN AT SAME LEVEL AS FINISHED GRADE.

BACKFILL WITH TOPSOIL AND PEATMOSS AT 3:1 RATIO BY VOLUME, IN 9" LAYERS.

3" OF SHREDDED HARDWOOD MULCH TO EXTEND OVER EDGE OF SAUCER.

PRUNE ⅓ OF NEW GROWTH - RETAIN NATURAL SHAPE.

DRIVE STAKES IN AT ANGLE AND DRAW VERTICAL.

TREE WRAP TO FIRST BRANCH WITH WATERPROOF TREE WRAP, SECURE WITH TWINE.

PROVIDE SAUCER AROUND TREE, FLOOD WITH WATER TWICE WITHIN 24 HOURS OF PLANTING.

REMOVE TWINE AND BURLAP FROM ROOT CROWN.

FINISHED GRADE

1'-0"

1'-0"

PLANTING AND GUYING DETAIL
FOR DECIDUOUS & EVERGREEN TREES

Figure 51

158

LEACHING The process by which soluble materials in the soil, such as nutrients, pesticide chemicals, or contaminants, are washed into a lower layer of soil and are dissolved and carried into the water.

LEASE A contractual agreement for the use of lands, structures, buildings, or parts thereof for a fixed time and consideration.

LEAST COST HOUSING Housing built in accordance with local codes and ordinances that have been carefully screened to eliminate cost-generating provisions and any requirements not related to health, safety, and welfare and that sells for prices substantially below median housing prices in an area. *See* MANUFACTURED HOUSING.

Comment: Some of the requirements found to be unrelated to health, safety, and welfare are large lot zoning, unrealistic densities for various housing types, minimum building areas, garages, and oversized utilities or infrastructures (thirty-six-feet-wide local streets, for example). However, the appropriate minimum standards for lot size, density, utilities, and other requirements may vary between and even within a municipality depending upon existing natural and created constraints and the character of local development.

Many of the impediments to least cost housing are identified in the 1991 report of the President's Advisory Committee on Regulatory Barriers to Affordable Housing, *Not in My Back Yard: Removing Barriers to Affordable Housing* (Kemp Report).

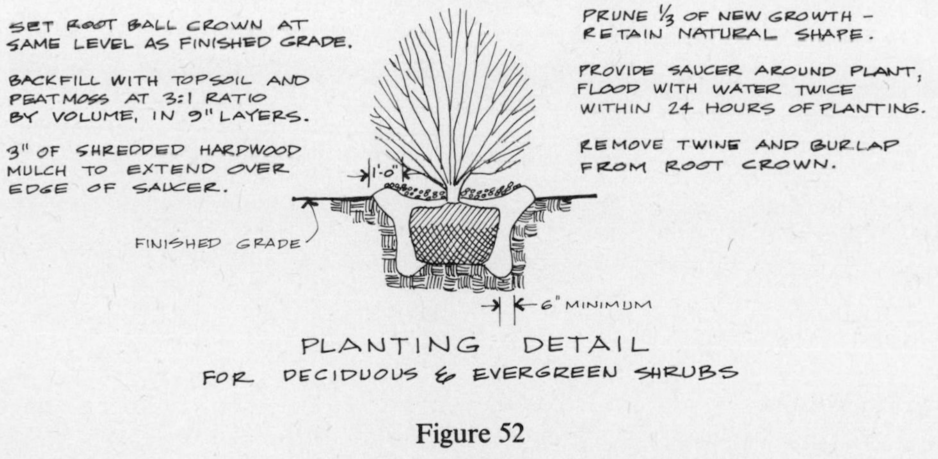

SET ROOT BALL CROWN AT SAME LEVEL AS FINISHED GRADE.

BACKFILL WITH TOPSOIL AND PEATMOSS AT 3:1 RATIO BY VOLUME, IN 9" LAYERS.

3" OF SHREDDED HARDWOOD MULCH TO EXTEND OVER EDGE OF SAUCER.

FINISHED GRADE

PRUNE ⅓ OF NEW GROWTH – RETAIN NATURAL SHAPE.

PROVIDE SAUCER AROUND PLANT, FLOOD WITH WATER TWICE WITHIN 24 HOURS OF PLANTING.

REMOVE TWINE AND BURLAP FROM ROOT CROWN.

1'-0"

6" MINIMUM

PLANTING DETAIL
FOR DECIDUOUS & EVERGREEN SHRUBS

Figure 52

LEISURE SERVICES

Activities for people other than employment or mandatory functions and including activities relating to recreation, social and cultural events, religion, and education.

LESS-THAN-FEE ACQUISITION

See EASEMENT.

LEVEL OF SERVICE

A description of traffic conditions along a given roadway or at a particular intersection.

Comment: The level of service ranges from "A" (free flow of traffic with minimum intersection delay), which is the best, to "F" (forced flow, jammed intersections, long delays), which is the worst. It reflects factors such as speed, travel time, freedom to maneuver, traffic interruptions, and delay (*Highway Capacity Manual* 1985). *See* comment under CAPACITY, ROADWAY.

LIFE CYCLE

The phases, changes, or stages an organism passes through during its lifetime.

LIFE-CARE COMMUNITIES

See CONTINUING CARE RETIREMENT COMMUNITY (CCRC).

LIFT

In a sanitary landfill, a compacted layer of solid waste and the top layer of cover material.

LIGHT INDUSTRY

See INDUSTRY, LIGHT.

LIGHT PLANE

See SKY EXPOSURE PLANE.

LIGHTING PLAN

See FOOTCANDLE.

LIMITED ACCESS HIGHWAY

A highway, especially designed for through traffic, over which abutting lot owners have no right to light, air, or direct access.

Comment: Interstate highways, parkways, and freeways are considered limited access highways.

LIMNOLOGY

The study of the physical, chemical, meteorological, and biological aspects of freshwaters.

LINES

See LOT LINE.

LINKAGE PROGRAMS

Developer contributions, either by construction, actually providing the service, or in-lieu fees, toward community

160

amenities and needs, such as affordable housing, open space, child-care facilities, transit improvements, and/or related community services, in return for obtaining development approval.

Comment: Linkage programs require developers to contribute money for or to actually build housing, transit improvements, recreation, or other amenities as a prerequisite for approvals. In some cases, the linkage programs allow for an increase in allowable density or intensity of development in return for providing the amenity. In order for linkage to work, there should be some relationship to what is being built and what is required—a rational nexus. For example, a new office building may generate a demand for more transit capacity, child care, and affordable housing. The impact can be determined and the linkage computed. Linkage formulas must be permitted by state law, be based on a local ordinance with clear and equitable requirements, and be applied fairly and uniformly.

However, a recent New Jersey Supreme Court case—*Holmdel Builders Association v. Township of Holmdel,* 583 A.2d 277 (1990) (Holmdel II)—appears to reject the rational nexus test for linkage programs relating to affordable housing. The court noted that the rational nexus test was not an appropriate standard to determine compliance with constitutional regional general welfare standards.

LITTORAL

Pertaining to the shore of seas and oceans.

LITTORAL DRIFT

The transportation of grains of sand due to water action produced by winds and currents.

LITTORAL LAND

Land that abuts a large body of water, such as an ocean or sea.

LOADING SPACE

An off-street space or berth used for the loading or unloading of cargo, products, or materials from vehicles.

LOCAL AUTHORITY

Any city, town, village, or other legally authorized agency charged with the administration and enforcement of land use regulations. *See* MUNICIPALITY.

Comment: In many states, the county or regional planning agencies are charged with the administration and enforcement of land use regulations.

161

LOCAL HOUSING AUTHORITY

Any public body authorized to engage in the development or administration of subsidized or public housing.

LOCAL IMPROVEMENT

A public improvement provided to a specific area that benefits that area and that is usually paid for by special assessment of the benefiting property owners.

LOCAL ROAD

See STREET, LOCAL.

LODGE

(1) A building or group of buildings under single management containing both rooms and dwelling units available for temporary rental to transient individuals or families; (2) the place where members of a local chapter of an association or a fraternal, cultural, or religious organization hold their meetings; (3) the local chapter itself. *See* BOARDING HOUSE; PRIVATE CLUB.

LODGER

A transient renter whose meals may or may not be included in the cost of his or her rent. *See* BOARDER.

LODGING HOUSE

A facility in which rental sleeping accommodations are provided and in which meals also may be supplied as part of the fee. *See* BOARDING HOUSE.

LONG-TERM CARE FACILITY

An institution or a distinct part of an institution that is licensed or approved to provide health care under medical supervision for twenty-four or more consecutive hours to two or more patients who are not related to the governing authority or its members by marriage, blood, or adoption.

Comment: A long-term care facility may be either a skilled nursing facility, where patients receive a minimum number of hours of nursing care daily (New Jersey requires 2.75 hours), or an intermediate care facility, where patients receive less than the specified number of hours of nursing care daily. In addition to a nursing home, other long-term care facilities are governmental medical institutions or nursing units in a home for the aged. Long-term care facilities can provide, in addition to maintenance care, restorative services. Hospices are also examples of long-term care facilities. *See* EXTENDED CARE FACILITY; INTERMEDIATE CARE FACILITY.

LOT

A designated parcel, tract, or area of land established by plat, subdivision, or as otherwise permitted by law, to be

162

separately owned, used, developed, or built upon. *See Figure 2.*

LOT, CORNER

A lot or parcel of land abutting upon two or more streets at their intersection or upon two parts of the same street forming an interior angle of less than 135 degrees. *See Figure 10.*

Comment: The major problem with corner lots is the designation of the yards opposite the street frontages. Most ordinances require that the minimum front yard be maintained on both frontages for purposes of providing adequate sight distances, safety, air and light to abutting residences, and aesthetics. There remains the question of how to treat the two remaining yards. Some ordinances call them side yards and require them to meet the minimum required side yard dimension. Unfortunately, this deprives the corner lot of any adequate backyard area and encroaches on one or both adjacent residences. A better approach is to permit the applicant to designate one of the street frontages as the front, require the house to be built facing the front, and then require the yard opposite the designated front to meet the minimum rear yard requirement. Both street frontages would still meet the minimum required front yard setback, one yard would meet side yard standards, and the lot would have a rear yard. The corner lot would have to be larger than the interior lots to provide the minimum required setbacks.

LOT, DEVELOPED

See LOT, IMPROVED.

LOT, DOUBLE FRONTAGE

See LOT, THROUGH.

LOT, FLAG

A large lot not meeting minimum frontage requirements and where access to the public road is by a narrow, private right-of-way or driveway. *See Figures 10 and 53.*

Comment: Flag lots are usually permitted in rural and developing municipalities to allow development of backland areas while still maintaining their rural character. The usual requirements for a flag lot are as follows: minimum lot area at least twice the area of standard lots in the zone where located exclusive of the staff connecting the lot to the public road; minimum setbacks from property lines as opposed to the usual front, side, and rear yard requirements; all setbacks measured from the

163

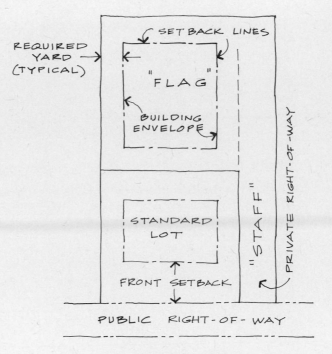

REQUIRED YARD (TYPICAL)

SET BACK LINES

"FLAG"

BUILDING ENVELOPE

STANDARD LOT

FRONT SETBACK

"STAFF"

PRIVATE RIGHT-OF-WAY

PUBLIC RIGHT-OF-WAY

FLAG LOT

Figure 53

projected right-of-way; minimum of twenty feet and maximum of fifty feet for the right-of-way; not more than one flag lot for each private right-of-way; and minimum distance between flag lot right-of-ways at least equal to the minimum lot frontage in the particular zone.

While flag lots can assist in retaining the rural character of an area, they are subject to abuses. The most prevalent is when the flag lot owner wants to further subdivide and use the private right-of-way for access. The municipality then has a major subdivision without adequate access. Many towns do not permit flag lots where the flag lot can be further subdivided.

LOT, IMPROVED

(1) A lot upon which a building can be constructed and occupied; (2) a lot with buildings or structures.

Comment: The principal definition of an improved lot is one for which a building permit can be issued to construct a building. This usually requires that the lot has frontage on, or access to, an improved street, and all utilities (such as water, sewer, and electric) are available to the lot. The second definition has largely been superseded by the term "developed lot."

164

LOT, INTERIOR	A lot other than a corner lot. *See Figure 10.*
LOT, ISOLATED	*See* ISOLATED LOT.
LOT, MINIMUM AREA OF	The smallest lot area established by the zoning ordinance on which a use or structure may be located in a particular district.
LOT, REVERSE FRONTAGE	A through lot that is not accessible from one of the parallel or nonintersecting streets upon which it fronts. *See Figures 25 and 54.*

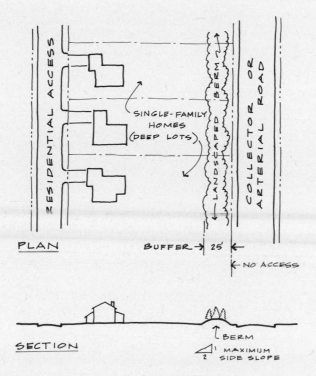

REVERSE FRONTAGE LOTS

Figure 54

LOT, SUBSTANDARD	A parcel of land that has less than the minimum area or minimum dimensions required in the zone in which the lot is located.
LOT, THROUGH	A lot that fronts upon two parallel streets or that fronts upon two streets that do not intersect at the boundaries of the lot. *See Figure 10.*

LOT, TRANSITION

(1) A lot in a transition zone; (2) a lot in one zoning district abutting another district and designated as a transition lot. *See Figure 55.*

Comment: Transition lots (or lots in transition zones) serve as logical "change" lots between two zones. For example, a lot between a business and residential zone might permit parking for the business use (with adequate setbacks and landscaping) or a higher density residential use. The zoning ordinance normally also establishes an intermediate size for the transition lot. For instance, if located between a forty thousand-square-foot residential zone and a twenty thousand-square-foot residential zone, the transition lot might be required to have a minimum of thirty thousand square feet. The transition lot also might be part of a lot averaging design.

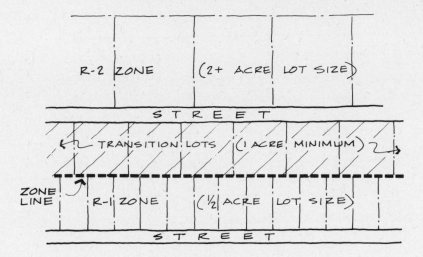

TRANSITION LOT
(RESIDENTIAL EXAMPLE)

Figure 55

LOT AREA

The total area within the lot lines of a lot, excluding any street rights-of-way.

LOT AVERAGING

A design technique permitting one or more lots in a subdivision to be undersized, providing the same number of lots in the same subdivision are oversized by an equal or greater area.

166

Comment: Lot averaging is similar to clustering except there is no common open space. It is particularly useful where topography or other environmental constraints affect the land. The ordinance should establish a maximum permitted reduction, such as not more than 25 percent of the minimum required lot area.

LOT COVERAGE

That portion of the lot that is covered by buildings. *See* Building Coverage.

Comment: Some definitions expand this to include all other created improvements on the ground that are more impervious than the natural surface, such as paving, patios, pools, and driveways. This all-inclusive coverage is usually defined as "impervious coverage," which includes all buildings and structures. *See* Impervious Surface.

LOT DEPTH

The average distance measured from the front lot line to the rear lot line. *See Figure 10.*

Comment: For lots where the front and rear lot lines are not parallel, the lot depth should be measured by drawing several evenly separated lines from the front to rear lot lines, at right angles to the front lot line, and averaging the length of these lines.

LOT FRONTAGE

The length of the front lot line measured at the street right-of-way line. *See Figure 10.*

Comment: On corner lots, each side abutting the street is considered the frontage, and in many ordinances, such lots have two front yards, two side yards, and no rear yards. *See Comment under* Corner Lot.

LOT LINE

A line of record bounding a lot that divides one lot from another lot or from a public or private street or any other public space. *See Figure 11.*

LOT LINE, FRONT

The lot line separating a lot from a street right-of-way. *See Figure 11.*

LOT LINE, REAR

The lot line opposite and most distant from the front lot line. In the case of triangular or otherwise irregularly shaped lots, a line ten feet in length entirely within the lot, parallel to and at a maximum distance from the front lot line. *See Figure 11.*

167

Comment: The ten-foot minimum length is not sacrosanct. On wider lots, it could be a percentage of the minimum lot width, say 10 percent.

LOT LINE, SIDE

Any lot line other than a front or rear lot line. *See Figure 11.*

LOT OF RECORD

A lot that exists as shown or described on a plat or deed in the records of the local registry of deeds.

LOT WIDTH

The horizontal distance between the side lines of a lot measured at right angles to its depth along a straight line parallel to the front lot line at the minimum required building setback line. *See Figure 10.*

LOW-INCOME HOUSING

Housing that is economically feasible for families whose income level is categorized as low within the standards promulgated by the U.S. Department of Housing and Urban Development (HUD) or the appropriate state housing agency.

Comment: Generally speaking, low income is defined as 50 percent or less of the median family income in a particular market area. Economically feasible is defined as housing costs between 28 and 30 percent of gross family income. HUD now uses the term ''very low'' to identify families earning up to 50 percent of the area median family income; ''lower,'' 50 to 80 percent; and ''moderate,'' 80 to 120 percent.

LOW-SPEED RURAL HIGHWAY

The access classification for roadways in rural environments where the posted speed limit is 45 miles per hour (mph) or less.

LOW-SPEED URBAN HIGHWAY

The access classification for roadways in urban environments where the posted speed limit is 40 mph or less.

M

MADE LAND

Land previously unsuitable for development because of a high water table, open waters, flooding, unstable subsurface conditions, or similar impairments and made suitable by corrective action. *See* FILLING; LAND RECLAMATION.

Comment: Reclaiming land unsuitable for development usually involves filling and draining, activities that require state and often federal permits.

MAGNET STORE

The largest retail establishment in a shopping center that draws customers and thereby generates business for the remaining stores in the center. *See* ANCHOR TENANT.

Comment: In a regional center, the department store is the magnet. In neighborhood centers, the supermarket is the magnet.

MAINTENANCE GUARANTEE

Any security that may be required and accepted by a governmental agency to assure that necessary improvements will function as required for a specific period of time. *See* PERFORMANCE GUARANTEE.

Comment: The maintenance guarantee takes effect after the municipality has accepted the improvements. The maintenance guarantee usually runs for a period of one to two years. If something malfunctions, the obligor is required to correct the deficiency.

MAJOR LIFE ACTIVITIES

Functions such as caring for one's self, performing manual tasks, walking, seeing, hearing, breathing, learning, and working. *See* AMERICANS WITH DISABILITIES ACT.

MAJOR TRAFFIC GENERATOR

The use or uses that generate a total of five hundred or more vehicle trips per day to and from the use or uses.

Comment: The five hundred-vehicle trip is the standard established by the New Jersey Department of Transportation. A proposed use classified as a major traffic generator is required to undertake impact studies on intersections and roadways surrounding the proposed use.

MALL

(1) A shaded walk or public promenade; (2) a shopping center where stores front on both sides of a pedestrian way, which may be enclosed or open.

MANUFACTURED HOUSING

Factory-built, single-family structures that meet the National Manufactured Home Construction and Safety Standards Act (42 U.S.C. Sec. 5401), commonly known as the HUD (U.S. Department of Housing and Urban Development) code.

Comment: Such houses have long been called "mobile homes," a term that was originally coined to describe trailers that were equipped to function as truly mobile homes. Recreational vehicles serve this purpose today, and the "mobile home" of years past has long since become a fixed in-place house that is mobile only at the time it is moved from the factory to the site. Besides losing its mobility, the "mobile home" has also become larger, and the safety and quality have been significantly improved as a result of the passage of the National Manufactured Home Construction and Safety Standards Act in 1976. Units built to this code are properly referred to as "manufactured homes" as a result of congressional action and, in New Jersey, state legislation.

Along with the name change, the appearance of manufactured housing has also changed. Many new manufactured units are designed to look like site-built housing and have pitched roofs and conventional roofing and siding materials. Additionally, many manufactured houses are "customized" with site-built amenities, such as patios, garages, and decks.

As manufactured housing has become less mobile, there has been a gradual shift in development approaches from the mobile home park system, where land was available on a long-term lease basis, to subdivisions, where lots are purchased. Although some manufactured housing subdivisions have comparatively large lot sizes, attractive developments can be created at densities typical of multifamily housing development if creative design techniques are used. The combined cost savings of manufactured housing and small lot sizes can produce single-family housing at least cost.

Manufactured housing developments usually require special zoning provisions. In New Jersey, though, the state planning and zoning enabling legislation was amended in 1983 to make double-wide manufactured units on permanent foundations a permitted use in all areas zoned for residential development.

MANUFACTURING

Establishments engaged in the mechanical or chemical transformation of materials or substances into new products, including the assembling of component parts, the creation of products, and the blending of materials, such as lubricating oils, plastics, resins, or liquors.

Comment: The term manufacturing covers all mechanical or chemical transformations, whether the new product is finished or semifinished as raw material in some

170

other process. Manufacturing production usually is carried on for the wholesale market rather than for direct sales, although retail sales to the ultimate consumer is becoming more prevalent. Processing on farms is not usually classified as manufacturing if the raw material is grown on the farm. The manufacturing is accessory to the major use of farming.

MAP, CONTOUR

A map that displays land elevations in graphic form with lines connecting areas of equal elevation.

MAP, OFFICIAL

See OFFICIAL MAP.

MAPPED STREET

A street appearing on the official map of the municipality or county.

Comment: Mapped streets are planned streets. By placing them on the official map, the integrity of the right-of-way is preserved since most enabling acts prevent the issuance of a building permit for a structure in the bed of a mapped street.

MARINA

A facility for the storing, servicing, fueling, berthing, and securing of boats and that may include eating, sleeping, and retail facilities for owners, crews, and guests.

MARKETABILITY STUDY

A study that measures the need for a particular land use or activity within a defined geographic area.

Comment: The market study, also referred to as market demand, usually involves a proposal to locate a specific use on a specified site. The study determines how many people can be expected to patronize the facility and how many similar facilities are located in the market area.

MARQUEE

Any hood, canopy, awning, or permanent construction that projects from a wall of a building, usually above an entrance.

Comment: Marquees are usually exempt from setback requirements and are allowed to project over the sidewalk, particularly in central business districts. Consideration should be given, however, to potential problems with fire fighting and the need to get ladders and equipment above the first floor. Also, there is the matter of aesthetics, and any permanent marquee extending along the sidewalk in the central business district should be

171

undertaken only in accordance with an overall plan to assure design continuity.

MARSHLANDS

Low-lying tracts of land characterized by high water tables, soils, and extensive vegetation peculiar to and characteristic of wet places. *See* WETLANDS, FRESHWATER.

MASKING

Covering over of one sound or element by another.

Comment: Masking is the amount the audibility threshold of one sound is raised by the presence of a second masking sound. Also used in regard to odors.

MASS GATHERING

Any outdoor event, or one held in a temporary structure or tent, attended by more than two thousand persons over an eight-hour period and that includes music festivals, concerts, theatrical exhibitions, public shows, entertainment, amusement, speeches, swap and shop markets, and flea markets. *See* TEMPORARY OUTDOOR ACTIVITY.

Comment: The two thousand threshold is somewhat arbitrary but assumes about two hundred and fifty persons in approximately eighty cars per hour. Temporary mass gatherings should be licensed (separate from zoning) and careful consideration given to parking, health and sanitary facilities, safety, fire danger, circulation, and impact on surrounding uses from amplifying systems, noise, litter, and lights.

MASS TRANSIT

A public common carrier transportation system for people having established routes and fixed schedules.

MASTER DEED

A legal instrument under which title to real estate is conveyed and by which a condominium is created and established.

Comment: The master deed is the key document in establishing a condominium. It is required to be filed in the office of the county recording officer. The contents of the master deed are usually prescribed by the appropriate state legislation covering condominium ownership. Master deeds usually contain the following information: a statement placing the land described in the master deed under the provisions of the condominium act; the official title of the condominium; a legal description of the land;

a survey of the land showing the improvements to be erected, common elements, and units to be sold, in sufficient detail and shown in their respective locations with dimensions; identification of each unit; a description of the common elements and limited common elements, if there are any; the proportion of the undivided interests in the common elements, including rights of owners; bylaws; methods of amending and supplementing the master deed; the name and nature of the association; the manner of sharing common expenses; and whatever other provisions may be desired, such as restrictions or limitations of use, occupancy, transfer leasing, or other disposition of a unit or the limitations on the use of common elements.

MASTER PLAN

A comprehensive, long-range plan intended to guide the growth and development of a community or region that typically includes inventory and analytic sections leading to recommendations for the community's future economic development, housing, recreation and open space, transportation, community facilities, and land use, all related to the community's goals and objectives for these elements.

Comment: The term "master plan" (also known as the general or comprehensive plan) has almost become a word of art. The principle underlying its analysis and preparation is the comprehensive nature of the document, integrating all of the various parts into a single, unified coherent plan that includes implementation proposals.

State enabling legislation specifies the legal requirements of a master plan, including its preparation, contents, modifications, adoption, and implementation. Although certain plan elements may be required, there are no limits to the number or type of plan elements, area, or subplans that may comprise a master plan. In many states, zoning ordinances must be based on the master plan, and where discrepancies occur, the master plan takes precedence.

MEAN

The average of a series of figures computed by adding up all the figures and dividing by the number of figures.

MEAN HIGH WATERLINE

The line formed by the intersection of the tidal plane of mean high tide with the shore.

173

MECHANICAL TURBULENCE

The erratic movement of air caused by local obstructions, such as buildings.

MEDIAN

(1) The middle number in a series of items in which 50 percent of all figures are above the median and 50 percent are below; (2) an island in the center of a highway that separates opposing traffic flows.

MEDIAN ISLAND

A barrier placed between lanes of traffic flowing in opposite directions. *See* BARRIER. *See Figure 70.*

MEDICAL BUILDING

A building that contains establishments dispensing health services. *See* HEALTH SERVICES.

MEGALOPOLIS

An extended metropolitan area created from the merging of once separate and distinct metropolitan areas.

MEMBERSHIP ORGANIZATION

An organization with preestablished formal membership requirements, bylaws, and with the objective of promoting the interests of its members.

Comment: Membership organizations include trade associations, professional organizations, unions, and political and religious organizations. From a zoning perspective, they usually operate out of office buildings and are treated like other office uses. However, periodic membership meetings may generate large traffic volumes. *See* CLUB; FRATERNAL ORGANIZATION.

MERGED LOTS

Two or more contiguous lots, in single ownership, that individually do not conform to zoning ordinance bulk standards.

Comment: In many states, the doctrine of merger treats separate lots under the same ownership as a single lot if either of the lots fails to meet the zoning requirement for area or frontage. The fact that the lots may have been purchased separately and may have been legally conforming lots at some time does not vest development rights in perpetuity.

MESOTROPHIC LAKES

Lakes that are intermediate in characteristics between oligotrophic (clear waters and relatively free of nutrients) and eutrophic (high levels of growth and nutrients) lakes. *See* EUTROPHIC LAKES; OLIGOTROPHIC LAKES.

METER

A metric scale measure equal to 3.28 feet.

174

METES AND BOUNDS	A method of describing the boundaries of land by directions (bounds) and distances (metes) from a known point of reference.
METROPOLIS	The major city in a designated area; generally, any large city.
METROPOLITAN AREA	An area whose economic and social life is influenced by and whose boundaries are roughly defined by the commuting limits to the center city. *Comment:* While commuting patterns usually define a metropolitan area, other factors can be used, such as newspaper circulation and retail trade areas.
METROPOLITAN STATISTICAL AREA (MSA)	A geographic area consisting of a large population nucleus together with adjacent areas having a high degree of economic and social integration. *Comment:* The major purpose of the MSA is to provide federal agencies with a common real base in tabulating and publishing data for metropolitan areas. Data are available for individual metropolitan areas on population, housing, industry, trade, employment, payrolls, and labor markets. To that end, MSAs are defined in terms of counties and the smallest geographical unit for which a wide range of statistical data can be obtained.
MEZZANINE	An intermediate level between the floor and ceiling of any story and covering not more than 33 percent of the floor area of the room in which it is located. *See Figure 6.*
MGD	Millions of gallons per day.
MID-RISE	A building of three to seven stories. *See* DWELLING, MID-RISE. *See Figure 30.*
MIGRATION	The movement of people from one domicile to another. *Comment:* The key word is domicile. It implies a permanent as opposed to a temporary movement, such as daily commuting to a job.
MILE	A linear measure equal to 5,280 feet, 1,760 yards, or 1.6 kilometers.

MILL

One-tenth of a cent.

Comment: The term is still used in matters relating to taxes.

MINE

(1) A cavity in the earth from which minerals and ores are extracted; (2) the act of removing minerals and ores.

MINERAL RIGHTS

One of a number of distinct and separate rights associated with real property that gives the owner of rights certain specified privileges, such as to extract, sell, and receive royalties with respect to the minerals.

Comment: The holder of mineral rights, in some cases, may be able to exercise those rights to the detriment of all other rights. For example, if the mineral rights owner has the right to explore or mine the minerals, it could severely affect the remainder of the land.

MINI-MALL

A shopping center of between 80,000 to 150,000 square feet on a site of eight to fifteen acres where tenants are located on both sides of a covered walkway with direct pedestrian access to all establishments from the walkway. *See* SHOPPING CENTER; SHOPPING MALL; SPECIALTY SHOPPING CENTER.

MINI-WAREHOUSE

See SELF-SERVICE STORAGE FACILITY.

MINIMAL ACCESSIBILITY

An environment that will afford a handicapped person access with difficulty. Some assistance may be required.

MINING

The extraction of minerals, including solids, such as coal and ores; liquids, such as crude petroleum; and gases, such as natural gases.

Comment: The term also includes quarrying; groundwater diversion; soil removal; milling, such as crushing, screening, washing, and flotation; and other preparation customarily done at the mine site or as part of a mining activity.

MINOR SUBDIVISION

See SUBDIVISION, MINOR.

MINOR TRAFFIC GENERATOR

The use or uses that generate less than a total of five hundred vehicle trips per day. *See* MAJOR TRAFFIC GENERATOR.

176

MIST   Liquid particles suspended in air and formed by condensation of vaporized liquids.

MITIGATION   Methods used to alleviate or lessen the impact of development.

                                        Comment: One of the purposes of requiring an environmental impact statement is to determine the potential impacts from any development proposal and to propose mitigation methods to alleviate and minimize the impacts. These might include soil erosion measures and buffers, replacement of wetlands, or contributions for expanded public facilities.

MIXED-USE DEVELOPMENT   The development of a tract of land, building, or structure
(MXD)   with a variety of complementary and integrated uses, such as, but not limited to, residential, office, manufacturing, retail, public, or entertainment, in a compact urban form.

                                        Comment: Central business districts are examples of MXD, but generally developed over a long period of time and often without a plan. An early example of a planned MXD is Rockefeller Center in New York City. The appearance of developments with several mutually supporting activities in a single, compactly configured, integrated project is a relatively recent innovation in urban land use, dating only from the mid-1950s. Examples are Penn Center in Philadelphia (1953), Midtown Plaza in Rochester (1956), and Charles Center in Baltimore (1957) (*Mixed-Use Development Handbook,* 1987).

                                        MXDs are often cited as ways to reduce traffic generation, particularly where homes and jobs are planned and developed within easy commuting distance and shopping is located close to residences.

MIXED-USE ZONING   Regulations that permit a combination of different uses within a single development.

MOBILE HOME   *See* MANUFACTURED HOUSING.

MOBILE HOME PARK   A site containing spaces with required improvements and utilities that are leased for the long-term placement of manufactured houses and that may include services and facilities for the residents. *See* MANUFACTURED HOUSING.

Comment: Mobile home parks, frequently referred to as manufactured housing parks or subdivisions, often are licensed by the municipality or county, and compliance with local regulations is a prerequisite to annual license renewal. The regulations may specify a minimum area for the house pad, such as four thousand to five thousand square feet, and other required amenities. The spaces may be rented, owned individually, or sold as condominiums. Mobile home parks usually ban recreational vehicles, campers, or trailers.

MOBILE HOME SPACE

A plat of land for placement of a single mobile home within a mobile home park. *See* PAD.

MOBILE SOURCE

A moving source of pollution, such as an automobile.

MODAL SPLIT

The breakdown of how people get to work, shop, travel to recreational activities, or other origin or destination by type of conveyance.

Comment: The description of a modal split of commuting traffic might indicate 85 percent private auto, 10 percent bus, and 5 percent pedestrian.

MODE

In statistics, the value or number that occurs most frequently in a given series.

MODERATE-INCOME HOUSING

Housing that is economically feasible for families whose income level is categorized as moderate within the standards promulgated by HUD or the appropriate state housing agency.

Comment: Generally speaking, moderate income is defined as between 50 and 80 percent of the median family income in a particular market area. Economically feasible is defined as housing costs between 28 and 30 percent of gross family income. HUD now uses the term "very low" to identify families earning 50 percent or less of area median family income; "lower," 50 to 80 percent; and "moderate," 80 to 120 percent.

MODULAR HOUSING

See MANUFACTURED HOUSING.

MORATORIUM

The legally authorized delay of new construction or development.

MORBIDITY RATE

The incidence of a specific disease per specified unit of population.

MORGUE

A place for the storage of human bodies prior to autopsy, burial, or release to survivors.

MORTALITY RATE

The annual number of deaths per thousand population.

MORTUARY

A place for the storage of human bodies prior to their burial or cremation.

MOTEL

An establishment providing sleeping accommodations with a majority of all rooms having direct access to the outside without the necessity of passing through the main lobby of the building.

Comment: The distinction between hotels and motels is narrowing. Traditionally, the motel (motor-hotel) was a one- or two-story, less-expensive accommodation catering to the automobile traveling public. Today, rentals range across the entire economic spectrum, multistory structures are common, and motels may offer a full range of services. Guests usually register at the main desk and then drive their cars to a parking space closest to their room to unload and store their car.

MOTION PICTURE THEATER

A place where motion pictures are shown to the public for a fee.

MOTOR FREIGHT TERMINAL

See FREIGHT HANDLING FACILITIES.

MULCH

A layer of wood chips, dry leaves, straw, hay, plastic, or other material placed on the surface of the soil around plants to retain moisture, to prevent weeds from growing, to hold soil in place, and to aid in plant growth.

MULCHING

The application of mulch.

MULTIFAMILY DWELLING

See DWELLING, MULTIFAMILY

MULTIPHASE DEVELOPMENT

A development project that is constructed in stages, each stage being capable of existing independently of the others.

MULTISERVICE CENTER

A building containing a variety of social services convenient and readily available to the residents of the neighborhood where located.

Comment: Such services may include education, counseling, legal aid, recreation, and health care. It is often

179

associated with and may be located in a church, school, or similar facility (Schultz and Kasen 1984).

MULTIUSE BUILDING

A building containing two or more distinct uses.

Comment: A multiuse building might include retail stores on the first floor and apartments on the upper floors.

MUNICIPALITY

The political subdivision that can adopt and enforce the development ordinances if so empowered by state legislation.

Comment: The development regulations would, under this definition, note the specific legal name of the municipality. In some states, the county or the state itself may adopt and enforce development regulations. *See* LOCAL AUTHORITY.

N

NATIONAL AMBIENT AIR QUALITY STANDARDS

Standards promulgated by the federal Environmental Protection Agency for specified air pollutants, including suspended particulates, sulfur dioxide, carbon monoxide, nitrogen dioxide, ozone, hydrocarbons, and lead (Schultz and Kasen 1984).

NATIONAL FLOOD INSURANCE PROGRAM

A federal program that provides for flood insurance.

NATIONAL HISTORIC AREA

Parts of the National Park System that commemorate historic events, activities, or persons associated with the history of the United States.

Comment: National historic areas include battlefields, monuments, battlefield sites, historical parks, and national memorials.

NATIONAL HISTORICAL LANDMARK

A site with national historic significance included on the National Register of Historic Places. *See* NATIONAL REGISTER OF HISTORIC PLACES.

NATIONAL HISTORIC PRESERVATION ACT

A 1966 federal law that established a National Register of Historic Places and the Advisory Council on Historic

Preservation and authorized grants-in-aid for historic properties preservation.

NATIONAL REGISTER OF HISTORIC PLACES

The official list, established by the National Historic Preservation Act, of sites, districts, buildings, structures, and objects significant in the nation's history or whose artistic or architectural value is unique.

Comment: Listing on the National Register does not restrict any activities or actions of the property owner. It does, however, place limits on any actions of the federal government that might damage the historic nature of the property. Some states have a similar register. Only local historic district ordinances can place limits on the actions of a private property owner with respect to a property in that district. *See* HISTORIC AREA; HISTORIC BUILDING; HISTORIC BUILDING STYLES; HISTORIC PRESERVATION; HISTORIC SITE; NATIONAL HISTORIC PRESERVATION ACT.

NATURAL DRAINAGE FLOW

The pattern of surface and stormwater drainage from a particular site before the construction or installation of improvements or prior to any regrading.

NATURAL GRADE

See GRADE, NATURAL.

NATURAL GROUND SURFACE

The ground surface in its original state before any grading, excavation, or filling. *See* GRADE, NATURAL.

NATURAL MONUMENT

(1) A natural feature or object used to define or mark a boundary; (2) any large, remarkable natural feature.

NATURAL RECHARGE

Adding water to an aquifer by natural means, such as precipitation, or from lakes and rivers.

NATURAL RESOURCES INVENTORY (NRI)

A survey of existing natural elements relating to land, water, air, plant, and animal life of an area or a community and the interrelationship of these elements. The NRI usually includes data on soils, geology, topography (including watershed and flood areas), and vegetation.

Comment: The NRI (also known as the environmental resources inventory) is an important input to master plan preparation and is useful in the review of subdivision and other development plans. Such studies primarily indicate which areas are environmentally suitable for development and which are not. Depending on study detail, they

181

also can provide: (1) indices of development capacity; (2) background information useful in the preparation of environmental impact statements; (3) disclosure of current imbalances between development and the environment; and (4) information to residents on the environmental impacts of development.

The NRI is an areawide inventory and, as such, its data may not be sufficiently precise for use in the preparation or detailed review of specific development projects. One of the initial steps in the design review procedure, though, is a check of the proposed plans against the findings of the natural resources inventory. This check may provide some design direction or at least alert the reviewing authority of potential environmental problems. This review also may suggest that an environmental impact statement may be necessary.

NATURAL SELECTION

The natural process by which organisms best adapted to their environment survive and those less well adapted are eliminated.

NATURE PRESERVE

Areas in which human activities are very limited and where the natural environment is protected from man-made changes.

Comment: Nature preserves may be large holdings protected by governmental ownership or small parcels restricted by conservation easements. Nature preserve uses are usually limited to hiking and walking trails.

NEGATIVE EASEMENT

See EASEMENT, NEGATIVE.

NEIGHBORHOOD

An area of a community with characteristics that distinguish it from other areas and that may include distinct ethnic or economic characteristics, housing types, schools, or boundaries defined by physical barriers, such as major highways and railroads or natural features, such as rivers.

Comment: Historically, the neighborhood was defined as the area served by an elementary school, with shopping and recreation facilities to serve neighborhood residents. While the description is probably dated, the neighborhood designation is useful in analyzing the adequacy of facilities and services and in identifying factors affecting the quality of the built environment. In addition, as a distinct and identifiable area, often with its own name, neighborhoods are recognized as fostering community spirit and a sense of place, factors recognized as important in community planning.

NEIGHBORHOOD BUSINESS AREA

A commercial area of approximately fifty thousand square feet, often located on an arterial or collector street, providing convenience goods and services for residents of the surrounding area. *See* STRIP COMMERCIAL DEVELOPMENT.

Comment: The neighborhood business area usually serves residents within five minutes driving time. The stores include food, drugs, hardware, clothing, and sundries; services include barber and beauty parlors, cleaners, and so on. The major characteristic of the neighborhood business area is its scale. It usually does not contain any large stores designed to serve several neighborhoods. Zoning can protect the scale of such areas by placing upper limits on the size of permitted uses.

NEIGHBORHOOD PARK

An open area of two to five acres in size and including lawn area, trees, shrubbery, walks, benches, a focal point, such as a fountain or statue, sandbox, play apparatus, and table game area.

Comment: A neighborhood park may also include baseball or softball fields, basketball courts, and other activities.

NEIGHBORHOOD SHOPPING CENTER

See NEIGHBORHOOD BUSINESS AREA; SHOPPING CENTER.

NEIGHBORING DWELLING

Any first or second lot in either direction along the same side of the street from the subject lot, or any lot that fronts directly across from the subject lot or first or second lot adjacent thereto.

Comment: The phrase is used in zoning to establish a prevailing setback line.

NET AREA OF LOT (NET ACREAGE)

The area of the lot excluding those features or areas that the development ordinance excludes from the calculations.

Comment: A development ordinance might exclude, for density or area calculation purposes, undevelopable or critical areas of land, such as floodways, wetlands, areas with steep slopes, or other constrained areas or easements. However, in recent years, court cases have sharply restricted the ability to exclude these lands, particularly where a state land use law defines terms differently. *See* CRITICAL AREA; DENSITY.

NEW CAR AGENCY *See* AUTOMOBILE SALES.

NEW TOWN A planned community, usually developed on largely vacant land and containing housing, employment, shopping, industry, recreation and open space, and public facilities.

Comment: The term new town implies a predetermined population level and phased development over a relatively short period. Examples of new towns include Reston, Virginia, and Columbia, Maryland.

NEWSRACK A self-service, coin-operated dispenser installed, used, or maintained for the display and sale of newspapers.

Comment: Great care must be used in adopting standards to control the location of newsracks located on sidewalks and along public streets. Unreasonable controls, not related to safety, run afoul of First Amendment (freedom of speech) criteria.

NEWSSTAND A portable structure usually not exceeding one hundred square feet from which newspapers, magazines, and other printed material are sold.

Comment: Newsstands usually do not have water or sanitary facilities but may have electricity. They are frequently located on sidewalks at busy intersections, typically in the right-of-way. They are often licensed by the municipality.

NIGHTCLUB An establishment dispensing liquor and meals and in which music, dancing, or entertainment is conducted.

NOISE Any undesired audible sound.

NOISE POLLUTION Continuous or episodic excessive noise in the human environment.

Comment: Noise pollution usually is defined in terms of a maximum decibel level by frequency range.

NONAMBULATORY HANDICAP	An impairment that, regardless of cause or manifestation, for all practical purposes confines individuals to wheelchairs. *See* AMERICANS WITH DISABILITIES ACT.
NONCONFORMING LOT	A lot, the area, dimensions, or location of which was lawful prior to the adoption, revision, or amendment of the zoning ordinance but that fails by reason of such adoption, revision, or amendment to conform to the present requirements of the zoning district.
NONCONFORMING SIGN	Any sign lawfully existing on the effective date of an ordinance, or amendment thereto, that renders such sign nonconforming because it does not conform to all the standards and regulations of the adopted or amended ordinance.
NONCONFORMING STRUCTURE OR BUILDING	A structure or building, the size, dimensions, or location of which was lawful prior to the adoption, revision, or amendment to the zoning ordinance but that fails by reason of such adoption, revision, or amendment to conform to the present requirements of the zoning district.
NONCONFORMING USE	A use or activity that was lawful prior to the adoption, revision or amendment of the zoning ordinance but that fails by reason of such adoption, revision, or amendment to conform to the present requirements of the zoning district.
NONPOINT RUNOFF	Surface water entering a channel from no definable discharge source.
NONSLIP	A surface that is tested or approved to be slip resistant by a nationally recognized testing laboratory. *See* AMERICANS WITH DISABILITIES ACT.
NUISANCE	An interference with the enjoyment and use of property.
NUISANCE ELEMENT	Any environmental pollutant, such as smoke, odors, liquid wastes, solid wastes, radiation, noise, vibration, glare, or heat.
NURSERY	Land or greenhouses used to raise flowers, shrubs, and plants for sale. *See* GREENHOUSE.
NURSERY SCHOOL	*See* CHILD-CARE CENTER.

185

NURSING HOME   *See* EXTENDED CARE FACILITY; INTERMEDIATE CARE FACILITY; LONG-TERM CARE FACILITY.

O

OBSTRUCTION   Any dam, wall, embankment, levee, dike, pile, abutment, soil, material, bridge, conduit, culvert, building, wire, fence, refuse, fill, structure, or other matter in, along, across, or projecting into any channel, watercourse, or flood plain that may impede, retard, or change the direction of the flow of water, either in itself or by catching debris carried by such water, or that is placed where the flow of water might carry the same downstream.

OCCUPANCY or OCCUPIED   The residing of an individual or individuals overnight in a dwelling unit or the storage or use of equipment, merchandise, or machinery in any public, commercial, or industrial building.

OCCUPANCY PERMIT   A required permit allowing the use of a building or structure after it has been determined that all the requirements of applicable ordinances have been met.

Comment: The occupancy permit may be a temporary one for a given period of time to permit completion of certain improvements. For example, installation of landscaping may be delayed because of weather. Obviously, a temporary permit would not be granted if the unfinished or incomplete improvement is essential to the use or affects health or safety.

One of the problems in granting temporary permits is the difficulty in halting operations or evicting tenants if the temporary permit expires. Consequently, many jurisdictions grant temporary permits reluctantly or not at all.

OCCUPANCY RATE   The ratio of occupied space or dwelling units to total space or dwelling units.

OCCUPANT   The individual, individuals, or entity in actual possession of a premises.

OCCUPATION   Gainful employment in which an individual engages to earn compensation.

ODD-LOT DEVELOPMENT

The development of new housing or other buildings on scattered vacant sites in a built-up area. *See* INFILL DEVELOPMENT.

ODOROUS MATTER

Any material that produces an olfactory response in a human being.

Comment: This is a difficult nuisance element to monitor and enforce. For some odorous chemicals or elements, research has determined minimum levels at which the chemical can be detected by smell.

OFFER

A proposal to enter into an agreement with another party.

OFFICE

A room or group of rooms used for conducting the affairs of a business, profession, service, industry, or government and generally furnished with desks, tables, files, and communication equipment.

Comment: The term "office" is almost generic without the necessity of spelling out all the functions that may be carried out in an office. Indeed, as modern technology expands, office functions include tasks that in the past would have been considered production, industrial, or commercial. For example, desktop publishing, high-speed data transmission, and large varieties of research are now carried out in offices.

OFFICE BUILDING

A building used primarily for conducting the affairs of a business, profession, service, industry, or government, or like activity, and may include ancillary services for office workers, such as a restaurant, coffee shop, newspaper or candy stand, and child-care facilities.

Comment: Typical controls for offices include floor area ratios (FAR), height, setback requirements, building and impervious surface coverage, and parking requirements. A typical suburban office building FAR may range from .15 to .30. Town and small city FARs range from 1 to 5, with FARs in major cities running as high as 15.

OFFICE PARK

A development on a tract of land that contains a number of separate office buildings, accessory and supporting uses, and open space designed, planned, constructed, and managed on an integrated and coordinated basis.

OFFICE AT HOME

A home occupation in which a part of a dwelling unit is used as the resident's office. *See* HOME OCCUPATION.

187

OFFICIAL MAP

An ordinance in map form adopted by the governing body that conclusively shows the location and width of proposed streets, public facilities, public areas, and drainage rights-of-way.

Comment: State regulations vary as to what may be shown on an official map. The purpose is to prevent private development from encroaching on sites for proposed public improvements. However, most states require that governmental entities move to acquire the land within a relatively short period of time (often one year) after an application for development is received that encroaches on the proposed public facility. In addition, an option fee may be required for the year. There is often a waiver of taxes on the property during the option period.

OFFICIAL SOIL MAP

Maps that are part of a Soil Conservation Service soil survey that delineates various soil types.

Comment: Soil surveys contain information on soil characteristics, including depth to bedrock, height of water table, slopes, permeability, size of rocks, erodability, and other characteristics. The soil surveys also contain aerial photographs on which the locations of the various types of soil within a particular geographic area are shown. More detailed on-site surveys and investigations may be needed to verify the types and locations of soils prior to preparing a development plan.

OFFICIAL SOILS INTERPRETATION

The written description of soil types and their characteristics and accompanying maps that are part of a recognized soil survey.

OFF-ROAD VEHICLE

See VEHICLE, OFF-ROAD.

OFF-SITE

Located outside the lot lines of the lot in question but within the property (of which the lot is a part) that is the subject of a development application or within a contiguous portion of a street or other right-of-way. *See Figure 56.*

OFF-SITE IMPROVEMENT

Improvements required to be made off-site as a result of an application for development and including, but not limited to, road widening and upgrading, stormwater facilities, and traffic improvements.

188

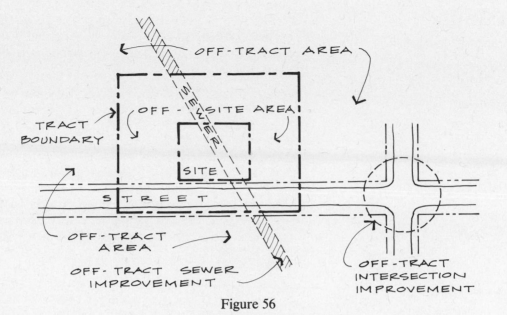

Figure 56

Comment: Off-site improvements are imposed as a condition of development approval. The type and extent of the improvements should be spelled out in the development ordinance. Typically, a proposed development adjacent to a narrow road would be required to widen and improve the road, on the development side, and install curbs and drains. When the property across from the development is not expected to be improved in the immediate future, though, municipalities often opt for requiring the developer to improve the entire width of the road to a somewhat lesser extent than normally required rather than have one-half the width totally improved and one-half in relatively poor condition.

OFF-SITE PARKING

Parking provided for a specific use but located on a site other than the one on which the specific use is located.

Comment: Many ordinances permit off-site parking provided it is located reasonably close to the use it is designed to serve. A distance of three hundred to four hundred feet is considered the maximum. Off-site parking offers an advantage in that it encourages a grouping of parking for more than one use. In some cases, shared parking can result in having to provide for fewer spaces than for the sum of individual uses.

189

OFF-STREET LOADING

Designated areas located adjacent to buildings where trucks may load and unload cargo.

Comment: A minimum dimension of fourteen by forty feet is needed to accommodate modern tractor-trailers. Site design should provide adequate circulation—wide aisles, large turning radii, and back-up space—for the tractor-trailer. Since many load and unload throughout the night or early in the morning, and many are refrigerator trucks requiring noisy machinery to be kept going at all times, the nature and location of adjacent uses should be taken into consideration in locating the off-street loading areas.

OFF-STREET PARKING SPACE

A temporary storage area for a motor vehicle that is directly accessible to an access aisle and that is not located on a dedicated street right-of-way. *See Figure 59.*

OFF-TRACT

Not located on the property that is the subject of a development application or on a contiguous portion of a street or other right-of-way. *See Figure 56.*

OFF-TRACT IMPROVEMENT

Improvements required to be made off-tract as a result of an application for development.

Comment: The payment of off-tract improvements can be complicated. Most state land use laws permit only a proportionate share assessment and require the facility to be improved to have a "rational nexus" to the project. Consequently, a developer cannot be required to pay for the entire improvement of an intersection, for example, that is seriously congested even without the new project. The developer could be made to provide his or her fair share of any improvement needed to accommodate the traffic impact of the new development.

Rational nexus means that the project has a discernible impact on the facility proposed to be improved. The impact of a major traffic generator on adjacent intersections is obvious. The impact on one ten miles away probably does not meet the rational nexus test.

OLIGOTROPHIC LAKES

Deep lakes that have a low supply of nutrients, contain little organic matter, and are characterized by high water transparency and high dissolved oxygen.

ON-SITE

Located on the lot that is the subject of an application for development. *See Figure 56.*

ON-STREET PARKING SPACE   A temporary storage area for a motor vehicle that is located on a dedicated street right-of-way. *See Figure 59.*

ON-TRACT   Located on the property that is the subject of a development application or on a contiguous portion of a street or other right-of-way.

ONE HUNDRED PERCENT LOCATION   A real estate term identifying the prime business location usually able to command the highest commercial and office rentals for a particular area or municipality.

OPACITY   Degree of obscuration of light.

Comment: The range is from 0 to 100 percent. For instance, a window has 0 percent opacity and a wall is 100 percent opacity. The Ringelmann system of evaluating smoke density is based on opacity.

OPEN BURNING   Uncontrolled burning of wastes in an open area.

OPEN MEETING OR HEARING   A meeting open to the public.

Comment: Open meetings may be required by statute under a "sunshine law." However, the fact that a meeting is required to be open to the public does not necessarily mean that the public can participate. Public participation usually is permitted only at a public hearing, duly noticed and advertised.

OPEN SPACE   Any parcel or area of land or water essentially unimproved and set aside, dedicated, designated, or reserved for public or private use or enjoyment or for the use and enjoyment of owners, occupants, and their guests of land adjoining or neighboring such open space.

Comment: Open space may include active recreational facilities, such as swimming pools, play equipment for youngsters, ball fields, court games, and picnic tables. The improved recreation facilities, though, would be only a small part of the overall open space.

OPEN SPACE, COMMON   Land within or related to a development, not individually owned or dedicated for public use, that is designed and intended for the common use or enjoyment of the residents and their guests of the development and may include such complementary structures and improvements as are necessary and appropriate. *See Figure 16.*

OPEN SPACE, GREEN   An open space area not occupied by any structures or impervious surfaces. *See* GREEN AREA; GREENBELT.

OPEN SPACE, PRIVATE   Common open space, the use of which is normally limited to the occupants of a single dwelling or building or property.

Comment: In a multifamily development, the land immediately surrounding a building for a distance of perhaps twenty-five feet would be considered private open space and limited for use by the occupants of the building.

OPEN SPACE, PUBLIC   Open space owned by a public agency and maintained by it for the use and enjoyment of the general public.

OPEN SPACE RATIO   Total area of open space divided by the total site area in which the open space is located. *See Figure 57.*

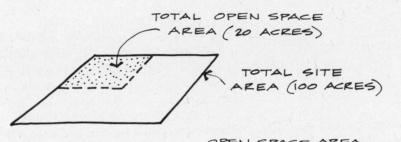

OPEN SPACE RATIO CALCULATION

Figure 57

OPTION   An exclusive right to purchase, rent, or sell a property usually at a stipulated price and within a specified time.

ORDINANCE   A municipally adopted law or regulation.

ORGANIC   Referring to or derived from living organisms.

ORGANISM   Any living human, plant, or animal.

ORIGIN AND DESTINATION STUDY   A transportation study that records the location from where a trip begins and where it will end.

ORNAMENTAL TREE

A deciduous tree planted primarily for its ornamental value or for screening purposes; tends to be smaller at maturity than a shade tree (Planning Advisory Service Report No. 431 1990).

OUTBUILDING

A separate accessory building or structure not physically connected to the principal building.

Comment: Outbuildings tend to be smaller than the principal structure and may be used for storage or ancillary use. On estates, outbuildings are often the living quarters for employees.

OUTDOOR RETAIL SALES

See RETAIL SALES, OUTDOOR.

OUTDOOR STORAGE

The keeping, in an unenclosed area, of any goods, junk, material, merchandise, or vehicles in the same place for more than twenty-four hours. *See* RETAIL SALES, OUTDOOR.

Comment: Many ordinances prohibit outdoor storage entirely. Others ban it in any required yard areas unless the outdoor storage is screened from public view by a fence or wall. There are uses that typically and traditionally include outdoor storage. These include new and used vehicles, agriculture, plant and landscaping establishments, and long-term parking lots. Hardware stores and gas stations often display merchandise outdoors. Ordinances should establish controls over these uses to ensure they do not become nuisances, safety problems, and aesthetic disasters. These controls should include minimum setbacks from street rights-of-way and property lines, landscaping requirements, maximum height of outdoor material, and, for especially obnoxious outdoor storage, such as junkyards, fences to screen the material.

OUTFALL

The mouth of a sewer, drain, or conduit where an effluent is discharged into the receiving waters.

OUTLET STORE

See RETAIL OUTLET STORE.

OVERFLOW RIGHTS

An easement that allows an owner to run excess water onto another's land.

OVERFLOWED LAND

A flood plain or land subject to frequent flooding. *See* FLOOD PLAIN.

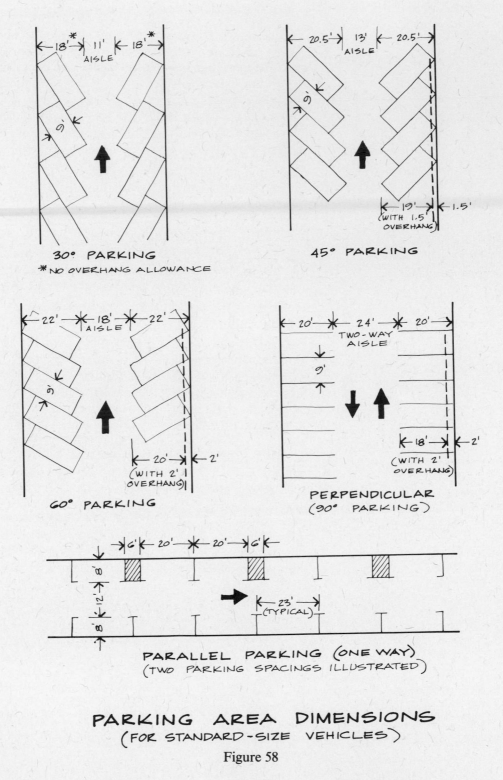

18' * | 11' AISLE | 18' *

9'

30° PARKING

* NO OVERHANG ALLOWANCE

20.5' | 13' AISLE | 20.5'

9'

19' (WITH 1.5' OVERHANG) | 1.5'

45° PARKING

22' | 18' AISLE | 22'

9'

20' (WITH 2' OVERHANG) | 2'

60° PARKING

20' | 24' TWO-WAY AISLE | 20'

9'

18' (WITH 2' OVERHANG) | 2'

PERPENDICULAR (90° PARKING)

6' | 20' | 20' | 6'

8'

8' | 12' | 8'

23' (TYPICAL)

PARALLEL PARKING (ONE WAY)
(TWO PARKING SPACINGS ILLUSTRATED)

PARKING AREA DIMENSIONS
(FOR STANDARD-SIZE VEHICLES)

Figure 58

OVERHANG

(1) The part of a roof or wall that extends beyond the facade of a lower wall *(see Figure 14);* (2) the portion of a vehicle extending beyond the wheel stops or curb *(see Figure 58).*

Comment: In parking lot design, the depth of the parking stall can be reduced by two feet if curbing is used for wheel stops and allowance is made for the overhang. However, the overhanging car can interfere with pedestrian travel if it encroaches on an adjacent sidewalk. If the sidewalk is placed two or more feet from the curb, the intervening space is generally not appropriate for planting due to the difficulty in caring for the plants and because of fluid leakage from car engines.

OVERLAY ZONE

A zoning district that encompasses one or more underlying zones and that imposes additional requirements above that required by the underlying zone.

Comment: Overlay zones deal with special situations in a municipality that are not appropriate to a specific zoning district or apply to several districts. For example, in all business zones, an overlay provision might require impact fees to provide for traffic improvements or an historic district overlay may cover parts of several zones. An overlay provision covering an entire municipality or specific zoning districts might require that all properties over a certain acreage proposed for higher density development also provide a percentage of lower income housing.

OWNER

An individual, firm, association, syndicate, partnership, or corporation having sufficient proprietary interest to seek development of land.

OXIDATION POND

A man-made lake or pond in which organic wastes are reduced by bacterial action.

OZONE

A pungent, colorless, toxic gas.

Comment: Ozone is one component of photochemical smog and is considered a major air pollutant.

P

PACKAGE TREATMENT PLANT

Small, self-contained sewage treatment facilities built to serve developed areas beyond the service area of larger regional plants.

195

PAD

A paved space in a mobile home park for the parking of a mobile home and usually containing utility connections. *See* MOBILE HOME SPACE.

Comment: The term pad is also used by developers of shopping centers to designate an area reserved for the future development of a freestanding commercial use; typically, a bank, fast-food outlet, or similar drive-up use.

PAPER STREET

See STREET, PAPER.

PARAPET

The extension of the main walls of a building above the roof level. *See Figure 14.*

Comment: Parapet walls often are used to shield mechanical equipment and vents. Many ordinances do not include the height of the parapet wall as part of the maximum height limit.

PARCEL

A contiguous lot or tract of land owned and recorded as the property of the same persons or controlled by a single entity. *See Figure 2.*

PARK

A tract of land, designated and used by the public for active and passive recreation.

PARK AND RIDE FACILITY

A parking lot designed for drivers to leave their cars and use mass transit facilities beginning, terminating, or stopping at the park and ride facility.

Comment: Park and ride facilities are often called intercept facilities.

PARKING, SHARED

Joint use of a parking area for more than one use.

Comment: Shared parking involves parking spaces that are used at different times by different uses. A shared parking space serves several stores so that a vehicle does not have to be moved from place to place. The classic example is the movie theater in a mall that, because of off-peak hour use, may not generate any additional parking demand.

Each type of joint use reduces the total number of spaces needed. Shopping center parking is an example of a shared parking facility. Instead of computing the parking requirement for each use, a ratio of parking spaces to square footage is used. This may vary between four

196

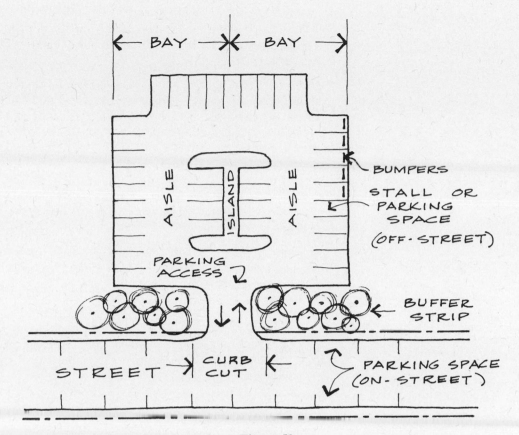

Figure 59

spaces per one thousand square feet to five per one thousand square feet depending on the size of the center.

PARKING ACCESS

The area of a parking lot that allows motor vehicles ingress and egress from the street. *See Figure 59.*

PARKING AREA

Any public or private area, under or outside of a building or structure, designed and used for parking motor vehicles including parking lots, garages, private driveways, and legally designated areas of public streets. *See GARAGE.*

PARKING AREA, PRIVATE

A parking area for the exclusive use of the owners, tenants, lessees, or occupants of the lot on which the parking area is located or their customers, employees, or whomever else they permit to use the parking area.

197

PARKING AREA, PUBLIC

A parking area available to the public, with or without payment of a fee.

PARKING BAY

The parking module consisting of one or two rows of parking spaces and the aisle from which motor vehicles enter and leave the spaces. *See Figure 59.*

PARKING LOT

An off-street, ground-level open area, usually improved, for the temporary storage of motor vehicles. *See* GARAGE; PARKING AREA.

PARKING SPACE

A space for the parking of a motor vehicle within a public or private parking area. *See* OFF-STREET PARKING SPACE; ON-STREET PARKING SPACE; STALL. *See Figure 58.*

PARKING STRUCTURE

A building or structure consisting of more than one level and used to store motor vehicles.

PAROCHIAL SCHOOL

See SCHOOL, PAROCHIAL.

PARTIAL DESTRUCTION

A building or structure that because of fire, flood, explosion, or other calamity, requires the rebuilding of less than half of its floor area.

Comment: The rebuilding of partially destroyed buildings becomes an issue when the building or use did not conform to current development regulations. Most ordinances stipulate that if a substantial part of a building or structure is damaged and requires rebuilding, then the new structure must meet current requirements. It is difficult to arrive at an enforceable and easily applicable standard that describes the extent of destruction beyond which a nonconforming structure may not be rebuilt. Some ordinances base it on value; others on the amount of floor area that has to be replaced. Many municipalities require a conforming structure when 50 percent of the value or floor area is destroyed. Others permit any damaged or destroyed building to be rebuilt, regardless of the amount of area or percent of value. In the process of application review, the approving authority will often attempt to mitigate some of the zoning deficiencies.

PARTIAL TAKING

The condemnation of part of a property.

PARTICULATES

Finely divided solid or liquid particles in the air or in an emission, including dust, smoke, fumes, mist, spray, and fog.

198

PARTY DRIVEWAY A single way providing vehicular access to two or more properties. See COMMON PASSAGEWAY. *See Figure 2.*

PARTY IMMEDIATELY CONCERNED For purposes of notice, party immediately concerned means any applicant for development, the owners of the subject property, and all owners of property and government agencies entitled to notice under a zoning ordinance, subdivision regulations, or other development controls.

PARTY WALL A common shared wall between two separate structures, buildings, or dwelling units. *See Figure 2.*

PASSENGER VEHICLE *See* VEHICLE, PASSENGER.

PASSIVE RECREATION *See* RECREATION, PASSIVE.

PATH A cleared way for pedestrians and/or bicycles that may or may not be paved or otherwise improved.

PATHOGENIC Causing or capable of causing disease.

PATIO *See* TERRACE.

PATIO HOME *See* DWELLING, PATIO HOME.

PAVEMENT (1) A created surface, such as brick, stone, concrete, or asphalt, placed on the land to facilitate passage; (2) that part of a street having an improved surface.

PAVERS Preformed paving blocks that are installed on the ground to form patterns while at the same time facilitate pedestrian and vehicular travel.

Comment: Pavers are particularly appropriate for overflow parking or occasional parking or light use areas.

PEAK-HOUR TRAFFIC The largest number of vehicles passing over a designated section of a street during the busiest one-hour period during a twenty-four-hour period.

PEAT Partially decomposed organic material.

PEDESTRIAN An individual who travels on foot.

PEDESTRIAN SCALE The proportional relationship between an individual and his or her environment.

199

Comment: Pedestrian scale is an informal and subjective standard. It suggests that the relationship between the person and his or her environment, whether natural or created, is comfortable, intimate, and contributes to the individual's sense of accessibility.

PEDESTRIAN TRAFFIC COUNT   The number of people who walk past a single point during a specified period of time.

PENINSULA   A projection of land surrounded on three sides by water.

PENTHOUSE   A roofed structure located on the roof of a building. *See Figure 14.*

Comment: Penthouses may be used for a variety of purposes, such as offices, dwelling units, or mechanical equipment associated with a building. Mechanical equipment penthouses are often excluded from building height requirements.

PEOPLE MOVER   A conveyor system designed for carrying pedestrians.

PERCOLATING AREA   That portion of soil utilized as the effective disposal media for sewage.

PERCOLATION   Downward flow or infiltration of water through the pores or spaces of rock or soil.

PERCOLATION TEST   A test designed to determine the ability of ground to absorb water and used to determine the suitability of soil for drainage or for septic system use.

PERFORMANCE GUARANTEE   Any security that may be accepted by a municipality to assure that improvements required as part of an application for development will be satisfactorily completed.

Comment: Performance guarantees may be a surety bond or letter of credit. In fact, they may be any security permitted by state or local ordinance to serve as a performance guarantee. *See* MAINTENANCE GUARANTEE.

PERFORMANCE STANDARDS   A set of criteria or limits relating to certain characteristics that a particular use or process may not exceed.

Comment: The standards may be established by state or federal law or by the municipality and may vary by zone or use. The standards usually cover noise, vibration, glare, heat, air or water contaminants, and traffic. As noted in Planning Advisory Service Report No. 322 (1976):

> It is a more precise way of defining compatibility. . . . The performance standard approach is based on the technical ability to identify activities numerically . . . and to measure them to see if they meet ordinance requirements. The most advanced work in performance standards has been in the area of industrial emissions.

PERIMETER

The boundaries or borders of a lot, tract, or parcel of land.

PERMAFROST

A permanently frozen soil layer.

PERMEABILITY

The ease with which air, water, or other fluids can move through soil or rock.

PERMIT

Written governmental permission issued by an authorized official, empowering the holder thereof to do some act not forbidden by law but not allowed without such authorization.

PERMITTED USE

Any use allowed in a zoning district and subject to the restrictions applicable to that zoning district.

PERMITTEE

Any person to whom a permit is issued.

PERSON

A corporation, company, association, society, firm, partnership, or joint stock company, as well as an individual, a state, and all political subdivisions of a state or any agency or instrumentality thereof.

PERSONAL SERVICES

Establishments primarily engaged in providing services involving the care of a person or his or her personal goods or apparel.

Comment: Personal services usually include the following: laundry, including cleaning and pressing service, linen supply, diaper service, beauty shops, barbershops, shoe repair, funeral services, steam baths, reducing salons and health clubs, clothing rental, locker rental, porter service, and domestic services.

PERVIOUS SURFACE

Any material that permits full or partial absorption of stormwater into previously unimproved land. See IMPERVIOUS SURFACE. *See Figure 49.*

201

PESTICIDE

An agent used to control pests.

Comment: Pesticides include insecticides for use against harmful insects; herbicides for weed control; fungicides for control of plant disease; rodenticides for killing rats, mice, and such; and germicides used in disinfectant products, algaecides, slimicides, and so forth. Some pesticides, particularly if they are misused, can contaminate water, air, or soil and accumulate in humans, animals, and the environment.

PESTICIDE TOLERANCE

A scientifically and legally established limit for the amount of chemical residue that can be permitted to remain in or on a harvested food or feed crop as a result of the application of a chemical for pest-control purposes.

pH

A measure of the acidity or alkalinity of a material, liquid, or solid.

Comment: A pH of 7 is considered neutral. Below 7 is acidic; above 7 is alkaline.

PHARMACY

A place where drugs and medicines are prepared and dispensed. *See* Drugstore.

PHASING

Development undertaken in a logical time and geographical sequence.

Comment: Phasing of large developments is not uncommon. The approving authority must ensure that each phase can exist as a separate entity if the project does not continue to buildout. Improvements for any phase that are geographically located in other phases must be installed and maintained prior to or coincident with construction of the phase to be served. Both objectives can be assured by establishing deadlines and requiring performance guarantees.

PHOTOCHEMICAL SMOG

Air pollution associated with oxidants rather than with sulfur oxides, particulates, or similar materials.

PHYSICAL HANDICAP

A physical impairment that confines a person to a wheelchair; causes a person to walk with difficulty or insecurity; affects the sight or hearing to the extent that a person functioning in a public area is insecure or exposed to danger; causes faulty coordination, or reduces mobil-

202

ity, flexibility, coordination, and perceptiveness to the extent that facilities are needed to provide for the safety of that person. *See* AMERICANS WITH DISABILITIES ACT.

PICNIC AREA

A place equipped with tables, benches, grills, and trash receptacles for people to assemble, cook, eat, and relax.

Comment: Picnic areas are passive recreation areas and could include rest rooms, play facilities, and open shelters.

PIER

A column, usually concrete, poured into holes to support large structures.

PIERHEAD LINE

A line beyond which no structure may extend out into navigable waters.

PILE

A nuclear reactor.

PILOT PLANT

An establishment or part thereof used to test out concepts and ideas and determine physical layouts, material flows, type of equipment required, costs, and secure other information prior to full-scale production.

Comment: The pilot plant is usually an intermediate step between the research laboratory and full-scale production. It requires monitoring and supervision by other than the usual production personnel and may involve frequent changes in physical layout, natural flow, or even processes. Pilot plants may produce production-grade goods, especially during the latter stages of the pilot process. However, if the pilot plant is switched to full production and operation and used for other than testing, it should be treated as a principal permitted use. Most development ordinances allow some percentage of research facilities, usually not more than 25 percent of the floor area, to be used for pilot plant operations.

PLACE OF WORSHIP

(1) A church, synagogue, temple, mosque, or other facility that is used for prayer by persons of similar beliefs; (2) a special purpose building that is architecturally designed and particularly adapted for the primary use of conducting on a regular basis formal religious services by a religious congregation.

Comment: For planning purposes, places of worship may include accessory uses that could have significant impacts on surrounding uses, such as schools, dormitories, recreational facilities, assembly halls, and catering facilities. (*See* comment under CHURCH.)

PLANNED COMMERCIAL DEVELOPMENT (PCD)

An area of a minimum contiguous size, as specified by ordinance, to be planned, developed, operated, and maintained as a single entity and containing one or more structures to accommodate retail, service, commercial, or office uses, or a combination of such uses, and appurtenant common areas and accessory uses incidental to the predominant uses.

PLANNED DEVELOPMENT

An area of a minimum contiguous size, as specified by ordinance, to be planned, developed, operated, and maintained according to plan as a single entity and containing one or more structures with appurtenant common areas.

PLANNED INDUSTRIAL DEVELOPMENT (PID)

A planned development consisting primarily of industrial uses.

Comment: Most PIDs now include retail service uses as well as recreational facilities to accommodate the work force.

PLANNED RESIDENTIAL DEVELOPMENT (PRD)

An area of a minimum contiguous size, as specified by ordinance, to be planned, developed, operated, and maintained as a single entity and containing one or more residential clusters; appropriate commercial, public, or quasi-public uses may be included if such uses are primarily for the benefit of the residential development.

PLANNED UNIT DEVELOPMENT (PUD)

An area of a minimum contiguous size, as specified by ordinance, to be planned, developed, operated, and maintained as a single entity and containing one or more residential clusters or planned unit residential developments and one or more public, quasi-public, commercial, or industrial areas in such ranges or ratios of nonresidential uses to residential uses as specified in the ordinance.

PLANNING BOARD

The duly designated planning board of the municipality, county, or region.

Comment: The planning board (also known as planning agency or commission) is created by ordinance with responsibility for reviewing and approving applications for development and preparation of master plans. Membership and duties are usually specifically delineated in the state enabling act.

PLAT

(1) A map representing a tract of land showing the boundaries and location of individual properties and streets; (2) a map of a subdivision or site plan.

PLAT, FINAL

A map of all or a portion of a subdivision or site plan that is presented to the approving authority for final approval.

Comment: Approval of the final plat usually is granted only upon the completion or installation of all improvements or the posting of performance guarantees assuring the completion or installation of such improvements. In many states, final approval is required before property can be transferred or building permits issued.

PLAT, PRELIMINARY

A map indicating the proposed layout of the subdivision or site plan that is submitted to the approving authority for preliminary approval.

PLAT, SKETCH

A concept, informal map of a proposed subdivision or site plan of sufficient accuracy to be used for the purpose of discussion and classification.

PLAYGROUND

An active recreational area with a variety of facilities, including equipment for younger children as well as court and field games.

Comment: The playground is usually located next to an elementary school and serves the neighborhood (a half-mile radius). Depending on the type of equipment and games, playgrounds can vary in size from ten thousand square feet to twenty-five thousand square feet.

PLAZA

An open space that may be improved and landscaped; usually surrounded by streets and buildings. *See* COURT; SQUARE. *See Figure 14*.

PLOT

(1) A single unit parcel of land; (2) a parcel of land that can be identified and referenced to a recorded plat or map.

PLUME

The visible emission from a flue or chimney.

POINT OF TANGENCY

The point at which a curved line meets a straight line. *See Figure 24*.

205

POINT SOURCE

A stationary source of a large individual emission, generally of an industrial nature. *See* AREA SOURCE; STATIONARY SOURCE.

POLLUTANT

Any introduced gas, liquid, or solid that makes a resource unfit for a specific purpose.

POLLUTION

The presence of matter or energy whose nature, location, or quantity produces undesired environmental effects.

PORCH

A roofed open area, which may be screened, usually attached to or part of and with direct access to or from a building. *See Figure 7.*

Comment: A porch becomes a room when the enclosed space is heated or air-conditioned and when the percentage of window area to wall area is less than 50 percent.

POROSITY

A measure of the amount of space between the grains or the cracks that can fill with water.

POROUS PAVEMENT SYSTEM

An arrangement of interlocking, prefabricated, perforated blocks, laid on a soil base and providing a stable pervious surface for low-volume vehicular use.

Comment: This product is useful in providing, for example, roadway-type support for emergency access lanes around buildings without the water runoff and appearance problems a paved surface can create.

POTABLE WATER

Water suitable for drinking or cooking purposes.

PPM

Parts per million.

Comment: A measurement commonly used to represent the amount of pollutant concentration in a liquid or gas.

PRECIPITATE

A solid that separates from a solution because of some chemical or physical change or the formation of such a solid.

PRECIPITATION

In pollution control work, any of a number of air pollution control devices, usually using mechanical/electrical means, to collect particulates from an emission.

PREEMPTIVE RIGHT

The right of a riparian owner to a preference in the acquisition of lands under tidewaters adjoining the owners upland. *See* RIPARIAN LAND.

206

PREEXISTING USE

The use of a lot or structure prior to the time of the enactment of a zoning ordinance.

Comment: Most municipalities, at the time a new zoning or development ordinance is proposed, will attempt to survey existing uses in order to provide an accurate record of preexisting nonconforming uses. The preexisting nonconforming use, legal prior to the time of the passage of the ordinance but made nonconforming as a result of the ordinance, has a legal right to continue. Future problems arise because of confusion as to the extent and nature of the uses at the time of passage. Hence, an inventory is often necessary to ensure that nonconforming uses do not expand illegally.

PRELIMINARY APPROVAL

Preliminary approval means the conferral of certain rights, prior to final approval, after specific elements of a development have been approved by the approving authority and agreed to by the applicant.

Comment: Preliminary approval generally freezes the terms and conditions required of an applicant for a specified period of time, often three to five years. It protects against any changes in zoning or other conditions of approval during the period. Preliminary approval usually involves public hearings and serious planning board input into the design. All specific conditions of approval are spelled out during the preliminary approval phase.

PRELIMINARY FLOOR PLANS AND ELEVATIONS

Architectural drawings prepared during early and introductory stages of the design of a project illustrating in schematic form the scope, scale, and relation of the project to its site and immediate environs.

PRELIMINARY PLAN

See PLAT, PRELIMINARY.

PREMISES

A lot, parcel, tract, or plot of land together with the buildings and structures thereon.

PRESCRIPTION

The acquisition of land by right of continuous use without protest from the owner.

Comment: The time period for a prescription is usually twenty years. *See* CONDEMNATION; DEDICATION; RESERVATION.

PRESERVATION, HISTORIC

See HISTORIC PRESERVATION.

207

PRETREATMENT	In wastewater treatment, any process used to reduce the pollution load before the wastewater is introduced into a main sewer system or delivered to a treatment plant.
PRIMARY TREATMENT	The first stage in wastewater treatment in which substantially all floating or settleable solids are removed by screening and sedimentation.
PRINCIPAL BUILDING	*See* BUILDING, PRINCIPAL.
PRINCIPAL ENTRANCE	The place of ingress and egress used most frequently by the public.
PRINCIPAL USE	The primary or predominant use of any lot or parcel.
PRIVATE CLUB	A building and related facilities owned or operated by a corporation, association, or group of individuals established for the fraternal, social, educational, recreational, or cultural enrichment of its members and not primarily for profit and whose members pay dues and meet certain prescribed qualifications for membership. *See* LODGE.
PRIVATE SCHOOL	*See* SCHOOL, PRIVATE.
PROBABILITY	A statistical method that calculates the chance a prescribed event will occur.
PROCESS WEIGHT	The total weight of all materials, including fuels, introduced into a manufacturing process.
	Comment: The process weight is used to calculate the allowable rate of emission of pollutant matter from the process.
PROCESSING	A series of operations, usually in a continuous and regular action or succession of actions, taking place or carried on in a definite manner.
	Comment: The term processing usually is associated with the chemical transformation of materials or substances into new products and may include the blending and combining of gases and liquids. However, the term also may be applied to a specific industrial or manufacturing operation.
PROCESSING AND WAREHOUSING	The storage of materials in a warehouse or terminal and where such materials may be combined, broken down,

or aggregated for transshipment or storage and where the original material is not chemically or physically changed.

Comment: "Processing and warehousing" is a single term and must be defined as such. Otherwise, the word "processing," which is akin to manufacturing, describes a manufacturing facility, which could also contain warehousing space, not uncommon in a manufacturing operation. The term processing and warehousing as defined is essentially a storage and shipment place as opposed to a manufacturing establishment.

PROFESSIONAL OFFICE

The office of a member of a recognized profession maintained for the conduct of that profession. *See* HOME OCCUPATION; HOME PROFESSIONAL OFFICE.

PROGRAM ACCESSIBILITY

Refers to ensuring nondiscrimination and equal opportunities for individuals with disabilities so they may participate in programs and activities.

PROHIBITED USE

A use that is not permitted in a zone district.

Comment: Older zoning ordinances usually listed those uses specifically prohibited in each zone. New technology often resulted in uses that were clearly inappropriate for certain zones but because they were not listed had to be permitted. Most ordinances today are permissive ordinances, and a use not specifically permitted is prohibited.

PROJECT

A development with the necessary site improvements on a particular parcel of land.

PROJECTION

(1) A prediction of a future state based on an analysis of what has happened in the past; (2) part of a building or structure that is exempt from the bulk requirements of the zoning ordinance.

Comment: Usually bay windows, driveways, and steps may project into required yards, and parapet walls and mechanical equipment on roofs may exceed the height limitation.

PROPERTY

A lot, parcel, or tract of land together with the building and structures located thereon.

PROPERTY LINE

See LOT LINE.

209

PROSPECTIVE NEED A projection of low- and moderate-income housing needs based on the development and growth that are reasonably likely to occur in a region or municipality.

PROTECTIVE COVENANT *See* RESTRICTIVE COVENANT.

PUBLIC ADMINISTRATION Legislative, judicial, administrative, and regulatory activities of federal, state, local, and international governmental agencies.

Comment: Government owned and operated business establishments are excluded from this category and are classified in accordance with the major activity.

PUBLIC AREAS Parks, playgrounds, trails, paths, and other recreational areas and open spaces; scenic and historic sites; schools and other buildings and structures; and other places where the public is directly or indirectly invited to visit or permitted to congregate.

Comment: Historically, all public areas were owned by a governmental agency. This is not necessarily the case any longer. For example, malls and shopping areas and private plazas with benches are public areas in the sense that they invite the public in to browse, sit, walk, and congregate. Shopping malls, for instance, are the downtowns of suburbia and have become popular meeting places for people. While technically and legally private property, they are functionally public areas.

PUBLIC ASSEMBLY AREA Any area where large numbers of individuals collect to participate or to observe programs of participation.

Comment: The most common public assembly areas are auditoriums, stadia, gymnasiums, or comparable facilities under different names, for example, "field house," "banquet room," and "theater."

PUBLIC BUILDING Any building, structure, facility, or complex used by the general public, whether constructed by any state, county, or municipal government agency or instrumentality or any private individual, partnership, association, or corporation, including, but not limited to, assembly buildings, such as auditoriums, libraries, public eating places, schools, and theaters; business buildings, such as offices; and factories and industrial buildings.

PUBLIC DEVELOPMENT PROPOSAL

A master plan, capital improvement program, or other proposal for land development and any amendment thereto adopted by the appropriate public body.

PUBLIC DOMAIN

All lands owned by the government.

PUBLIC DRAINAGE WAY

Land owned or controlled by a governmental agency reserved or dedicated for the installation of stormwater sewers or drainage ditches or required along a natural stream or watercourse for preserving the channel and providing for the flow of water so as to safeguard the public against flood damage, sedimentation, and erosion.

PUBLIC GARAGE

See GARAGE, PUBLIC.

PUBLIC HEARING

A meeting announced and advertised in advance and open to the public, with the public given an opportunity to talk and participate.

Comment: Public hearings often are required before adoption or implementation of a master plan, project, ordinance, or like activity that will have an effect on the public.

PUBLIC HOUSING

Housing that is constructed, bought, owned, or rented and operated by a local housing authority for households meeting designated income limits. *See* LOCAL HOUSING AUTHORITY; LOW-INCOME HOUSING.

PUBLIC IMPROVEMENT

Any improvement, facility, or service together with its associated site or right-of-way necessary to provide transportation, drainage, utilities, or similar essential services and facilities and that are usually owned and operated by a governmental agency.

Comment: The requirement that public improvements are owned and operated by a governmental agency may be changing. Public improvements may be owned by a governmental agency and leased to a private entity to provide the service or operate a facility. Conversely, the government may lease a private facility to carry out a governmental function. In both situations, the improvement, facility, or service would still be considered public improvements.

PUBLIC NOTICE

The advertisement of a public hearing in a paper of general circulation, and through other media sources,

211

indicating the time, place, and nature of the public hearing and where the application and pertinent documents may be inspected.

PUBLIC SERVICE

Relating to the health, safety, and welfare of the population.

Comment: The term is often used in defining inherently beneficial uses or public utilities.

PUBLIC SEWER AND WATER SYSTEM

Any system, other than an individual septic tank, tile field, or individual well, that is operated by a municipality, governmental agency, or a public utility for the collection, treatment, and disposal of wastes and the furnishing of potable water.

PUBLIC TRANSIT SYSTEM

Any vehicle or transportation system, owned or regulated by a governmental agency, used for the mass transport of people.

PUBLIC UTILITY

A closely regulated enterprise with a franchise for providing to the public a utility service deemed necessary for the public health, safety, and welfare.

Comment: All states regulate public utilities, but the kind of uses that get classified as a public utility differs from state to state. For example, cellular telephone service is classified as a public utility in New York but not in New Jersey. The threshold questions as to whether a use is a public utility is whether it is so defined in the applicable state legislation. If it is, it obviously must be considered a public utility; even if it is not, it still may be a public utility for zoning purposes if it has the following characteristics:

1. Provides a service that is essential to the public health, safety, and general welfare. This critical criterion rules out radio stations, which, while important, are not essential to public health, safety, and general welfare.
2. Regulated by a governmental agency. The regulatory agency may be a federal or state agency. (In the example of cellular phones, the Federal Communications Commission is the regulatory agency, regardless of whether the state also regulates them.)
3. Granted an exclusive or near exclusive franchise for a specific geographic area. (At one time, public utili-

212

ties were given exclusive rights to provide the service in the franchised area. In recent years, more than one utility may be permitted to operate in a geographic area.)

4. Required to provide service to all who apply within their franchised area.
5. May have the right of condemnation.
6. Are usually exempt from local development requirements or can appeal such requirements to an administrative agency.

Utility service to the public has been defined broadly to mean all consumers—industrial, commercial, or residential.

PUBLIC UTILITY FACILITIES

Building, structures, and facilities, including generating and switching stations, poles, lines, pipes, pumping stations, repeaters, antennas, transmitters and receivers, valves, and all buildings and structures relating to the furnishing of utility services, such as electric, gas, telephone, water, sewer, and public transit, to the public.

PULVERIZATION

The crushing or grinding of material into small pieces.

PUMPING STATION

A building or structure containing the necessary equipment to pump a fluid to a higher level.

PUTRESCIBLE

Capable of being decomposed by microorganisms with sufficient rapidity to cause nuisances from odors or gases.

Q

QUADRUPLEX

See DWELLING, QUADRUPLEX.

QUARRY

A place where rock, ore, stone, and similar materials are excavated for sale or for off-tract use. *See* GRAVEL PIT; SAND PIT.

Comment: Quarries may include rock crushing, asphalt plants, and similar activities. Approving authorities should consider the eventual use of the property when the quarry use ceases.

213

QUARTER SECTION

A tract of land one-half-mile square, 2,640 feet by 2,640 feet, or 160 acres.

QUASI-PUBLIC USE

A use owned or operated by a nonprofit, religious, or eleemosynary institution and providing educational, cultural, recreational, religious, or similar types of programs.

Comment: The term is somewhat antiquated. A quasi-public use should be included under the definition of institutional or public uses.

QUENCH TANK

A water-filled tank used to cool incinerator residues.

QUORUM

A majority of the full authorized membership of a board or agency.

R

RACQUET SPORTS

Court games played with a racquet and ball and played either indoors or outdoors on various surfaces.

RADIAL STREET SYSTEM

A pattern of streets in which the streets converge on a central point or area. *See Figure 60.*

RADIATION

The emission of atomic particles or rays by the nucleus of an atom.

Comment: Some elements are naturally radioactive while others become radioactive after bombardment with neutrons or other particles. The three major forms of radiation are alpha, beta, and gamma.

RADIATION STANDARDS

Regulations that include exposure standards, permissible concentrations, and regulations for transportation of radioactive material.

RADIO AND TELEVISION BROADCASTING STATION

An establishment engaged in transmitting oral and visual programs to the public and that consists of a studio, transmitter, and antennas.

Comment: The studio for a radio or television broadcasting station may be located some distance from the transmitter and antenna. The transmitter and antennas must be located close to each other.

214

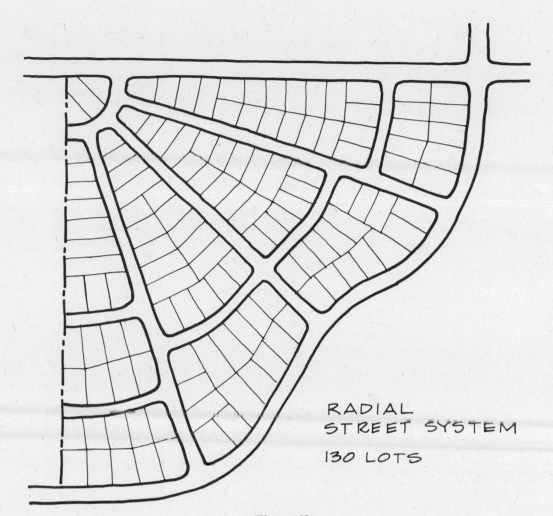

RADIAL
STREET SYSTEM

130 LOTS

Figure 60

RADIOACTIVE WASTES

The by-products of nuclear reactors and military, industrial, and medical activities using radioactive material.

Comment: Disposal and storage of radioactive wastes are a major concern and problem. Storage sites should be safe from natural disasters (such as hurricanes and earthquakes), away from population centers, and accessible without traversing heavily populated areas (Schultz and Kasen 1984).

RAILROAD YARD

An open area for the storage and repair of trains.

Comment: Railroad yards may include warehouses for freight operations.

215

RAINFALL, EXCESS The portion of rainfall that becomes direct surface runoff.

RAMP (1) A sloping walkway, roadway, or passage used to join and provide a smooth transition between two levels of different elevations; (2) driveways leading to parking aisles.

Comment: For ramps accessible to the handicapped, a maximum pitch of 8.33 percent is often specified.

RANCH A place where livestock is bred and/or raised.

RASP A device used to grate solid waste into a more manageable material, ridding it of much of its odor.

RATABLE PROPERTY Real property subject to tax by a municipality or other taxing district.

RATABLES Improvements producing taxes to the taxing authority where the real estate tax is applied.

RATIONAL NEXUS A clear, direct, and substantial relationship between a particular development and the public improvement needs generated by the development.

Comment: Rational nexus remains an important validation for off-tract improvements. The rational nexus criteria differentiate the impact fee from general taxes in which there may not be any relationship between the development and the tax.

RAVINE A long, deep hollow in the earth's surface; a valley with sharply sloping walls created by the action of stream waters.

RAW LAND Unimproved land without buildings, structures, utilities, or streets.

RAW SEWAGE Untreated domestic or commercial wastewater.

REALLOCATED PRESENT NEED That part of a municipality's present affordable housing need that is redistributed to other municipalities in the region.

Comment: Affordable housing need consists of a municipality's indigenous or existing need, reallocated present need, and prospective need. The reallocated present need

216

is that part of a region's present need that has been proportionally reallocated from municipalities with obligations in excess of the regional average.

REAR LOT LINE   *See* LOT LINE, REAR.

REAR YARD   *See* YARD, REAR.

REASONABLE USE DOCTRINE   A common law principle that no one has the right to use his or her property in a way that deprives others of the lawful enjoyment of their property.

RECEIVING MUNICIPALITY   A municipality that agrees to assume a portion of another municipality's fair share obligation.

Comment: Some states permit one municipality to transfer part of its lower income obligation to another, willing municipality for a fee. In New Jersey, these transfers are permitted as part of a "regional contribution agreement" (RCA).

RECEIVING WATERS   Rivers, lakes, oceans, or other water bodies, including underground aquifers, that receive treated or untreated wastewaters.

RECHARGE   The addition to, or replenishing of, water in an aquifer.

RECLAIMED LAND   *See* MADE LAND.

RECREATION, ACTIVE   Leisure-time activities, usually of a formal nature and often performed with others, requiring equipment and taking place at prescribed places, sites, or fields.

Comment: The term active recreation is more a word of art than one with a precise definition. It obviously includes swimming, tennis and other court games, baseball and other field sports, track, and playground activities. There is a legitimate difference of opinion as to whether park use per se may be considered active recreation, although obviously some parks contain activity areas that would qualify.

RECREATION, PASSIVE   Activities that involve relatively inactive or less energetic activities, such as walking, sitting, picnicking, card games, chess, checkers, and similar table games.

Comment: The reason for the differentiation between active and passive recreation is their potential impacts

217

on surrounding land uses. Passive recreation can also mean open space for nature walks and observation.

RECREATION FACILITY

A place designed and equipped for the conduct of sports and leisure-time activities. *See* HEALTH CLUB.

Comment: The National Recreation and Park Association publishes general standards for a variety of recreation facilities (see column (a) in *Table 1*). These standards can be used in all types of jurisdictions. A selective survey of municipalities in New Jersey and the standards they use are shown in column (b) of *Table 1*. These two sets of standards provide benchmarks, but the specific recreation preferences of residents based on current experience need to be analyzed as well. Most importantly, the amount of space must be tempered by accessibility and convenience. In addition, smaller municipalities with fewer than five thousand persons may have many of the listed facilities.

RECREATION FACILITY, COMMERCIAL

A recreation facility operated as a business and open to the public for a fee.

RECREATION FACILITY, PERSONAL

A recreation facility provided as an accessory use on the same lot as the principal permitted use and designed to be used primarily by the occupants of the principal use and their guests.

RECREATION FACILITY, PRIVATE

A recreation facility operated by a nonprofit organization and open only to bona fide members and guests of such nonprofit organization.

RECREATION FACILITY, PUBLIC

A recreation facility open to the general public.

Comment: Public recreation facilities are usually owned and operated by a governmental agency, but not necessarily so. For example, ball fields owned by industry might be available for public use at certain times.

RECREATIONAL DEVELOPMENT

A residential development planned, maintained, operated, and integrated with a major recreation facility, such as a golf course, ski resort, or marina.

RECREATIONAL VEHICLE

A vehicular-type portable structure without permanent foundation that can be towed, hauled, or driven and primarily designed as a temporary living accommodation for recreational, camping, and travel use and including,

218

TABLE 1
General Standards for Recreational Facilities

	(a) *National Recreation* *and* *Park Standards**	*(b)* *Outdoor Recreation* *Facility Standards***
Softball fields	1/5,000 population	1/1,500 population
Little League fields	1/5,000 population	1/3,000 population
Soccer fields	1/10,000 population	1/4,000 population
Paddle tennis courts	No standard	1/5,000 population
Field hockey fields	1/20,000 population	1/20,000 population
Basketball courts	1/5,000 population	1/2,000 population
Baseball fields	1/5,000 population	1/5,000 population
Volleyball courts	1/5,000 population	1/3,000 population
Football fields	1/20,000 population	1/10,000 population
Tennis courts	1/2,000 population	1/1,500 population
Trails	1 system per region	1 mi./3,000 population
Swimming pools	1/20,000 population	1/20,000 population
Running track (quarter mile)	1/20,000 population	1/20,000 population
Community centers	1/25,000 population***	1/20,000 population
Playgrounds/tot lots	No population-based standard	1/1,000 population

*Source: National Recreation and Park Association, *Recreation, Park and Open Space Standards and Guidelines*. Alexandria, Virginia: NRPA, 1983.

**Standards derived from a variety of municipalities.

***Source: Joseph DeChiara and Lee Koppelman, *Urban Planning and Design Criteria*, 1982, p. 405.

but not limited to, travel trailers, truck campers, camping trailers, and self-propelled motor homes.

RECREATIONAL VEHICLE PARK

Any lot or parcel of land upon which two or more recreational vehicle sites are located, established, or maintained for occupancy by recreational vehicles of the general public as temporary living quarters for recreation or vacation purposes. *See* CAMPGROUND.

Comment: Many ordinances define "temporary" in terms of the length of continuous occupancy permitted in order to avoid these facilities becoming permanent home sites. Some planned developments also contain recreational vehicle parking areas for the use of their residents.

RECTILINEAR STREET SYSTEM

A pattern of streets that is characterized by right-angle roadways, grid pattern blocks, and four-way intersections. *See* Gridiron Pattern. *See Figure 61.*

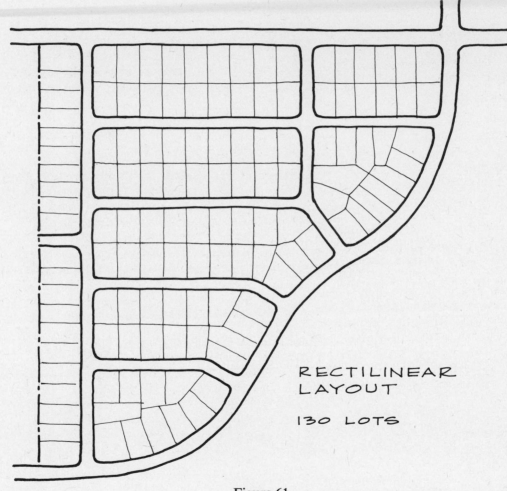

RECTILINEAR
LAYOUT

130 LOTS

Figure 61

RECYCLABLE

A waste product capable of being reused or transformed into a new product.

RECYCLING

The process by which waste products are reduced to raw materials and transformed into new and often different products.

Comment: Recycling also has a broader meaning referring to all activities related to recycling, including the collection, separation, and storage of materials.

RECYCLING CENTER

A lot or parcel of land, with or without buildings, upon which used materials are separated and processed for shipment for eventual reuse in new products.

Comment: Most recycling centers are publicly owned. If privately owned, it may become difficult to distinguish recycling centers from junkyards, with all their attendant problems. All recycling centers should be planned with adequate buffers, unloading areas, and safe and convenient access. Larger ones probably belong in industrial zones.

RECYCLING COLLECTION POINT

An incidental use that serves as a neighborhood drop-off point for temporary storage of recyclables.

Comment: No processing of recyclables takes place at the collection point. Approving authorities should determine and approve recycling collection points as part of their review of major development applications.

RECYCLING PLANT

A facility in which recyclables, such as newspapers, magazines, books, and other paper products; glass; metal cans; and other products, are recycled, reprocessed, and treated to return such products to a condition in which they may again be used in new products.

Comment: Recycling plants are intensive uses that generate truck traffic, noise, and waste. They should be located in the heavy (or intensive) industrial district.

REFUSE

See SOLID WASTE.

REFUSE RECLAMATION

The process of converting solid waste to salable products.

Comment: An example of refuse reclamation is the composting of organic solid waste to yield a salable soil conditioner.

REGION

A geographic area defined by some common feature, such as a river basin, housing market, commutershed,

221

economic activity, or political jurisdiction. *See* HOUSING REGION.

REGIONAL SHOPPING CENTER   *See* SHOPPING CENTER.

REGULATORY BASE FLOOD   *See* FLOOD, REGULATORY BASE.

REGULATORY BASE FLOOD DISCHARGE   *See* FLOOD, REGULATORY BASE DISCHARGE.

REGULATORY FLOODWAY   *See* FLOODWAY; FLOODWAY, REGULATORY.

REHABILITATION   The upgrading of a building previously in a dilapidated or substandard condition for human habitation or use.

RELIGIOUS USE   A structure or place in which worship, ceremonies, rituals, and education pertaining to a particular system of beliefs are held.

RELOCATE   To move an individual, household, use, or building from its original place to another location.

REMODEL   To construct an addition or alter the design or layout of a building or make substantial repairs or alterations so that a change or modification of the entrance facilities, toilet facilities, or vertical access facilities is achieved.

Comment: The above definition is from a New Jersey State Code relating to barrier-free access. When a public building is remodeled, barrier-free devices and construction are required.

RENT   A periodic payment, made by a tenant, to a landlord for the use of land, buildings, structures, or other property, or portions thereof.

RENTAL HOUSING   Housing occupied by a tenant paying rent to an owner and no part of the rent is used to acquire equity in the property.

REPAIR GARAGE   *See* GARAGE, REPAIR.

REPLACEMENT COST   The cost of replacing a building or structure with its functional equivalent.

222

Comment: The equivalent is not necessarily an exact replica of the original. The cost of providing a replica with the same or very similar materials is called reproduction cost.

RESEARCH LABORATORY

An establishment or other facility for carrying on investigation in the natural, physical, or social sciences, which may include engineering and product development.

Comment: Research laboratories imply physical activities usually associated with "wet" labs or places with running water, gases, special ventilation devices, chemicals, special heating and electrical or electronic equipment, or use of animals or human subjects under controlled conditions.

Research facilities often include pilot plant operations, and development ordinances usually permit a certain percentage of the floor area (25 percent, for example) for pilot plant use.

RESERVATION

(1) A provision in a deed or other real estate conveyance that retains a right for the existing owner even if other property rights are transferred; (2) a method of holding land for future public use by designating public areas on a plat, map, or site plan as a condition of approval.

RESERVOIR

A pond, lake, tank, or basin, natural or man-made, used for the storage, regulation, and control of water.

RESIDENCE

A home, abode, or place where an individual is actually living at a specific point in time.

Comment: A domicile is the place one intends to maintain as his or her permanent home. One may have a number of residences but the permanent home is called the domicile. *See* DOMICILE.

RESIDENTIAL CLUSTER

A form of planned residential development to be developed as a single entity according to a plan and containing residential housing units that have a private or public open space area as an appurtenance. *See* CLUSTER.

Comment: The open space may be used for agricultural activities, parks, recreation, or open space.

RESIDENTIAL DENSITY

The number of dwelling units per acre of residential land.

Comment: The density must be further defined in terms of net or gross. *See* DENSITY.

223

RESIDENTIAL HEALTH CARE FACILITY (RHCF)

Residences usually occupied by the frail elderly that provide rooms, meals, personal care, and health monitoring services under the supervision of a professional nurse and that may provide other services, such as recreational, social, and cultural activities, financial services, and transportation.

Comment: RHCFs may be independent facilities but are most often developed in conjunction with long-term, bed-care facilities. In fact, in New Jersey, certificates of need, which are required for a RHCF, are issued only when the RHCF is part of a long-term care facility, although not necessarily on the same lot as the RHCF. RHCFs are almost always licensed by the state and most have communal dining rooms and other communal space. The professional nurse may be a registered or licensed professional practical nurse. In New Jersey, all residents must be ambulatory and free of communicable diseases. Rooms and baths may be either private or shared.

RESIDENTIAL UNIT

See HOUSEHOLD.

RESORT

A facility for transient guests where the primary attraction is generally recreational features or activities.

RESOURCE RECOVERY

The process of obtaining materials or energy, particularly from solid waste.

REST HOME

See NURSING HOME.

RESTAURANT

An establishment where food and drink are prepared, served, and consumed primarily within the principal building. *See* RESTAURANT, TAKE-OUT; RETAIL FOOD ESTABLISHMENT.

RESTAURANT, DRIVE-IN

See RESTAURANT, TAKE-OUT.

RESTAURANT, TAKE-OUT

An establishment where food and/or beverages are sold in a form ready for consumption, where all or a significant portion of the consumption takes place or is designed to take place outside the confines of the restaurant, and where ordering and pickup of food may take place from an automobile.

Comment: Take-out restaurants also encompass restaurants that sell food from drive-up windows. The zoning problem with these types of restaurants is when the

224

proprietor decides to add tables for on-premises consumption of food. The additional parking area required is often not available or is otherwise inadequate. In addition, since such uses have drive-up and pickup lanes, circulation, stacking, and safety are major considerations.

The term drive-in restaurant applies to older fast-food places where the food was served and eaten in cars on the premises. Many municipalities banned drive-in restaurants because of their nuisance characteristics including litter, glare, noise, hangouts, and garish architecture. Most of the former "drive-ins" now resemble standard restaurants and are regulated as such.

RESTORATION

The replication or reconstruction of a building's original architectural features.

Comment: Restoration is usually used to describe the technique of preserving historic buildings. Rehabilitation, which also accomplishes building upgrading, does not necessarily retain the building's original architectural features. *See* REHABILITATION.

RESTRICTION

A limitation on property that may be created in a property deed, lease, mortgage, through certain zoning or subdivision regulations, or as a condition of approval of an application for development.

RESTRICTIVE COVENANT

A restriction on the use of land usually set forth in the deed.

Comment: Restrictive covenants usually run with the land and are binding upon subsequent owners of the property. However, some restrictive covenants run for specific periods of time.

RESUBDIVIDE

The further division of lots or the relocation of lot lines of any lot or lots within a subdivision previously approved and recorded according to law; or the alteration of any streets or the establishment of any new streets within any such subdivision, but not including conveyances, made so as to combine existing lots by deed or other instrument.

RETAIL FOOD ESTABLISHMENT

Any fixed facility in which food or drink is offered or prepared primarily for retail sale.

225

Comment: A retail food establishment is a grocery store or supermarket. Some markets now prepare and serve meals at lunch counters or tables as accessory to the principal use.

RETAIL FOOD ESTABLISHMENT, MOBILE

A vehicle, normally a van, truck, towed trailer, or push-cart, from which food and beverages are sold.

Comment: Many municipalities choose to regulate these uses by licensing them with rules dealing with sanitation, traffic safety, and where they may operate; for instance, job sites and places of assembly, such as colleges or sports events.

RETAIL OUTLET STORE

A retail establishment selling a single manufacturer's product.

Comment: A traditional or conventional retail establishment normally handles a number of different product lines of the same product. An outlet store differs in that it handles a single manufacturer and is usually owned by that manufacturer. From a planning and zoning perspective, the major difference is that outlet stores draw from a much larger service area than a typical retail establishment. The service area may vary between five to fifty miles. Consequently, much of the traffic generation takes place on weekends as opposed to the more typical evening traffic flow generated by conventional retail stores.

RETAIL SALES

Establishments engaged in selling goods or merchandise to the general public for personal or household consumption and rendering services incidental to the sale of such goods.

Comment: Some of the important characteristics of retail sales establishments are: (1) the establishment is usually a place of business and is engaged in activity to attract the general public to buy; (2) the establishment buys and receives as well as sells merchandise; (3) it may process or manufacture some of the products, such as a jeweler or bakery, but such processing or manufacturing usually is incidental or subordinate to the selling activities; and (4) retail establishments sell to customers for their own personal or household use.

An important characteristic of a retail trade establishment is that it buys goods for resale. A farmer, for example, selling goods grown on his own property would not be classified as a retailer. A farm stand that brings in goods from other farmers would be classified as a retail outlet. Eating and drinking places also may be classified as retail establishments although more often they are classified under retail services.

Lumber yards, paint, glass, and wallpaper stores usually are included as retail trade even though a substantial portion of their business may be to contractors. Establishments selling office supplies, typewriters, and similar products are usually classified as retail although they sell to offices and other business establishments.

Finally, there are categories of retail trade that manufacture products and sell them on premises, such as bakeries. If the bulk of the products made in the bakery is sold on premises, it would still be classified as retail trade. If the baking includes a large wholesale operation, selling to other stores, or supplying their own outlets, the operation would probably more accurately be classified as manufacturing.

RETAIL SALES, OUTDOOR

The display and sale of products and services primarily outside of a building or structure, including vehicles, garden supplies, gas, tires and motor oil, food and beverages, boats and aircraft, farm equipment, motor homes, burial monuments, building and landscape materials, and lumber yards.

Comment: The major characteristic of outdoor retail sales establishments is that the material sold is usually stored outdoors and customers and salespersons examine and inspect the materials outside of a building or structure. Obviously, outdoor retail establishments usually have buildings in which sales may be consummated or products displayed; however, most of the items are too large or there are too many of them to be stored indoors or they require light, air, and water.

From a planning and zoning perspective, site plan considerations include the visual impact of the stored materials, outdoor lighting, noise generation (including amplifiers), banners and attention gathering devices, and traffic.

The outdoor area where the material is stored should be paved or dust free, except for plant materials. The stored material should be kept a reasonable distance from all lot lines and less "tidy" items, such as building materials and lumber stacks, could be restricted to rear

227

or side yards with adequate screening or fencing. The maximum height of the stored material should be specified.

RETAIL SERVICES

Establishments providing services or entertainment, as opposed to products, to the general public for personal or household use, including eating and drinking places, hotels and motels, finance, real estate and insurance, personal service, motion pictures, amusement and recreation services, health, educational, and social services, museums, and galleries.

Comment: Services may involve some products, for example, restaurants. The difference, though, is that the products are part of the overall service and are usually consumed on the premises. Retail services may also involve processing, such as cleaners, shoemakers, and beauty parlors. Services to businesses or industry are not usually included under retail services. *See* PERSONAL SERVICES; SERVICES.

RETAIL WAREHOUSE OUTLET

Retail operation from a warehouse as an accessory use to the principal warehouse use.

Comment: The individual terms are easily understood —a retail store in a warehouse. The major problem is how to regulate these uses since they can cause relatively low-intensity warehouse uses and districts to become high-traffic, very intensive retail centers. Reasonable controls include:

1. The retail establishment is accessory to and incidental to the principal warehouse use;
2. The maximum area within the warehouse that can be used for retail sales is a small percentage of the warehouse and a small area (10 percent and twenty-five hundred square feet, whichever is less, for example);
3. The hours of operation are coincident with warehouse operations;
4. The items on sale in the retail establishment are actually part of the stock of the warehouse; and
5. Adequate parking, in accordance with retail standards, is required for the retail space (often five spaces/one thousand square feet of retail space).

228

RETAINING WALL

A structure constructed and erected between lands of different elevations to protect structures and/or to prevent erosion. *See Figure 13.*

RETENTION BASIN

A pond, pool, or basin used for the permanent storage of water runoff.

Comment: Retention basins differ from detention basins in that the latter are temporary storage areas. Retention basins have the potential for water recreation and water-oriented landscaping since the water remains. Both types of basins provide for controlled release of the stored water and groundwater recharge.

RETIREMENT COMMUNITY

Any age-restricted development, which may be in any housing form, including detached and attached dwelling units, apartments, and residences, offering private and semiprivate rooms.

Comment: The 1988 amendments to the Federal Fair Housing Act provide guidance on age restrictions. These amendments stipulate that a community will be considered to be "housing for the elderly," and therefore exempt from lawsuits for discriminating against children, if the minimum age for all residents is sixty-two years or fifty-five years for one resident of each of 80 percent of the units, provided that "significant facilities and services for the elderly are provided." The term "significant facilities and services" is not specifically defined in the regulations that implement the amendments and, therefore, has been determined on a case-by-case basis as litigation has arisen.

Housing in retirement communities always provides one-level living and usually includes other features designed to increase safety and amenity for the elderly, such as grab bars in the bathrooms, nonskid flooring, and higher levels of lighting. The housing may also be adaptable to use by the physically impaired and, accordingly, may be built with features such as wider doorways and elevators that can accommodate wheelchairs.

Retirement communities vary from those that provide only one type of housing and one level of service to communities that provide a range, from apartments for independent living to residences for assisted living (which includes meals, personal care, housekeeping, and some health services) to long-term bed care. *See* ADULT RETIREMENT COMMUNITY; ASSISTED LIVING FACILITY;

229

CONGREGATE RESIDENCES; CONTINUING CARE RETIRE-
MENT COMMUNITY; HOUSING FOR THE ELDERLY; RESI-
DENTIAL HEALTH CARE FACILITY.

RETURN The line between the mean high waterline and the sea-
ward extension of a permitted structure, such as a bulkhead.

REUSE *See* ADAPTIVE REUSE.

REVERBERATION The persistence of sound in an enclosed or confined
space after the sound source has stopped.

REVERSE FRONTAGE *See* LOT, REVERSE FRONTAGE.

REVERSE OSMOSIS An advanced method of wastewater treatment relying on
a semipermeable membrane to separate waters from pol-
lutants.

REVERSION The return of real estate to its original owner or owner's
heirs.

Comment: Many donations of land to a governmental
agency specify that if the property is not used for the
purpose for which it was donated, it reverts back to the
owner. Another type of reversion is a street that may
have been platted but never constructed and that is
subsequently vacated by the municipality. The unused
right-of-way reverts back to abutting land owners.

REZONE To change the zoning classification of particular lots or
parcels of land.

RIDE SHARING The cooperative effort between two or more people to
travel together, usually to and from work.

Comment: Car pools, van pools, and bus pools are all
examples of ride sharing.

RIDGE LINE (1) The intersection of two roof surfaces forming the
highest horizontal line of the roof; (2) the highest elevation of a mountain chain or line of hills. *See Figure 62.*

RIDING ACADEMY An establishment where horses are boarded and cared
for and where instruction in riding, jumping, and showing
is offered and where horses may be hired for riding.

230

RIGHT OF ACCESS   The legal authority to enter or leave a property.

Comment: In privately owned property, right of access usually means access to a public road. In rented property, right of access also could mean the landlord's right to enter the property to make repairs.

RIGHT-OF-WAY   (1) A strip of land acquired by reservation, dedication, forced dedication, prescription, or condemnation and intended to be occupied by a road, crosswalk, railroad, electric transmission lines, oil or gas pipeline, water line, sanitary storm sewer, and other similar uses; (2) generally, the right of one to pass over the property of another. *See Figure 1.*

RIGHT-OF-WAY LINES   The lines that form the boundaries of a right-of-way. *See Figure 1.*

RINGELMANN CHART   A device used to measure the opacity of smoke emitted from stacks and other sources.

Comment: The chart has a series of illustrations ranging from light gray to black. The shades of gray simulate various smoke densities and are assigned numbers ranging from one to five. Ringelmann No. 1 is equivalent to 20 percent dense; No. 5 is 100 percent dense. Ringelmann charts are used in the setting and enforcement of emission standards.

RIPARIAN GRANT   The grant by the state of lands below the mean high waterline usually beginning at the shore and extending outward to the center of the stream or some predetermined line.

Comment: Riparian grants mainly affect tidal waters.

RIPARIAN LAND   Land that is traversed or bounded by a natural watercourse or adjoining tidal lands.

RIPARIAN RIGHTS   Rights of a landowner to the water on or bordering his or her property, including the right to make use of such waters and to prevent diversion or misuse of upstream water.

RIVER   A natural stream of water, of greater volume than a creek, flowing in a more or less permanent bed or chan-

231

nel, between defined banks or walls, with a current that either may be continuous in one direction or affected by the ebb and flow of the tide.

RIVER BASIN　　　　The total area drained by a river and its tributaries. *See* BASIN.

ROAD　　　　*See* STREET.

ROD　　　　A lineal measure equal to 16.5 feet or 5.5 yards.

　　　　Comment: This surveyor's measure is no longer used. Four rods equal one chain. Ten chains by ten chains equals ten acres. *See* CHAIN.

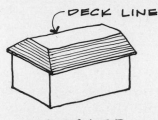

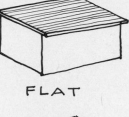

MANSARD　　　HIP　　　FLAT

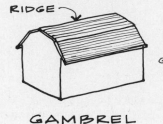
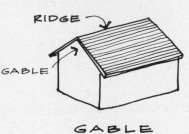

GAMBREL　　　GABLE　　　SHED

ROOF TYPES

Figure 62

ROOF　　　　The outside top covering of a building. *See Figure 62.*

ROOF, FLAT　　　　A roof that is not pitched and the surface of which is generally parallel to the ground. *See Figure 62.*

ROOF, GABLE　　　　A ridged roof forming a gable at both ends of the building. *See Figure 62.*

232

ROOF, GAMBREL	A gabled roof with two slopes on each side, the lower steeper than the upper. *See Figure 62.*
ROOF, HIP	A roof with sloping ends and sides. *See Figure 62.*
ROOF, MANSARD	A roof with two slopes on each of four sides, the lower steeper than the upper. *See Figure 62.* *Comment:* In current use, the upper slope may be flat.
ROOF, SHED	A roof with one slope. *See Figure 62.*
ROOMER	*See* BOARDER.
ROOMING HOUSE	*See* BOARDING HOUSE.
ROOMING UNIT	Any habitable room or group of rooms forming a single habitable unit, used or intended to be used for living and sleeping but not for cooking or eating.
ROW HOUSE	An attached dwelling separated from others in a row by a vertical unpierced wall extending from basement to roof. *See* DWELLING, TOWNHOUSE. *Comment:* Row houses are urban housing types, usually on their own lots.
RUBBISH	A general term for solid waste, excluding food waste and ashes, taken from residences, commercial establishments, and institutions.
RUN WITH THE LAND	A covenant or restriction to the use of land contained in a deed and binding on the present and all future owners of the property. *Comment:* For example, a promise never to divide the land into more lots is incorporated in a deed and the prohibition against subdivision is said to "run with the land" since future owners also are bound by the restriction.
RUNOFF	The portion of rainfall, melted snow, irrigation water, and any other liquids that flows across ground surface and eventually is returned to streams. *See Figure 4.*
RURAL AREA	A sparsely developed area, with a population density of less than one hundred persons per square mile and where

the land is undeveloped or primarily used for agricultural purposes.

S

SALE

The exchange of goods or property for money or some other consideration.

SALINE LAND

Land with a high salt content that makes it unsuitable for agricultural cultivation.

SALINITY

The degree of salt in water.

SALT WATER INTRUSION

The invasion of salt water into a body of fresh water, occurring in either surface or groundwater bodies. *See Figure 4*.

Comment: Salt water intrusion or infiltration is generally caused by overpumping or overdrawing fresh water from an aquifer.

SALVAGE

The utilization of waste materials. *See* REFUSE RECLAMATION.

SAME OWNERSHIP

Properties owned by the same individual, corporation, partnership, or other entity, or if one property is owned by any corporation that controls, is controlled by, or is under common control with the owner of the other property, or is owned by any corporation resulting from a merger or consolidation with the other property owner, or is owned by any subsidiary or affiliate of the other property owner, or is owned by any joint venture of which the other property owner is a partner.

Comment: Certain bulk controls usually do not apply to multibuilding developments, such as office and research parks, shopping centers, and semipublic uses. However, the property may be subdivided in several corporate names or owned by subsidiaries of the parent company. This definition clarifies the intent by broadening the definition of same ownership.

SAMPLING

A statistical technique of selecting a small random, stratified percentage of a group, analyzing it, and being able to draw certain conclusions about the group.

SAND PIT	A surface mine or excavation used for the removal of sand, gravel, or fill dirt for sale or for use off-tract. *See* GRAVEL PIT; QUARRY.
SANITARY LANDFILL	A site for solid waste disposal. *See* DUMP.
SANITARY LANDFILLING	A planned method of solid waste disposal in which the solid waste is spread in thin layers, compacted to reduce its volume, and covered with earth at the end of each working day.
SANITARY SEWAGE	Any liquid waste containing animal or vegetable matter in suspension or solution or the water-carried waste resulting from the discharge of water closets, laundry tubs, washing machines, sinks, dishwashers, or any other source of water-carried waste of human origin or containing putrescible material.
SANITARY SEWERS	Pipes that carry domestic or commercial sanitary sewage and into which storm, surface, and ground waters are not intentionally admitted. *See* COMBINED SEWERS; SEWER.
SANITATION	The control of all the factors in the physical environment that exercise or can exercise a deleterious effect on human physical development, health, and survival.
SANITORIUM	A hospital used for treating chronic and usually long-term illnesses.
SATELLITE EARTH STATION ANTENNA	A parabolic or dish-shaped antenna or any other apparatus or device that is designed for the purpose of receiving radio waves.

Comment: Many local ordinances have attempted to control the location and size of satellite antennas for aesthetic reasons. Recent court cases have ruled that Federal Communications Commission regulations have preempted local control over these devices or at least require them to be treated as any other antenna (*Alsan Technology v. Zoning Board of Adjustment*, 235 N.J. Super. 471; *Nationwide v. Zoning Board of Adjustment*, 243 N.J. Super. 18).

Local control of satellite antennas may be upheld if the local ordinance is crafted to meet the following three-point test:

235

1. The ordinance should not differentiate between satellite dish antennas and other types of antennas;
2. There should be a reasonable, clearly defined health, safety, and/or aesthetic objective as the basis for the ordinance; and
3. The ordinance should not impose unreasonable limitations on reception or impose costs on the user disproportionate to total investment in antenna equipment and installation.

SATELLITE OFFICE

(1) An office used by employees who are telecommuting; (2) a branch office or facility of a company or governmental agency.

Comment: It is a means of decentralizing part of a company's operations to another location. It can be a means of providing services to populations outside the area of the central office and, as such, may be an important part of a company's marketing efforts. Satellite offices may also be established as cost-saving devices, so that back-office operations can be established at locations where business costs are less. With respect to zoning, there is no reason to distinguish between satellite offices and any other types of office use.

SCALE

(1) The relationship between distances on a map and actual ground distances; (2) the proportioned relationship of the size of parts to one another. *See Figure 5.*

Comment: Map scale usually is represented by a graphic scale (by a visual bar) or by a ratio (or representative fraction), such as one inch (on the map) equals one mile (on the ground). Since maps are often enlarged or reduced photographically, the bar scale that is not affected by map enlargement or reduction should be used. *See* AREA SCALE.

SCALE OF DEVELOPMENT

The relationship of a particular project or development, in terms of size, height, bulk, intensity, and aesthetics, to its surroundings.

SCATTERED SITE HOUSING

New or rehabilitated subsidized dwellings located in substantially built-up areas.

Comment: The theory behind scattered site housing is to locate subsidized units throughout established neighborhoods as opposed to concentrating the units in one area. *See* ODD-LOT DEVELOPMENT.

236

SCENIC AREA

An open area the natural features of which are visually significant or geologically or botanically unique.

SCENIC CORRIDOR

An area visible from a highway, waterway, railway, or major hiking, biking, or equestrian trail that provides vistas over water, across expanses of land, such as farmlands, woodlands, or coastal wetlands, or from mountaintops or ridges.

Comment: Scenic vistas can also view the built environment, such as a famous urban skyline.

SCENIC EASEMENT

An easement the purpose of which is to limit development in order to preserve a view or scenic area. *See* EASEMENT, CONSERVATION.

SCENIC OVERLOOK

An area, usually at the side of a road, where persons can observe a scenic area.

SCHEMATIC DRAWING

A sketch, usually to scale, of a proposed development, building, or layout at an early stage in the design process.

Comment: Many planning boards encourage applicants to submit schematic drawings for conceptual review prior to the preparation of detailed plans for a formal application.

SCHOOL

Any building or part thereof which is designed, constructed, or used for education or instruction in any branch of knowledge.

Comment: The above definition includes business schools, trade schools, schools of dance and the martial arts, as well as academic institutions. Local ordinances can further define the kinds of schools that might be allowed in specific areas, for example, only elementary and secondary schools in residential areas. In many states, however, regulations affecting schools must be applied uniformly to private and public schools—See *Roman Catholic Diocese of Newark v. Borough of Ho-Ho-Kus,* 202 A.2d 161 (1964).

SCHOOL, ELEMENTARY

Any school licensed by the state and that meets the state requirements for elementary education.

SCHOOL, PAROCHIAL

A school supported and controlled by a church or religious organization. *See* SCHOOL, PRIVATE.

237

SCHOOL, PRIVATE

Any building or group of buildings the use of which meets state requirements for elementary, secondary, or higher education and which use does not secure the major part of its funding from any governmental agency.

SCHOOL, SECONDARY

Any school licensed by the state and that is authorized to award diplomas for secondary education.

SCHOOL, VOCATIONAL

See VOCATIONAL SCHOOL.

SCHOOL DISTRICT

A district that serves as a unit for state financing and administration of elementary and secondary schools.

SCRAP

Discarded or rejected materials that result from manufacturing or fabricating operations.

SCREENING

(1) A method of visually shielding or obscuring one abutting or nearby structure or use from another by fencing, walls, berms, or densely planted vegetation; (2) the removal of relatively coarse floating and/or suspended solids by straining through racks or screens.

SCRUBBER

An air pollution control device that uses a liquid spray to remove pollutants from a gas stream by absorption or chemical reaction.

SEA LEVEL

A reference or datum mark measuring land elevation using the level of the ocean between high and low tides.

SEASHORE

The area where the land meets the sea or ocean.

SEASONAL DWELLING UNIT

A dwelling unit that lacks one or more of the basic amenities or utilities required for all-year or all-weather occupancy.

Comment: In resort or seashore areas, municipalities may grant certificates of occupancy for dwelling units that place limits on their occupancy during certain periods of time. For example, houses that lack heating would not be certified for use during winter months.

Many municipalities also recognize that houses originally built for seasonal use eventually become all-year-round dwellings and require all dwellings to be fully certified.

SEASONAL STRUCTURE

A temporary covering erected over a recreational amenity, such as a swimming pool or tennis court, for the

238

purpose of extending its use to cold weather months or inclement conditions.

Comment: The problem with seasonal structures is that they often become permanent, and where an open tennis court, for instance, is acceptable, one with a plastic structure to extend the season may be visually objectionable and cut off light and air to surrounding properties.

SEASONAL USE A use carried on for only a part of the year, such as outdoor swimming during the summer months or skiing during the winter months.

SEAWALL A wall or embankment that acts as a breakwater and is used to prevent beach erosion.

SECOND-HOME COMMUNITY A development consisting of vacation homes or resort residences, not used as the principal domicile.

SECONDARY TREATMENT Wastewater treatment beyond the primary stage in which bacteria consume the organic parts of the wastes.

Comment: This biochemical action is accomplished by use of trickling filters or the activated sludge process. Effective secondary treatment removes virtually all floating and settleable solids and approximately 90 percent of both BOD (biological oxygen demand) and suspended solids. Customarily, disinfection by chlorination is the final stage of the secondary treatment process.

SECTION OF LAND Measured as 640 acres, 1 square mile, or one thirty-sixth of a township.

SEDIMENT Deposited silt that is being or has been moved by water or ice, wind, gravity, or other means of erosion. *See* SILT.

SEDIMENT BASIN A barrier or dam built across a waterway or at suitable locations to retain sediment.

SEDIMENTATION (1) The depositing of earth or soil that has been transported from its site of origin by water, ice, wind, gravity, or other natural means as a product of erosion; (2) in wastewater treatment, the settling out of solids by gravity.

SEDIMENTATION TANKS In wastewater treatment, tanks where the solids are allowed to settle or to float as scum.

239

Comment: The scum is skimmed off and settled solids are pumped to incinerators, digesters, filters, or other means of disposal.

SEEPAGE

Water that flows through the soil.

SEEPAGE PIT

A covered pit with open, jointed lining through which septic tank effluent or laundry waste may seep or leach into the surrounding soil.

SELF-SERVICE STORAGE FACILITY

A structure containing separate, individual, and private storage spaces of varying sizes leased or rented on individual leases for varying periods of time.

Comment: Self-service storage facilities, often referred to as mini-warehouses, are storage facilities designed to serve both residential and commercial establishments. Because they are relatively inexpensive to construct and maintain, they are often interim uses. The self-service storage facilities are very low traffic generators, thus requiring little permanent parking, often as little as one parking space per fifty to one hundred rental units for one-story units. Two-story units may require elevator access so that more parking spaces around the elevators may be needed. Many have resident managers in separate apartments on-site. The size of storage units varies between thirty and four hundred square feet.

Access is provided to the units from driveways so the width should be at least twenty feet between rows of buildings. Self-service storage facilities are not particularly attractive because they are usually flat-roofed, one-story structures arranged in long monotonous rows. Heavy perimeter landscaping may be the best way to break up the building appearance along with substantial setbacks from lot lines (twenty-five feet or more).

Local ordinances should address security, landscaping, fencing, lighting, and height. The use of the spaces should also be spelled out. Most ordinances specify that the use is for dead storage only, and flammable or hazardous chemicals and explosives are prohibited. Arlington, Texas, prohibits the following uses in self-service storage facilities:

1. Auctions, commercial, wholesale, or retail sales, or miscellaneous or garage sales;
2. The servicing, repair, or fabrication of motor vehi-

cles, boats, trailers, lawn mowers, appliances, or other similar equipment;

3. The operation of power tools, spray-painting equipment, table saws, lathes, compressors, welding equipment, kilns, or other similar equipment;

4. The establishment of a transfer and storage business; and

5. Any use that is noxious or offensive because of odors, dust, noise, fumes, or vibrations.

Some self-service storage facilities have areas where boats, vacant trailers, and recreation vehicles may be stored. The local ordinance should specify whether this type of storage is permitted (Planning Advisory Service Report No. 396 1986).

SEMIAMBULATORY HANDICAP

An impairment that causes individuals to walk with difficulty or insecurity. Individuals using braces or canes, arthritics, spastics, and those with pulmonary and cardiac ills may be semiambulatory.

SEMIDETACHED

See DWELLING, SINGLE-FAMILY SEMIDETACHED.

SEMIFINISHED PRODUCT

The end result of a manufacturing process that will become a raw material for an establishment engaged in further manufacturing.

Comment: The above definition, from the *Standard Industrial Classification Manual* (1987), includes the following illustration of a semifinished product: The product of the copper smelter is the raw material used in electrolytic refineries; refined copper is the raw material used by copper wire mills; and copper wire is the raw material used by electrical equipment manufacturers. In each case, the product serves as a raw material for subsequent manufacturing activities.

SENDING MUNICIPALITY

A municipality that transfers a portion of its fair share obligation to another willing municipality.

Comment: In New Jersey, a municipality (usually suburban towns) may transfer a part of its low- and moderate-income housing obligation (often up to 50 percent) to a willing municipality, usually an urban center. The transfer usually involves money to pay for the subsidy to construct a low- or moderate-income unit or to rehabilitate a substandard unit. In New Jersey, for example, that cost is now between $25,000 to $30,000 per unit. *See* RECEIVING MUNICIPALITY.

SENIOR CITIZEN HOUSING   *See* HOUSING FOR THE ELDERLY.

SENSE OF PLACE   The characteristics of a location that make it readily recognizable as being unique and different from its surroundings (Schultz and Kasen 1984).

SEPTIC SYSTEM   An underground system with a septic tank used for the decomposition of domestic wastes. *See Figure 26.*

Comment: Bacteria in the wastes decompose the organic matter and the sludge settles to the bottom. The effluent flows through drains into the ground. Sludge is pumped out at regular intervals.

SEPTIC TANK   A water-tight receptacle that receives the discharge of sewage from a building, sewer, or part thereof and is designed and constructed so as to permit settling of solids from this liquid, digestion of the organic matter, and discharge of the liquid portion into a disposal area. *See Figure 26.*

SERVICE STATION   *See* AUTOMOBILE SERVICE STATION.

SERVICES   Establishments primarily engaged in providing assistance, as opposed to products, to individuals, business, industry, government, and other enterprises, including hotels and other lodging places; personal, business, repair, and amusement services; health, legal, engineering, and other professional services; educational services; membership organizations; and other miscellaneous services. *See* BUSINESS SERVICES; PERSONAL SERVICES; RETAIL SERVICES; SOCIAL SERVICES.

Comment: The above definition includes all types of services and would be appropriate for intensive commercial and retail districts, such as the central business district of an urban area. Development ordinances may specify different types and scale of services appropriate for neighborhood or local business areas.

SET-ASIDE   The percentage of housing units devoted to low- and moderate-income households within an inclusionary development.

242

Comment: In New Jersey, the maximum required set-aside is usually 20 percent. In a one hundred-unit inclusionary development, twenty units are set aside for lower income families (ten for low income and ten for moderate income) in return for allowing a higher density of development. A higher set-aside is considered risky in terms of selling or renting the market units and a lower set-aside is one that provides too much of a bonus to the developer.

In other states, set-asides are different. In Florida, for example, the percentage is lower than 20 percent, and there is no requirement for a 50 percent low and 50 percent moderate split. *See* INCLUSIONARY DEVELOPMENT.

SETBACK

The distance between the building and any lot line. *See Figure 11.*

Comment: The minimum setbacks in a zoning ordinance define the building envelope and establish the required yards—front, rear, and side. The ordinance should also indicate what may be permitted in which yards: parking, fences, accessory buildings, patios, swimming pools, and so on. The setback may exclude certain projections, such as uncovered walks, chimneys, and bay windows.

SETBACK LINE

That line that is the required minimum distance from any lot line and that establishes the area within which the principal structure must be erected or placed. *See* BUILDING LINE. *See Figure 11.*

SETTLEABLE SOLIDS

Bits of debris and fine matter heavy enough to settle out of wastewater.

SETTLING CHAMBER

In air pollution control, a device used to reduce the velocity of flue gases, usually by means of baffles, promoting the settling of fly ash.

SETTLING TANK

In wastewater treatment, a tank or basin in which settleable solids are removed by gravity.

SEWAGE

The total of organic waste and wastewater generated by residential, industrial, and commercial establishments.

SEWER

Any pipe or conduit used to collect and carry away sewage or stormwater runoff from the generating source to treatment plants or receiving streams.

Comment: A sewer that conveys household, commercial, and industrial sewage is called a sanitary sewer; if it transports runoff from rain or snow, it is a storm sewer. If stormwater runoff and sewage are transported in the same system, then it is a combined sewer.

SEWER SYSTEM AND TREATMENT

Devices for the collection, treatment, and disposal of sewage. *See* COMBINED SEWERS; INTERCEPTOR SEWER; LATERAL SEWERS; OUTFALL; PACKAGE TREATMENT PLANT; PRIMARY TREATMENT; SANITARY SEWAGE; SANITARY SEWERS; SECONDARY TREATMENT; SEPTIC SYSTEM; SEWER; TERTIARY TREATMENT.

SEWERAGE

(1) All effluent carried by sewers whether it is sanitary sewage, industrial wastes, or stormwater runoff; (2) the entire system of sewage collection, treatment, and disposal.

SHADE TREE

A tree, usually deciduous, planted primarily for overhead canopy.

SHADOW PATTERN

(1) The impact of shade cast by a structure or building on surrounding areas during the day and over various seasons; (2) the pattern of light or shade cast by a nonsolid object.

SHARED DRIVEWAY

A single driveway serving two or more adjoining lots.

Comment: A shared driveway may cross a side lot line, enabling a lot without direct highway access to have access to the highway. Shared driveways require access easements.

SHARED PARKING

See PARKING, SHARED.

SHELTERED CARE FACILITY

See BOARDING HOME FOR SHELTERED CARE.

SHIELD

A wall that protects workers from harmful radiation released by radioactive materials.

SHOPPING CENTER

A group of commercial establishments planned, constructed, and managed as a total entity, with customer and employee parking provided on-site, provision for goods delivery separated from customer access, aesthetic considerations and protection from the elements, and landscaping and signage in accordance with an approved plan.

Comment: Shopping centers are further defined by size and the area their shoppers come from: (1) a super regional center includes retail, office, and service uses, occupies more than one hundred acres, has four or more anchor stores, and contains more than one million square feet of gross leasable space; (2) a regional shopping center contains a wide range of retail and service establishments, occupies fifty to one hundred acres of land, has at least one or more anchor stores, and contains more than 400,000 square feet of gross leasable space. It draws its clientele from as much as a forty-five-minute drive away; (3) a community shopping center features a junior department store and contains approximately 150,000 square feet of gross leasable area and has a site area of ten to twenty-five acres. Its clientele draw is approximately a ten-minute drive from the center; (4) a neighborhood shopping center generally offers goods necessary to meet daily needs, occupies up to ten acres, has up to 100,000 square feet of gross leasable area, and draws its clientele from a five-minute driving radius from the center. *See* Mini-Mall; Specialty Shopping Center.

SHOPPING MALL   A shopping center with stores on both sides of an enclosed or open pedestrian walkway.

SHOULDER   The area between the moving traffic lanes and curb used for emergency stopping of vehicles or parking.

SHRUB   A woody plant, smaller than a tree, consisting of several small stems from the ground or small branches near the ground; may be deciduous or evergreen (Planning Advisory Service Report No. 431 1990).

SIDE YARD   *See* Yard, Side.

SIDEWALK   A paved, surfaced, or leveled area, paralleling and usually separated from the street, used as a pedestrian walkway.

SIDEWALK AREA   That portion of the right-of-way that lies between the right-of-way and curb line, regardless of whether the sidewalk exists.

SIDEWALK CAFÉ   A restaurant with tables on the sidewalk in front of the premises.

245

Comment: Municipalities that permit outdoor cafés usually do so by special permit since the space occupied by tables is often part of the right-of-way. In considering outdoor cafés, the width of the sidewalk becomes a critical criterion to assure adequate pedestrian circulation.

SIGHT TRIANGLE

A triangular-shaped portion of land established at street intersections in which nothing is erected, placed, planted, or allowed to grow in such a manner as to limit or obstruct the sight distance of motorists entering or leaving the intersection. Also known as a sight easement. *See Figures 1 and 63.*

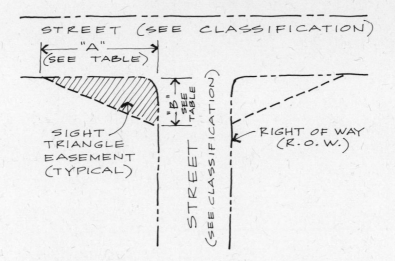

REQUIREMENT BY STREET CLASSIFICATION (MEASURED ALONG R.O.W.)

"A" (DISTANCE IN FEET)		"B" (DISTANCE IN FEET)		
		LOCAL STREET	COLLECTOR STREET	ARTERIAL STREET
30	LOCAL STREET	30	100	130-150
100	COLLECTOR STREET	30	100	130-150
130-150	ARTERIAL STREET	30	100	130-150

SIGHT TRIANGLE

Figure 63

246

SIGN

Any object, device, display, or structure, or part thereof, situated outdoors or indoors, which is used to advertise, identify, display, direct, or attract attention to an object, person, institution, organization, business, product, service, event, or location by any means, including words, letters, figures, design, symbols, fixtures, colors, illumination, or projected images. *See Figure 64.*

Comment: Ordinances usually exclude from the definition of signs national or state flags, window displays, graffiti, athletic scoreboards, or the official announcements or signs of government.

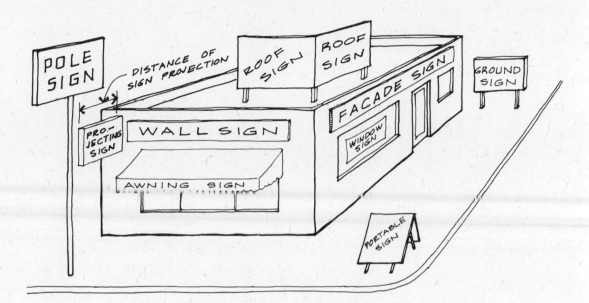

SIGN TYPES

Figure 64

SIGN, ANIMATED OR MOVING

Any sign or part of a sign that changes physical position or light intensity by any movement or rotation or that gives the visual impression of such movement or rotation.

SIGN, AWNING, CANOPY, OR MARQUEE

A sign that is mounted, painted, or attached to an awning, canopy, or marquee that is otherwise permitted by ordinance. *See Figures 64 and 65.*

247

Comment: Regulations usually specify that the sign shall not project above, below, or beyond the awning, canopy, or marquee. These are defined as suspended signs.

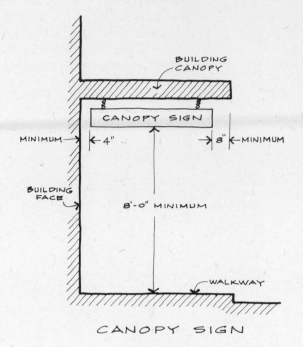

CANOPY SIGN

Figure 65

SIGN, BENCH

A sign painted, located on, or attached to any part of the surface of a bench, seat, or chair placed on or adjacent to a public place or roadway.

SIGN, BILLBOARD

A sign that directs attention to a business, commodity, service, or entertainment conducted, sold, or offered at a location other than the premises on which the sign is located.

SIGN, BULLETIN BOARD

A sign that identifies an institution or organization on the premises of which it is located and that contains the name of the institution or organization, the names of individuals connected with it, and general announcements of events or activities occurring at the institution or similar messages.

SIGN, BUSINESS

A sign that directs attention to a business or profession conducted, or to a commodity or service sold, offered,

248

or manufactured, or to an entertainment offered on the premises where the sign is located.

SIGN, CONSTRUCTION

A temporary sign erected on the premises on which construction is taking place, during the period of such construction, indicating the names of the architects, engineers, landscape architects, contractors or similar artisans, and the owners, financial supporters, sponsors, and similar individuals or firms having a role or interest with respect to the structure or project.

SIGN, DIRECTIONAL

Signs limited to directional messages, principally for pedestrian or vehicular traffic, such as "one-way," "entrance," and "exit."

SIGN, DIRECTORY

A sign listing the tenants or occupants of a building or group of buildings and that may indicate their respective professions or business activities. *See Figure 66.*

SIGN, FACADE

See SIGN, WALL.

SIGN, FACE

The area or display surface used for the message.

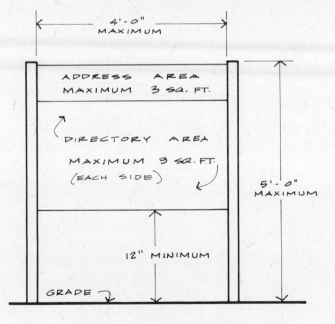

DIRECTORY GROUND SIGN

Figure 66

249

SIGN, FLASHING	Any directly or indirectly illuminated sign that exhibits changing natural or artificial light or color effects by any means whatsoever.
SIGN, FREESTANDING	Any nonmovable sign not affixed to a building. *Comment:* Usually pole signs, ground signs, and construction signs.
SIGN, GOVERNMENTAL	A sign erected and maintained pursuant to and in discharge of any governmental functions or required by law, ordinance, or other governmental regulation.
SIGN, GROUND	Any sign, other than a pole sign, in which the entire bottom is in contact with or is close to the ground and is independent of any other structure. *See Figure 64.*
SIGN, HOLIDAY DECORATION	Temporary signs, in the nature of decorations, clearly incidental to and customarily and commonly associated with any national, local, or religious holiday.
SIGN, HOME OCCUPATION	A sign containing only the name and occupation of a permitted home occupation.
SIGN, IDENTIFICATION	A sign giving the nature, logo, trademark, or other identifying symbol; address; or any combination of the name, symbol, and address of a building, business, development, or establishment on the premises where it is located.
SIGN, ILLUMINATED	A sign lighted by or exposed to artificial lighting either by lights on or in the sign or directed toward the sign.
SIGN, INFLATABLE	Any display capable of being expanded by air or other gas and used on a permanent or temporary basis to advertise a product or event.
SIGN, MEMORIAL	A sign, tablet, or plaque memorializing a person, event, structure, or site.
SIGN, NAMEPLATE	A sign, located on the premises, giving the name or address, or both, of the owner or occupant of a building or premises.
SIGN, OFF-PREMISES	*See* SIGN, BILLBOARD.

250

SIGN, ON-SITE INFORMATIONAL

A sign commonly associated with, and not limited to, information and directions necessary or convenient for visitors coming on the property, including signs marking entrances and exits, parking areas, circulation direction, rest rooms, and pickup and delivery areas.

SIGN, POLE

A sign that is mounted on a freestanding pole or other support so that the bottom edge of the sign face is six feet or more above grade. *See Figure 64.*

SIGN, POLITICAL

A temporary sign announcing or supporting political candidates or issues in connection with any national, state, or local election.

SIGN, PORTABLE

A sign that is not permanent, affixed to a building, structure, or the ground. *See Figure 64.*

SIGN, PRIVATE SALE OR EVENT

A temporary sign advertising private sales of personal property, such as "house sales," "garage sales," "rummage sales," and the like, or private not-for-profit events, such as picnics, carnivals, bazaars, game nights, art fairs, craft shows, and Christmas tree sales.

SIGN, PROJECTING

A sign that is wholly or partly dependent upon a building for support and that projects more than twelve inches from such building. *See Figure 64.*

Comment: Also known as a shingle sign.

SIGN, REAL ESTATE

A sign pertaining to the sale or lease of the premises, or a portion of the premises, on which the sign is located.

SIGN, ROOF

A sign that is mounted on the roof of a building or that is wholly dependent upon a building for support and that projects above the top walk or edge of a building with a flat roof, the eave line of a building with a gambrel, gable, or hip roof, or the deck line of a building with a mansard roof. *See Figure 64.*

SIGN, SUSPENDED

A sign hanging down from a marquee, awning, or porch that would exist without the sign.

SIGN, TEMPORARY

A sign or advertising display constructed of cloth, canvas, fabric, plywood, or other light material and designed or intended to be displayed for a short period of time.

SIGN, VEHICLE	A sign on a vehicle not customarily and regularly used to transport persons or properties.
SIGN, VENDING MACHINE	Any sign, display, or other graphic attached to or part of a coin-operated machine dispensing food, beverages, or other products.
SIGN, WALL	A sign fastened to or painted on the wall of a building or structure in such a manner that the wall becomes the supporting structure for, or forms the background surface of, the sign and that does not project more than twelve inches from such building or structure. *See Figure 64.*
SIGN AREA	The entire face of a sign, including the advertising surface and any framing, trim, or molding but not including the supporting structure. *See Figure 67.*

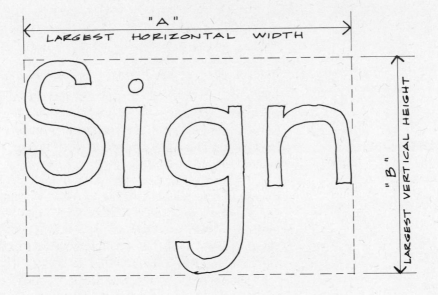

MEASUREMENT OF WALL SIGN AREA WHERE
THERE IS NO DEFINED SIGN BACKGROUND

"A" x "B" = SIGN AREA

Figure 67

252

SIGN CONTROL

Regulations on the number, size, location, height, color, materials, lighting, and content of signs.

Comment: Sign controls are difficult to prepare, enact, and enforce. There are legitimate questions on the extent of sign controls and their legality. All controls have to relate to the purposes of zoning: health, safety, and the welfare of the public. Aesthetics are also an important basis for sign controls. All controls have to be the minimum necessary to accomplish the stated purpose, otherwise the regulations run into serious constitutional questions (Planning Advisory Service Report No. 419 1989). Some of the more conventional controls are as follows:

1. *Number:* Most ordinances permit only one freestanding sign per lot, if they allow any, regardless of the number of establishments on the lot. If a lot has more than one frontage, a freestanding sign for each frontage might be appropriate.

Wall signs can also be limited in number, but a better approach is to limit the square feet of the sign based on the area or frontage of the facade on which it is located. The owner can then split up the permitted sign area into as many signs as desirable.

2. *Location:* The major problem of location is with pole signs, ground signs, and freestanding signs. If the signs are kept small in area and low in height, they have to be located closer to the roadway. A distance of ten to twenty-five feet off the right-of-way appears to be the general range.

3. *Area:* The maximum area of wall signs depends on the facade on which it is located. Most ordinances seem to set a maximum of between 5 and 10 percent of the facade as the maximum area permitted for wall signs. Window signs and temporary signs in windows are included in the 5 to 10 percent maximum.

The area of freestanding signs depends on the zone where located and the speed of traffic on the abutting road. On highways with relatively high speeds, a larger letter size, and consequently overall sign area, is needed due to increased travel during reaction time. Mandelker and Ewald (1988) developed the following chart relating size of signs, speed limits, and types of land use as follows:

253

Design Factors and Resulting Basic Design Elements

Highway (lanes)	Speed (mph)	Reaction Time (seconds)	Distance (feet)	Letter Height (inches)	Total Area of Sign (s.f.)	
					Commercial/ Industrial (surroundings)	Institutional/ Residential/ Rural (surroundings)
2	15–25	8	234	5	15	10
	30–40	8	410	8	35	20
	45–55	8	586	12	75	50
4	15–25	10	293	6	20	15
	30–40	10	510	10	50	35
	45–55	10	733	15	120	80
6	15–25	11	322	7	25	20
	30–40	11	564	11	65	40
	45–55	11	806	16	130	90
Expressway	50–55 +	12	1,056	21	200	150

Source: David R. Mandelker and William R. Ewald, *Street Graphics and the Law* (Chicago: Planners Press, American Planning Association, 1988), pp. 54–55.

4. *Height:* The maximum height of the top of signs should not be higher than the maximum height permitted in the zone. In addition, no signs should be permitted above the roof line of any building.

5. *Color, Material, Lighting, and Content:* Signs in multitenanted buildings, such as a shopping center, should be coordinated as part of an approved sign plan. The plan should include placement, sign area, materials, lighting, and content. On individual signs, lighting should be restricted so as to avoid glare to the traveling public and to avoid creating a nuisance to surrounding property owners.

6. *Flags, Banners, and Pennants:* Banners and pennants are designed for instant attention. They create a carnival-like atmosphere and should be banned except for carnivals, special temporary events, or the opening of new establishments.

National flags are another matter. Many businesses, particularly car dealers, are now featuring enormous garrison-size flags on very high flagpoles. No one would suggest that their motive is other than patriotism; however, there is no reason why the height of the pole cannot be restricted to the maximum height of all freestanding signs in the district. In addition, the forces resulting from high winds on flagpoles flying very large flags can cause structural failures.

SIGN PROJECTION

On a sign attached to a wall, the distance from the exterior wall surface to the sign element farthest distance from such surface. *See Figure 64.*

SIGNAL SPACING

The distance between traffic signals along a roadway.

SIGNIFICANT INCREASE IN TRAFFIC

Vehicular use exceeding the previously anticipated two-way traffic generated by a lot by the greater of:

1. One hundred movements during the peak hour of the highway or the development; or (by)
2. Ten percent of the previously anticipated daily movements.

Comment: The two standards (one hundred movements and 10 percent) are those established by the New Jersey State Highway Access Code. A significant increase in traffic triggers more study and possibly the need for improvements to the highway system.

SILT

Finely divided particles of soil or rock, often carried in cloudy suspension in water and eventually deposited as sediment.

SILVICULTURE

The development and/or maintenance of a forest or wooded preserve.

SIMILAR USE

A use that has the same characteristics as the specifically cited uses in terms of the following: trip generation and type of traffic, parking and circulation, utility demands, environmental impacts, physical space needs, and clientele. *See* CHANGE OF USE.

Comment: The term "same" refers to the range of impacts of all the previously cited uses as opposed to one specific standard for each characteristic.

SINGLE OWNERSHIP

Ownership by one or more persons, in any form of ownership, of more than one lot entirely in the same ownership.

Comment: The definition of single ownership becomes important since most ordinances permit the development of undersized isolated lots providing they are in single ownership. *See* ISOLATED LOT.

SINGLE-FAMILY DWELLING

See DWELLING, SINGLE-FAMILY DETACHED; DWELLING, SINGLE-FAMILY SEMIDETACHED.

SINGLE-ROOM OCCUPANCY (SRO)

A housing type consisting of one room, often with cooking facilities and with private or shared bathroom facilities.

Comment: The closest models to an SRO building are hotels and apartment buildings composed entirely of studio apartments. SROs may have the potential to meet some of the need for lower cost housing without the use of subsidies. The most appropriate locations for SROs are areas where low-cost retail and service establishments are in walking distance. Access to mass transit lines is another criterion that should be considered, so that travel to employment, services, and family is possible.

SINKING

A method of controlling oil spills that employs an agent to entrap oil droplets and sink them to the bottom of the body of water.

SITE

Any plot or parcel of land or combination of contiguous lots or parcels of land. *See Figure 56.*

SITE PLAN

The development plan for one or more lots on which is shown the existing and proposed conditions of the lot, including topography, vegetation, drainage, flood plains, wetlands, and waterways; landscaping and open spaces; walkways; means of ingress and egress; circulation; utility services; structures and buildings; signs and lighting; berms, buffers, and screening devices; surrounding development; and any other information that reasonably may be required in order that an informed decision can be made by the approving authority.

Comment: Many ordinances classify small site plans (five acres or less in rural areas, less in urban areas, or less than a specific square footage of building area) as minor site plans and relieve the applicant of some of the submission requirements.

SKATEBOARD PARK

A building, structure, or open area containing or developed with slopes, hills, passageways, and other challenges where people using skateboards may practice the sport for a fee; rental or sale of skateboards and related equipment may be included.

SKETCH PLAN

See PLAT, SKETCH.

256

SKI AREA

An area developed for snow skiing, with trails and lifts, and including ski rental and sales, instruction, and eating facilities.

SKI RESORT

A ski area that also includes sales, rental, and service of related equipment and accessories, eating places, residences, and hotels and motels. *See* Ski Area.

SKIMMING

The mechanical removal of oil or scum from the surface of water.

SKY EXPOSURE PLANE

A theoretical plane beginning at a lot line or directly above a street line at a height set forth in the ordinance and rising over a slope determined by an acute angle measured down from the vertical as set forth in the ordinance. *See Figure 68.*

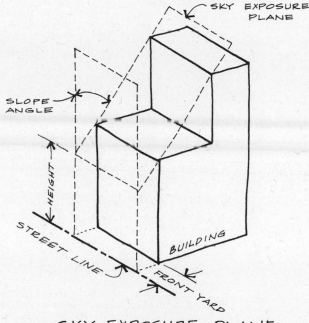

SKY EXPOSURE PLANE

Figure 68

SLOPE

The deviation of a surface from the horizontal, usually expressed in percent or degrees. *See* Grade. *See Figure 41.*

Comment: Slope percent is computed by dividing the

257

vertical distance by the horizontal distance times one hundred.

SLUDGE
Solids removed from sewage during wastewater treatment and then disposed of by incineration, dumping, or burial.

SLUM
See BLIGHTED AREA.

SMOG
Generally used as an equivalent of air pollution, particularly associated with oxidants.

SMOKE
Solid particles generated as a result of the incomplete combustion of materials containing carbon.

SOCIAL SERVICES
Establishments providing assistance and aid to those persons requiring counseling for psychological problems, employment, learning disabilities, and physical disabilities.

Comment: This major group also includes organizations soliciting funds for these and related services. They also include child day-care services, nurseries as well as residential care, and special categories for persons with limited ability for self-care but for whom medical care is not a major element.

SOIL
All unconsolidated mineral and organic material of whatever origin that overlies bedrock and can be readily excavated.

SOIL CONDITIONER
A biologically stable organic material, such as humus or compost, that makes soil more amenable to the passage of water and to the distribution of fertilizing material, providing a better medium for necessary soil bacteria growth.

SOIL CONSERVATION DISTRICT
A geographic area, usually a county, in which professionals provide advice to communities, agencies, and individuals within the jurisdiction and review development proposals for soil erosion and sedimentation control measures.

Comment: The soil conservation district concept was set up in 1936 and is used by the U.S. Department of Agriculture to administer its program relating to water and soil.

258

SOIL ENGINEER

A professional engineer who is qualified by education and experience to practice applied soil mechanics and foundation engineering.

SOIL EROSION

See EROSION.

SOIL EROSION AND SEDIMENT CONTROL PLAN

A plan that indicates necessary land treatment measures, including a schedule for installation, which will effectively minimize soil erosion and sedimentation.

SOIL MAP

A map indicating the names and spatial distribution of soil types on a site and including information relating to soil characteristics, such as slope, depth to seasonal high water, depth to bedrock, permeability, natural drainage class, stoniness, and flood and stream overflow hazard.

Comment: The data source for maps showing the soil types and locations on a given area is usually the official soil maps prepared by the Soil Conservation Service of the U.S. Department of Agriculture. The information provided in the official soil maps was field compiled by the Soil Conservation Service by testing at selected locations. However, soil maps developed from this base for use in development applications must be field checked for accuracy and adjusted if warranted, especially in cases involving the delineation of areas where development is precluded or limited.

SOLAR ACCESS

A property owner's right to have the sunlight shine on the owner's land.

Comment: The enforcement of this right is through the zoning ordinance that establishes height and setback requirements. Applicants may be asked to present sun shadow diagrams to permit an agency to determine if solar access will be impaired.

SOLAR ENERGY SYSTEM

A complete design or assembly consisting of a solar energy collector, an energy storage facility (where used), and components for the distribution of transformed energy.

Comment: Passive solar energy systems are usually included in this definition. Some judgment is required, though, when the passive systems also serve structural or recreational purposes. When they become predominantly structural or recreational, they are usually excluded from the definition.

SOLAR SKY SPACE

The space between a solar energy collector and the sun that must be free of obstructions that shade the collector to an extent that precludes its cost-effective operation.

Comment: Increasingly, planners will be asked to develop zoning requirements that protect the solar sky space. It can be done through minimum setback requirements and sky exposure planes. Site plan review might also require a shadow analysis to ascertain whether or not any proposed tree plantings, landscaping, or structures will block off solar collectors. For single-family and two-family homes that are usually excluded from site plan review, the construction code official or building inspector should be given guidelines as to what may be permitted and minimum setbacks in order to assure a functioning solar collector.

SOLAR SKY SPACE EASEMENT

A right, expressed as an easement, covenant, condition, or other property interest, in any deed or other instrument executed by or on behalf of any landowner that protects the solar sky space of an actual, proposed, or designated solar energy collector at a described location by forbidding or limiting activities or land uses that interfere with access to solar energy.

Comment: The solar sky space must be described either as the three-dimensional space in which obstruction is prohibited or limited, or as the times of day in which direct sunlight to the solar collector may not be obstructed, or as a combination of the two methods.

SOLID WASTE

Unwanted or discarded material, including waste material with insufficient liquid content to be free flowing.

Comment: Solid waste may be categorized as follows: (1) agricultural—solid waste that results from the raising and slaughtering of animals and the processing of animal products and orchard and field crops; (2) commercial—waste generated by stores, offices, and other activities that do not actually turn out a product; (3) industrial—waste that results from industrial processes and manufacturing; (4) institutional—waste originating from educational, health care, and research facilities; (5) municipal—residential and commercial solid waste generated within a community; (6) pesticide—the residue from the manufacturing, handling, or use of chemicals intended for killing plant and animal pests; (7) residential—waste

260

that normally originates in a residential environment, sometimes called domestic solid waste.

SOLID WASTE DISPOSAL

The ultimate disposition of solid waste that cannot be salvaged or recycled.

SOLID WASTE MANAGEMENT

A planned program providing for the collection, storage, and disposal of solid waste, including, where appropriate, recycling and recovery.

SOOT

Agglomerations of tar-impregnated carbon particles that form when carbonaceous material does not undergo complete combustion.

SORORITY HOUSE

See FRATERNITY HOUSE.

SPECIAL ASSESSMENT

A fee levied by a local authority for the financing of a local improvement that is primarily of benefit to the landowners who must pay the assessment.

SPECIAL DISTRICT

A district created by act, petition, or vote of the residents for a specific purpose with the power to levy taxes.

SPECIAL EXCEPTION USE

See CONDITIONAL USE.

SPECIAL USE PERMIT

A permit issued by the proper governmental authority that must be acquired before a special exception use can be constructed. *See* CONDITIONAL USE PERMIT.

SPECIALTY FOOD STORE

A retail store specializing in a specific type or class of foods, such as an appetizer store, bakery, butcher, delicatessen, fish market, or gourmet shop.

SPECIALTY SHOPPING CENTER

(1) A shopping center whose shops cater to a specific market and are linked together by an architectural, historical, or geographic theme or by a commonality of goods and services; also known as a theme or fashion center; (2) a retail center of between 100,000 to 200,000 square feet consisting mostly of small shops with distinctive, one-of-a-kind merchandise with emphasis on arts and crafts supplied locally. *See* MINI-MALL; SHOPPING CENTER.

SPECIFICATIONS

Detailed instructions that designate the quality and quantity of materials and workmanship expected in the construction of a structure.

SPECIMEN TREE

A particularly impressive or unusual example of a species due to its size, shade, age, or any other trait that epitomizes the character of the species (Planning Advisory Service Report No. 431 1990).

SPEED BUMP

A raised section of a paved surface or roadway designed to slow down vehicles.

Comment: Speed bumps can be hazardous and are used only on private roads and parking areas. They should be well marked with warning signs. Good road and parking area design can usually preclude the need for speed bumps.

SPEED-CHANGE LANE

An auxiliary lane, deceleration lane, or acceleration lane, including tapered areas, primarily for the deceleration or acceleration of vehicles entering or leaving the through traffic lanes.

SPOIL

Dirt, rock, or waste material that has been removed from its original location or materials that have been dredged from the bottoms of waterways.

SPOT ZONING

Rezoning of a lot or parcel of land to benefit an owner for a use incompatible with surrounding land uses and that does not further the comprehensive zoning plan.

Comment: Spot zoning per se may not be illegal; it may only be descriptive of a certain set of facts and consequently neutral with respect to whether it is valid or invalid. Hagman (1975) states that spot zoning is invalid only when all the following factors are present: (1) a small parcel of land is singled out for special and privileged treatment; (2) the singling out is not in the public interest but only for the benefit of the land owner; and (3) the action is not in accord with a comprehensive plan. See *Kozesnik's v. Twp. of Montgomery,* 24 N.J. 154, 131 A2 1 (1957); *Borough of Cresskill v. Borough of Dumont,* 15 N.J. 238, 104 A2d 441 (1954); and *Jones v. Zoning Board of Adjustment of Long Beach Twp.,* 32 N.J. Super. 397, 108, 498 (1954).

SPRAWL

Uncontrolled growth, usually of a low-density nature, in previously rural areas and some distance from existing development and infrastructure.

SQUARE

A public open space in a developed area. *See* COURT; PLAZA.

262

SQUATTER	A person who settled on land without the permission of the owner.
STABILIZATION	The process of converting active organic matter in sewage sludge or solid wastes into inert, harmless material.
STABLE	A structure that is used for the shelter or care of horses and cattle.
STACK	A smokestack, vertical pipe, or flue designed to exhaust gases and suspended particulate matter.
STADIUM	A large open or enclosed place used for games and major events and partly or completely surrounded by tiers of seats for spectators.
STAGGERED WORK HOURS	Work schedules that permit employees to arrive and leave at different hours, either individually or by department.
STALL	The parking space in which vehicles park. *See Figure 59.*

Comment: The size of stalls varies. The typical automobile stall is nine by twenty feet. However, where there is large turnover and drivers have packages, such as in a shopping center, a ten by twenty foot space may be appropriate. In addition, the wider stall will permit easier vehicular access for shoppers burdened with packages. In low turnover situations, an eight and a half by twenty foot stall may suffice. If spaces are assigned, then compact car parking can be as small as seven by seventeen feet. Where vehicles can overhang a curb, the stall depth can be reduced by two feet. *See* PARKING SPACE.

STANDARD OF LIVING	A measure of the adequacy of necessities and comforts in an individual's daily life in reference to the general populace.
STANDPIPE	*See* WATER TOWER.
STATIONARY SOURCE	A nonmobile emitter of pollution. *See* AREA SOURCE; POINT SOURCE.
STEEP SLOPE	Land areas where the slope exceeds 20 percent.

Comment: Use of the 20 percent figure is somewhat arbitrary. The major point is that construction on slopes in excess of 20 percent requires additional safeguards

263

against erosion and other potential problems. Some ordinances reduce the allowable intensity of development on steep slopes.

STORM SEWER A conduit that collects and transports runoff.

STORMWATER DETENTION Any storm drainage technique that retards or detains runoff, such as a detention or retention basin, parking lot storage, rooftop storage, porous pavement, dry wells, or any combination thereof. *See* DETENTION BASIN; RETENTION BASIN.

STORMWATER MANAGEMENT The control and management of stormwater to minimize the detrimental effects of surface water runoff.

Comment: For new development, stormwater management regulations usually apply only to any net increase in stormwater runoff generated by such development activity.

STORY That portion of a building included between the surface of any floor and the surface of the floor next above it, or if there is no floor above it, then the space between the floor and the ceiling next above it and including those basements used for the principal use. *See Figure 6.*

STORY, HALF A space under a sloping roof that has the line of intersection of the roof and wall face not more than three feet above the floor level and in which space the possible floor area with head room of five feet or less occupies at least 40 percent of the total floor area of the story directly beneath. *See Figure 69.*

STREAM A watercourse having a source and terminus, banks, and channel through which waters flow at least periodically.

Comment: Streams usually empty into lakes, other streams, or the ocean but do not lose their character as a watercourse even though the water may dry up.

STREAM CORRIDOR Any river, stream, pond, lake, or wetland, together with adjacent upland areas, that supports protective bands of vegetation that line the water's edge.

STREET Any vehicular way that: (1) is an existing state, county, or municipal roadway; (2) is shown upon a plat approved pursuant to law; (3) is approved by other official action;

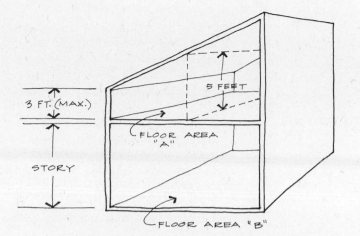

3 FT. (MAX.)

5 FEET

FLOOR AREA "A"

STORY

FLOOR AREA "B"

IF FLOOR AREA "A" IS AT LEAST
40% OF FLOOR AREA "B" -
THEN "A" IS A HALF STORY.

Figure 69

or (4) is shown on a plat duly filed and recorded in the office of the county recording officer prior to the appointment of a planning board and the grant to such board of the power to review plats; includes the land between the street lines, whether improved or unimproved.

STREET, COLLECTOR	A street that collects traffic from local streets and connects with minor and major arterials. *See Figure 70.*
STREET, CUL-DE-SAC	A street with a single common ingress and egress and with a turnaround at the end. *See Figures 18, 19, 20, 21, and 70.*
STREET, DEAD-END	A street with a single common ingress and egress. *See Figure 70.*
STREET, DUAL	A street with opposing lanes separated by a median strip, center island, or other form of barrier, which cannot be crossed except at designated locations.
STREET, EXPRESSWAY	A divided multilane major arterial street for through traffic with partial control of access and with grade separations at major intersections. *See Figure 70.*

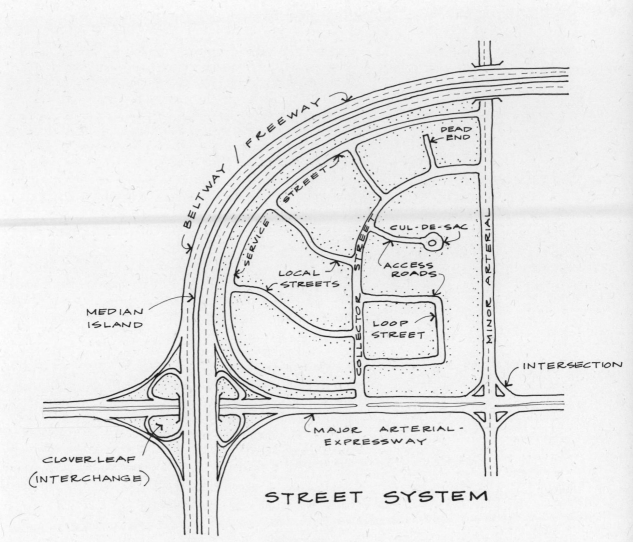

STREET SYSTEM

Figure 70

STREET, FREEWAY

A limited access highway with no grade crossings. *See Figure 70.*

STREET, LOCAL

A street designed to provide vehicular access to abutting property and to discourage through traffic. *See Figure 70.*

Comment: Cul-de-sacs and loop streets are both examples of local streets. *See* Cul-De-Sacs; Loop Streets.

STREET, LOOP

A local street that has its only ingress and egress at two points on the same collector street. *See Figure 70.*

266

STREET, MAJOR ARTERIAL   A street with access control, channelized intersections, restricted parking, and that collects and distributes traffic to and from minor arterials. *See Figure 70.*

STREET, MINOR ARTERIAL   A street with signals at important intersections and stop signs on the side streets and that collects and distributes traffic to and from collector streets. *See Figure 70.*

STREET, PAPER   A street that has never been built shown on an approved plan, subdivision plat, tax maps, or official map.

STREET, PRIVATE   A street that has not been accepted by the municipality or other governmental entity.

Comment: Private streets may be used by the public, often as access to a development, industrial plant, or shopping area. Some states permit the municipality to remove snow on private streets without affecting their status.

STREET, SERVICE   A street running parallel to a freeway or expressway and serving abutting properties. *See Figure 70.*

STREET BEAUTIFICATION   Improving the appearance of a street in accordance with a plan, including, but not limited to, the installation of landscaping, benches, street lighting, sidewalks, wastebaskets, and signage.

STREET CAPACITY   *See* Capacity, Roadway.

STREET FURNITURE   Constructed, aboveground objects, such as outdoor seating, kiosks, bus shelters, sculpture, tree grids, trash receptacles, fountains, and telephone booths, that have the potential for enlivening and giving variety to streets, sidewalks, plazas, and other outdoor spaces open to, and used by, the public.

Comment: Street furniture can include, but is generally distinct from, street hardware. *See* Street Hardware.

STREET HARDWARE   Mechanical and utility systems, usually located within a street right-of-way, such as hydrants, manhole covers, traffic signals, lighting standards, and directional signs.

STREET HIERARCHY   The system by which roads are classified according to their purpose and the travel demand they serve.

267

STREET LINE

See RIGHT-OF-WAY LINES.

STREETSCAPE

A design term referring to all the elements that constitute the physical makeup of a street and that, as a group, define its character, including building frontage, street paving, street furniture, landscaping, including trees and other plantings, awnings and marquees, signs, and lighting (Schultz and Kasen 1984).

STRIP COMMERCIAL DEVELOPMENT

Commercial or retail uses, usually one-story high and one-store deep, that front on a major street.

Comment: Strip commercial development is typically characterized by street frontage parking lots serving individual or strips of stores. Some older commercial strips, however, are dependent on on-street parking and, in some cases, parking lots interspersed among or positioned behind the buildings. Strip commercial differs from central business districts and shopping centers in at least two of the following characteristics: (1) there are no provisions for pedestrian access between individual uses; (2) the uses are only one-store deep; (3) the buildings are arranged linearly rather than clustered; and (4) there is no design integration among individual uses.

While they are universally criticized as ugly, the problem with strip commercial development may be inadequate local regulations. For example, landscaped parking lots, including trees and landscaped island separations between bays, can significantly improve the appearance and break up the building impact. Other requirements that significantly improve the aesthetics of their uses include peaked rather than flat roofs, wide sidewalks abutting the storefronts with canopy or roof overhangs over pedestrian areas, and controlled and integrated signing. Features such as kiosks, benches, and sculpture can help humanize and make more attractive these facilities.

In addition, adjacent residential areas can be shielded from strip commercial uses by requiring walls and berms with heavy landscape treatment.

STRIP MINING

A process of recovering ore or fuel deposits by mechanically scraping away the overhanging rock and strata.

Comment: Strip mining is also known as surface mining.

STRIP ZONING

See STRIP COMMERCIAL DEVELOPMENT.

268

STRUCTURAL ALTERATION

Any change in either the supporting members of a building, such as bearing walls, columns, beams, and girders, or in the dimensions or configurations of the roof or exterior walls.

STRUCTURE

A combination of materials to form a construction for use, occupancy, or ornamentation whether installed on, above, or below the surface of land or water.

Comment: By this definition, all buildings are structures; however, not all structures are buildings. *See* BUILDING.

STUD FARM

A farm where a stallion stands at stud and mares are bred to him, and where breeding, pasturing, and foaling may take place.

STUDIO

(1) The workshop of an artist, sculptor, photographer, or craftsperson; (2) a place for radio or television production; and (3) a place where movies are produced.

Comment: The studio for radio or television broadcasting is only that part of the station from which the signal originates. It could be an office or a home and is often separate and some distance from the transmitter and antennas.

From a zoning perspective, the local ordinance should clearly identify the type of studio being permitted. Workshops of craftspersons, for instance, would be appropriate for residential areas, as would small studios for radio production. Large-scale television or movie production studios clearly belong in nonresidential areas.

STUDIO APARTMENT

See DWELLING UNIT, EFFICIENCY.

SUBDIVIDER

Any person having an interest in land that is the subject of an application for subdivision. *See* APPLICANT.

SUBDIVISION

The division of a lot, tract, or parcel of land into two or more lots, tracts, parcels, or other divisions of land for sale, development, or lease.

Comment: Many state enabling laws exclude certain subdivisions from this definition. For example, in New Jersey, the following are not considered subdivisions, providing no new streets are created: (1) divisions of land for agricultural purposes where all resulting parcels are

269

five acres or larger in size; (2) divisions of property by testamentary or intestate provisions; (3) divisions of property upon court order, including, but not limited to, judgments of foreclosure; and (4) conveyances so as to combine existing lots by deed or other instruments.

SUBDIVISION, CLUSTER

See Cluster Subdivision.

SUBDIVISION, CONSOLIDATION

The combining of individual recorded lots to form a single tract in single ownership. *See* Assemblage; Consolidation.

SUBDIVISION, MAJOR

Any subdivision not classified as a minor subdivision.

SUBDIVISION, MINOR

A subdivision of land that does not involve any of the following: (1) the creating of more than the maximum number of lots specifically permitted by ordinance as a minor subdivision; (2) a planned development; (3) any new street; or (4) the extension of any off-tract improvements.

Comment: Many ordinances further restrict minor subdivisions to land incapable of further subdivision. Any parcel that could be further subdivided would be classified as a major. The purpose is to ensure that required improvements are installed and not avoided by a series of minor subdivisions.

SUBMERGED LAND

Those lands situated below the mean low waterline or all of the lands covered by the mean high waterline.

SUBSIDENCE

The gradual sinking of land as a result of natural or artificial causes.

SUBSIDIZED HOUSING

Housing priced below market cost as a result of the use of subsidies and limited to occupancy by households in specified income ranges. *See* Low-Income Housing; Moderate-Income Housing; Public Housing.

Comment: Subsidized housing is usually restricted to households earning 80 percent or less of the median income of the area in which the housing is located. Rental and sales prices are usually based on the income of the occupant. The U.S. Department of Housing and Urban Development regulations for rental housing stipulate that rents, including utilities, cannot exceed 30 percent of the occupant's gross annual income. In New Jersey, where

270

subsidized housing is made available on a sales basis, mortgage principal and interest, condo fees (if applicable), taxes, and insurance cannot exceed 28 percent of the occupant's income.

SUBSOIL

The layer of soil just below the surface of the ground.

SUBSTANDARD STRUCTURE/ DWELLING

A term used in the 1960s and preceding U.S. Censuses of Housing to indicate a lack of some or all plumbing facilities and/or the presence of physical inadequacies. *See* DEFICIENT UNIT.

SUBSTANTIAL IMPROVEMENT

Any extension, repair, reconstruction, or other improvement of a property, the cost of which equals or exceeds 50 percent of the fair market value of a property either before the improvement is started or, if the property has been damaged and is being restored, before the damage occurred.

Comment: Substantial improvement often is used to define the point where a nonconforming use or structure cannot be repaired. The Federal Insurance Administration also requires floodproofing measures to be installed when a structure in a floodway undergoes "substantial improvement."

SUBURBAN AREA

A predominantly low-density residential area located immediately outside of and physically and socioeconomically associated with an urban area or a city.

Comment: Suburban areas have population densities ranging from five hundred to one thousand persons per square mile.

SUITABLE SITE

A site that is adjacent to compatible land uses, has access to appropriate streets, and is consistent with state environmental policies.

Comment: The above is the New Jersey Council on Affordable Housing's definition for sites suitable for lower income housing. The broad criteria have been further refined in a series of court cases by judges and planners. In *Orgo Farms and Greenhouses v. Colts Neck Township,* 192 N.J. Super. 559 (1984), and *Orgo Farms and Greenhouses v. Colts Neck Township,* 204 N.J. Super. 585 (1985), the court cited the importance of state and regional planning designations for growth and limited

271

growth areas as criteria in determining suitable sites. The court-appointed planning master in the same case proposed five criteria as tests for suitable sites: (1) regional accessibility; (2) proximity to goods and services; (3) availability of water and sewers; (4) environmental suitability; and (5) land use compatibility.

Another special master added several more criteria as follows: (1) has access to appropriate streets; (2) avoids historic sites; (3) avoids restricted agricultural lands; (4) avoids wetlands and required buffers; (5) avoids flood hazard areas; (6) avoids steep slopes (in excess of 15 percent); (7) avoids reserved recreation, conservation, and open space; (8) has clear title, free of encumbrances that would preclude the development of low- and moderate-income housing; (9) lacks intangible factors likely to delay or hinder development of low- and moderate-income housing; and (10) is owned by, or under contract or sale to, a developer who is ready, willing, and able to build a substantial amount of low- and moderate-income housing.

SULFUR DIOXIDE (SO₂)

A heavy, pungent, colorless gas formed primarily by the combustion of fossil fuels that damage the respiratory tract as well as vegetation and certain materials and considered a major air pollutant.

SUMMER CAMP

A location away from home, often in a rural or country setting, where campers spend all or part of the summer living in tents, barracks, or dormitories, participating in organized activities, sports, and arts and crafts, and usually eating together in a central dining facility.

Comment: The term "summer camp" may be a misnomer since these facilities operate throughout the year in all seasons. Many are geared to the elderly or the physically or mentally handicapped. Housing includes "camp-type" dormitories and cabins.

SUMP

A depression or tank that serves as a drain or receptacle of liquids for salvage or disposal.

SUPERMARKET

A retail establishment primarily selling food as well as other convenience and household goods.

Comment: Supermarkets usually vary in size, from approximately thirty-five thousand square feet to seventy thousand square feet, and provide parking at a ratio of

272

about five to six off-street spaces per one thousand square feet of gross leasable space.

SURFACE WATER Water on the earth's surface exposed to the atmosphere as rivers, lakes, streams, and oceans. *See* GROUNDWATER.

SURFACTANT An agent used in detergents to cause lathering.

Comment: Composed of several phosphate compounds, surfactants are a source of external enrichment thought to speed the eutrophication of lakes.

SURGICAL CENTER A facility where outpatients come for simple surgical procedures.

Comment: Surgical centers are more elaborate than a doctor's office but less equipped and limited in the services they perform than a hospital.

SURROGATE A census indicator of deficient housing used in the calculation of present need.

Comment: Surrogates for deficient housing include age of structure, no elevators in mid-rise building, no central heat, overcrowding, nonexclusive use of complete plumbing facilities, inadequate kitchen facilities, and access. Usually any deficiency, together with age, constitutes evidence of deficient housing.

SURVEILLANCE SYSTEM A monitoring system to determine environmental quality or maintain security.

Comment: Surveillance systems are established to monitor all pollution and other aspects of progress toward attainment of environmental standards. Surveillance systems identify potential episodes of high pollutant concentrations in time to take preventive action.

SURVEY (1) The process of precisely ascertaining the area, dimensions, and location of a piece of land; (2) determining the characteristics of persons, land, objects, buildings, or structures by sampling, census, interviews, observations, or other methods.

SUSPENDED SOLIDS Small particles of solid pollutants in sewage that contribute to turbidity and that resist separation by conventional means.

273

Comment: The examination of suspended solids and the BOD (biological oxygen demand) test constitute the two main determinations for water quality performed at wastewater treatment facilities.

SWALE

A depression in the ground that channels runoff.

SWIMMING POOL

A water-filled enclosure, permanently constructed or portable, having a depth of more than eighteen inches below the level of the surrounding land, or an above-surface pool, having a depth of more than thirty inches, designed, used, and maintained for swimming and bathing.

Comment: The eighteen-inch exclusion would be effective in permitting landscaping and other shallow, not-for-swimming pools. The thirty-inch height for surface pools marks the usual break between portable and nonportable pools beyond which some codes require fencing and gates.

SYNDICATE

A group formed to combine capital or other assets for future investment.

SYNERGISM

The cooperative action of separate substances so that the total effect is greater than the sum of the effects of the substances acting independently.

T

TAILINGS

Second-grade or waste material derived when raw material is screened or processed.

TAKING

To take, expropriate, acquire, or seize property without compensation. *See* Eminent Domain; Just Compensation.

Comment: The question of taking has become increasingly more important in recent years as a result of a number of U.S. Supreme Court decisions, including *First English Evangelical Lutheran Church v. County of Los Angeles,* 482 U.S. 304 (1987); *Nollan v. California Coastal Comm'n,* 483 U.S. 825 (1987); and *Keystone Bituminous Coal Ass'n v. DeBenedictis,* 480 U.S. 470

(1987). The cases are complicated and in some cases contradictory. In the *Keystone* case, for example, the court appeared to suggest that if the regulations serve broad public purposes and permit reasonable economic use of property, they are legal. In the *Nollan* case, on the other hand, the court seemed to say that the broad public benefit is narrow and has to be carefully considered; finally, in the *Lutheran* case, the court indicated that if the regulations are too restrictive or excessive, then the entity harmed can secure damages for the time the regulations were in effect.

TANK FARM

An open-air facility containing a number of aboveground, large containers for the bulk storage of material in liquid, powder, or pellet form.

TAVERN

An establishment used primarily for the serving of liquor by the drink to the general public and where food or packaged liquors may be served or sold only as accessory to the primary use.

TAX ABATEMENT

Full or partial exemption for a defined period of time of real estate taxes.

Comment: Tax abatements can be used for a variety of purposes, including encouraging development, historic preservation, natural resource conservation, urban redevelopment, enterprise zones, or some other public objective. In many states, tax abatements are limited to those uses listed in applicable state legislation.

TAX-EXEMPT PROPERTY

Property that, because of its ownership or use, is not subject to property taxation.

TAX MAP

The recorded map of delineated lots or tracts in a municipality showing boundaries, bearings, sizes, and dimensions, including the block and lot numbers.

Comment: The tax map shows individual parcels of land that are duly recorded in the office of the county (usually) recording office. It may include ownership and use.

TELECOMMUTING

A work arrangement for performing work electronically, where employees work at a location other than the primary work location, such as at home or in a subordinate office.

TEMPORARY OUTDOOR ACTIVITY

Happenings that are carried out primarily out-of-doors for a fixed period of time and including flea markets, fireworks, displays, speeches, farm stands, seasonal sales, swap and shop markets, racing meets, circuses, carnivals, concerts, and parades. *See* MASS GATHERING.

Comment: Some forms of temporary outdoor activities are clearly addressed by zoning. These include weekend flea markets, farm stands, racing meets, and so forth. Others are more transitory, such as parades, carnivals, fireworks, and so on, and are probably best controlled by permit or license from the municipality.

TEMPORARY PROTECTION

Stabilization of erosive or sediment-producing areas by temporary measures until permanent measures are in place.

TEMPORARY RETAIL FOOD ESTABLISHMENT

A retail food establishment that operates at a fixed location for a temporary period of time in connection with a fair, carnival, circus, picnic, concert, public exhibition, or similar transitory gathering.

Comment: Temporary retail food establishments are accessory to the principal permitted use, for instance, a fair or carnival.

TEMPORARY STRUCTURE

A structure without any foundation or footings and that is removed when the designated time period, activity, or use for which the temporary structure was erected has ceased.

TEMPORARY USE

A use established for a limited duration with the intent to discontinue such use upon the expiration of the time period.

Comment: Temporary uses usually do not involve the construction or alteration of any permanent building or structure, although the authorization of the temporary use does not necessarily preclude such construction.

TENANT

An occupant of land or premises who occupies, uses, and enjoys real property for a fixed time, usually through a lease arrangement with the property owner and with the owner's consent.

TENEMENT HOUSE

A multifamily dwelling most commonly associated with low-income families and generally characterized as an aging, often substandard structure.

TENNIS COURT	An improved area used for playing tennis.
TERMINAL	(1) A place where transfer between modes of transportation takes place; (2) a terminating point where goods are transferred from a truck to a storage area or to other trucks or another form of transportation. *See* DISTRIBUTION CENTER; TRUCK TERMINAL; WAREHOUSE.
TERRACE	A level, landscaped, and/or surfaced area, also referred to as a patio, directly adjacent to a principal building at or within three feet of the finished grade and not covered by a permanent roof.
TERTIARY TREATMENT	Wastewater treatment, beyond the secondary, or biological stage, that includes removal of nutrients, such as phosphorus and nitrogen, and a high percentage of suspended solids.
TEXTURE	The quality of a surface, ranging from mirror finish, smooth, to coarse and unfinished.
THEATER	A building or part of a building devoted to showing motion pictures or for dramatic, dance, musical, or other live performances.
THEATER, DRIVE-IN	An open lot devoted primarily to the showing of motion pictures or theatrical productions on a paid admission basis to patrons seated in automobiles.
	Comment: Drive-in theaters are usually temporary uses until demand for other, more remunerative uses materialize. Drive-in theaters include refreshment stands and amusement rides. Since drive-in theaters operate only at night, many sites are used for other purposes during the day, such as flea markets.
THEME PARK	An entertainment or amusement facility built around a single theme that may be historical, architectural, or cultural.
THEORETICAL DRIVEWAY LOCATION (TDL)	The center of the highway frontage of any lot and used to calculate whether a lot is conforming.
	Comment: TDLs are used in highway access ordinances.
THERMAL POLLUTION	Degradation of water quality by the introduction of a heated effluent.

277

Comment: Thermal pollution is primarily the result of the discharge of cooling waters from industrial processes, particularly from electrical power generation.

THREATENED SPECIES Wildlife species who may become endangered if conditions surrounding them begin to or continue to deteriorate and so designated by a governmental agency.

THROUGH LOT *See* Lot, Through.

TIDE A periodic rise and fall of the surface of ocean waters caused by gravitational pull.

TIDE LAND Land between low and high tide. *See* Intertidal Area. *See Figure 8.*

TILLABLE LAND Fertile land that can be cultivated.

TIMBERLAND Land covered by harvestable trees and wooded areas.

T-INTERSECTION An at-grade intersection where one of the intersecting legs is perpendicular to the other two.

TOPOGRAPHIC MAP A map of a portion of the earth's surface showing its relative elevation.

Comment: Topographic maps often include natural and man-made features, such as structures, rivers, wooded areas, and so forth.

TOPSOIL The original upper layer of soil material to a depth of about six inches that is usually darker and richer than the subsoil.

TOT LOT An improved and equipped play area for small children usually up to elementary school age.

Comment: Tot lots may be small (one thousand square feet) and consist of swings and sandboxes, as well as benches and fences.

TOURISM The attracting and serving of people visiting an area for recreation and vacations.

TOURIST HOME An establishment in a private dwelling that supplies temporary accommodations to overnight guests for a fee. *See* Bed and Breakfast.

278

TOWER

A structure that is intended to send and/or receive radio and television communications.

TOWN

(1) A developed community, smaller than a city and larger than a village; (2) in some states, a description of the form of local government.

Comment: The New Jersey State Development and Redevelopment Plan defines a town as having an urban density of more than one thousand persons per square mile and interrelated mixed uses.

TOWN CENTER

See CENTRAL BUSINESS DISTRICT.

TOWN SQUARE

The traditional center of a village or town and usually surrounded by governmental and cultural buildings.

TOWNHOUSE

See DWELLING, TOWNHOUSE.

TOWNSHIP

(1) A unit of territory usually six miles square and containing thirty-six-mile-square sections; (2) in some states, a description of the form of local government.

TOXIC SUBSTANCES

Any combination of pollutants, including disease-carrying agents, that, after discharge and upon exposure, ingestion, inhalation, or assimilation into any organism, can cause death or disease, mutations, deformities, or malfunctions in such organisms or their offspring and that adversely affect the environment.

TOXICITY

The quality or degree of being poisonous or harmful to plant or animal life.

TRACE METALS

Metals, usually insoluble, found in small quantities or in the air, water, or other materials.

TRACT

An area, parcel, site, piece of land, or property that is the subject of a development application. *See Figure 56.*

TRAFFIC COUNT

A tabulation of the number of vehicles or pedestrians passing a certain point during a specified period of time.

TRAFFIC DEMAND MANAGEMENT

Strategies aimed at reducing the number of vehicle trips, shortening trip lengths, and changing the timing of trips out of peak hours.

Comment: These strategies encourage the use of mass

transit, car pools, van pools, bicycling, and walking and typically focus on the home-to-work commute. They also include efforts to provide housing close to jobs to shorten trip lengths. These strategies usually require the joint cooperation of developers, employers, and local governments.

TRAFFIC GENERATOR

A use in a particular geographic area that is likely to attract into the area substantial vehicular or pedestrian traffic.

TRAFFIC GROWTH RATE

The rate at which traffic volumes are projected to increase over a period of time, expressed as a percentage that is compounded annually.

TRAFFIC IMPACT STUDY

A report analyzing anticipated roadway conditions with and without an applicant's development.

Comment: The report may include an analysis of mitigation measures and a calculation of fair share financial contributions.

TRAILER

A structure standing on wheels, towed or hauled by another vehicle, and used for short-term human occupancy, carrying of materials, goods, or objects, or as a temporary office.

Comment: Development ordinances may allow for trailers on work sites to be used as temporary offices.

TRANSFER OF DEVELOPMENT RIGHTS (TDR)

The removal of the right to develop or build, expressed in dwelling units per acre or floor area, from land in one zoning district to land in another district where such transfer is permitted. *See* DENSITY TRANSFER. *See Figure 71.*

Comment: TDRs, or transfer of development credits, is a relatively new land development control tool used to preserve open space and farmland and to direct development to suitable areas. In urban areas, TDR has been used for historic preservation. TDR permits an owner of real property to sell or exchange the development rights associated with that property to another owner in return for compensation.

TRANSFER STATION

An intermediate destination for solid waste.

Comment: Transfer stations may include separation of different types of waste and aggregation of smaller ship-

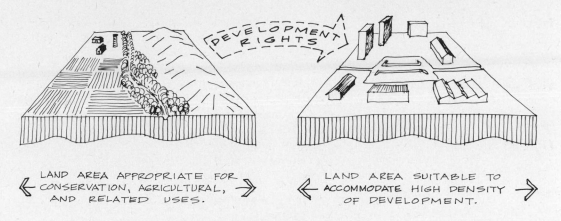

PRESERVATION ZONE
EXISTING PERMITTED LOW DEVELOPMENT DENSITY REDUCED FURTHER BY TRANSFER OF DEVELOPMENT RIGHTS TO TRANSFER ZONE.

TRANSFER ZONE
ZONING REGULATIONS ALLOW DENSITY INCREASE TO ACCOMMODATE DEVELOPMENT RIGHTS ACCEPTED FROM THE PRESERVATION ZONE.

DEVELOPMENT RIGHTS

LAND AREA APPROPRIATE FOR CONSERVATION, AGRICULTURAL, AND RELATED USES.

LAND AREA SUITABLE TO ACCOMMODATE HIGH DENSITY OF DEVELOPMENT.

TRANSFER OF DEVELOPMENT RIGHTS

Figure 71

ments with large ones. It may also include compaction to reduce the bulk of the waste. These facilities are intensive uses and are properly located in heavy industrial zones. They are usually necessary because garbage trucks that pick up from houses are unsuitable for long, over-the-road hauls to distant landfills.

TRANSITION ZONE

A zoning district that permits uses compatible with uses permitted in two adjacent zones that, without the transition zone, could be considered incompatible to each other. *See Figure 72.*

Comment: Examples of transition zones are low-density, multifamily zones between commercial and single-family zones. Transition zones may serve as buffers.

TRANSITIONAL AREA

(1) An area in the process of changing from one use to another or changing from one racial or ethnic occupancy to another; (2) an area that acts as a buffer between two land uses of different intensity and compatibility.

281

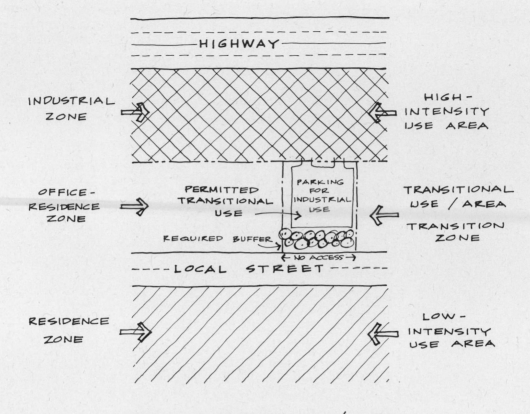

INDUSTRIAL ZONE →

HIGH-INTENSITY USE AREA

OFFICE-RESIDENCE ZONE →

← TRANSITIONAL USE / AREA

TRANSITION ZONE

PERMITTED TRANSITIONAL USE

PARKING FOR INDUSTRIAL USE

REQUIRED BUFFER →

← NO ACCESS →

----LOCAL STREET-----

RESIDENCE ZONE →

← LOW-INTENSITY USE AREA

TRANSITIONAL USE/AREA
TRANSITION ZONE

Figure 72

Comment: A transitional area, more specifically, a transitional use area, may be, for example, the land area between a business area along a street frontage and the adjacent residential area. Many development ordinances establish transitional districts that permit either residential or some less intensive commercial use to be located between the two different land uses. The less intensive commercial use might be a small office building or institutional use.

TRANSITIONAL CARE HOME

A facility in which individuals live for a short period while receiving physical, social, or psychological therapy and counseling to assist them in overcoming physical or emotional problems.

Comment: The transitional care home is a form of half-way house. Residents do not require segregation from society and require only short-term shelter away from their usual residences. Professional therapy and counseling are done on a more intensive basis than permitted by an outpatient status. In zoning, these facilities usually function as boarding homes. *See* Boarding Home for Sheltered Care.

TRANSITIONAL CLINIC CARE

A clinic operated as a subordinate use in connection with and on the premises of a transitional care home, solely for providing physical, social, and psychological therapy or counseling by qualified personnel whose patients are limited to those who have recently resided in the transitional care home or families of those who are residing in or have recently resided in a transitional care home.

TRANSITIONAL USE

A permitted land use or structure of an intermediate intensity by level of activity or scale between a more intensive and less intensive use. *See* Transitional Area. *See Figure 72.*

Comment: Some random examples of transitional uses include professional offices located between retail and residential uses; two-family and townhouse units located between single-family detached and apartment blocks; and private clubs or low-intensity recreational uses between industrial and residential uses.

TRANSPORTATION CORRIDOR

A combination of principal transportation routes involving a linear network of one or more highways of four or more lanes, rail lines, or other primary and secondary access facilities that support a development corridor.

TRANSPORTATION DEMAND MANAGEMENT PLAN

A system of actions and timetables to alleviate traffic problems through improved management of vehicle trip demand.

Comment: The plan is designed to reduce the use of single-occupancy vehicles and to encourage travel during less congested time periods. *See* Traffic Demand Management.

TRANSPORTATION MANAGEMENT ASSOCIATION (TMA)

(1) A group of employers, developers, building owners, and local government officials who work together to solve local transportation problems and establish transportation policies for their employees and the area; (2) a

nonprofit corporation that brokers transportation services, including, but not limited to, public transportation, van pools, car pools, bicycling, and pedestrian modes to corporations, employees, individuals, and other groups.

TRANSPORTATION SERVICES, ACCESSORY

Establishments furnishing services incidental to transportation, such as forwarding and packing services and the arranging of passenger or freight transportation.

TRANSPORTATION SERVICES, LOCAL

Establishments primarily engaged in furnishing local and suburban passenger transportation, including taxicabs, passenger transportation charter service, school buses, and terminal and service facilities for motor vehicle passenger transportation.

TRANSSHIPMENT

(1) The act of transferring freight between two modes of transport, such as from a truck to a railroad car; (2) the act of transferring freight from long-haul trucks to local delivery vehicles.

Comment: Transshipment may include aggregating or breaking down shipments into larger or smaller ones.

TRAP

A fitting or device so designed and constructed as to provide, when properly vented, a liquid seal that will prevent the back passage of air without materially affecting the flow of sewage or wastewater through it.

TRAVEL TRAILER

A recreation vehicle that is towed by a car or a truck. *See* RECREATIONAL VEHICLE.

TRAVELED WAY

That part of the roadway provided for the movement of vehicles, exclusive of shoulders and auxiliary lands.

TREE HOUSE

A structure built above ground level and not designed for continuous habitation, using a tree for part of its support.

TREE PROTECTION

Measures taken, such as temporary fencing and the use of tree wells, to protect existing trees from damage or loss during and after project construction. *See Figure 73.*

TRICKLING FILTER

A device for the biological or secondary treatment of wastewater consisting of a bed of rocks or stones that support bacterial growth and permit sewage to be trickled over the bed, enabling the bacteria to break down organic wastes.

284

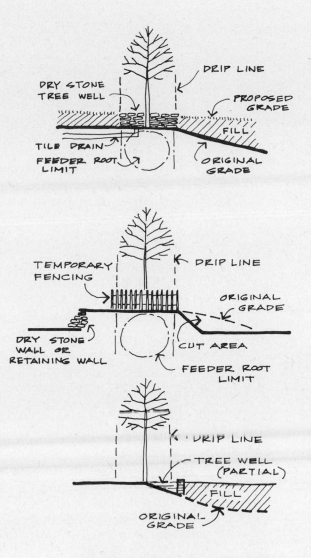

TREE PROTECTION

Figure 73

TRIP

A single or one-way motor vehicle movement either to or from a subject property or study area. *See Figure 50.*

TRIP DISTRIBUTION

The measure of the number of vehicles or passenger movements that are or will be made between geographic areas (Schultz and Kasen 1984).

TRIP ENDS

The total of trips entering and leaving a specific land use or site over a designated period of time. *See Figure 50.*

TRIP GENERATION

The total number of vehicle trip ends produced by a specific land use or activity.

Comment: The Institute of Transportation Engineers has undertaken more than three thousand trip generation studies and published their results in *Trip Generation* (1991). The book provides estimates on the number of vehicle trips likely to be generated by a particular land use in terms of a number of variables, such as the square footage of the structure, size of parcel, and number of employees. Approximately 120 land use types are analyzed.

TRIPLE-WIDE UNITS

Three manufactured housing components, attached side to side, to make one complete housing unit.

TRIPLEX

See DWELLING, TRIPLEX.

TRUCK CAMPER

A structure designed to fit into the bed of a pickup truck and used for temporary shelter and sleeping.

TRUCK SALES

The sale of vehicles primarily designed to carry cargo and material.

Comment: Truck sales often involve the assembly of chassis and cabs and may be more appropriate in an industrial zone.

TRUCK STOP

Any building, premises, or land in which or upon which a business, service, or industry involving the maintenance, servicing, storage, or repair of commercial vehicles is conducted or rendered, including the dispensing of motor fuel or other petroleum products directly into motor vehicles and the sale of accessories or equipment for trucks and similar commercial vehicles. A truck stop also may include overnight accommodations and restaurant facilities primarily for the use of truck crews.

TRUCK TERMINAL

An area and building where trucks load and unload cargo and freight and where the cargo and freight may be broken down or aggregated into smaller or larger loads for transfer to other vehicles or modes of transportation.

Comment: Truck terminals are basically transshipment facilities and often include the storage or parking of trucks awaiting cargo as well as facilities for servicing of trucks. Storage facilities, such as warehouses, incidental to the principal use may also be part of a truck terminal.

TURBIDITY	A thick, hazy condition of air or water due to the presence of suspended particulates or other pollutants.
TUTORING	The provision of instruction to not more than two students at any given time.
	Comment: Tutoring is usually considered a home occupation.
TWO-FAMILY DWELLING OR DUPLEX	*See* DWELLING, TWO-FAMILY.

UNDERGROUND UTILITIES	The placement of electric, telephone, cable, and other utilities customarily carried on poles in underground vaults or trenches.
UNDERUTILIZED LAND	Land parcels with any of the following characteristics: (1) more than 80 percent of the parcel in nonbuilding uses, such as surface parking or storage yard; (2) land parcels containing structures that are at least 50 percent vacant; (3) land parcels with buildings with a floor area ratio of less than 0.1; and (4) land parcels with buildings that are abandoned, dilapidated, or otherwise seriously impaired by physical deficiencies.
	Comment: This definition is useful in the preparation of surveys for redevelopment potential. The percentages should be adjusted to meet local needs and conditions.
UNDEVELOPED LAND	Land in its natural state before development.
UNDIVIDED HIGHWAY	A highway having access from both sides of the direction of travel.
UNIFORMITY	The requirement that all properties in a zoning district be treated alike.
UNIMPROVED LAND	Land in its natural state before development.
UNIQUE NATURAL FEATURE	That part of the natural environment that is rare or not duplicated in the community or region.

UNIVERSITY	*See* COLLEGE.
UNSIGHTLY AREAS	(1) Outside areas where machinery or equipment is repaired, stored, and/or serviced; (2) outside trash storage areas; (3) loading docks; (4) outdoor vehicle storage areas; and (5) utility facilities.
	Comment: This term must be specifically defined to meet local objectives where the regulation of such areas in terms of location and screening is desired.
UPLAND	(1) Land elevated above surrounding lands; (2) any non-wetland area.
UPZONE	To reduce the intensity of use by decreasing allowable density or lowering the floor area ratio or otherwise increasing bulk requirements.
	Comment: This phrase, and its counterpart, downzoning, is often misused and has certain class distinctions. It would be more accurate to use terms such as ''more restrictive,'' ''less restrictive,'' ''more intense,'' or ''less intense.'' *See* DOWNZONE.
URBAN AREA	A highly developed area that includes, or is appurtenant to, a central city or place and contains a variety of industrial, commercial, residential, and cultural uses.
	Comment: Densities of urban areas are usually two thousand persons per square mile and have central cities of fifty thousand persons or more.
URBAN CONTEXT	The combination of buildings, structures, and streetscape that form a distinct neighborhood or section of a city or urban place.
URBAN DESIGN	(1) The process of organizing the contextural elements of the built environment such that the end result will be a place with its own character or identity; (2) planning the development of the built environment in a comprehensive manner to achieve a unified, functional, efficient, and aesthetically appealing physical setting (Schultz and Kasen 1984).
URBAN HOMESTEADING	A program for selling vacant, usually substandard urban housing to people who will rehabilitate and occupy such housing.

URBAN RENEWAL	A program for the physical improvement of primarily urban areas through comprehensive planning and governmental assistance to effect rehabilitation and redevelopment.
URBAN RUNOFF	Stormwater from city streets, gutters, and paved surfaces. *Comment:* Urban runoff usually contains a great deal of litter and organic and bacterial wastes. *See* RUNOFF.
URBAN SERVICE BOUNDARY	A defined region, not always coincidental with a municipality's corporate boundary, that defines the geographical limit of government-supplied public facilities and services.
USE	The purpose or activity for which land or buildings are designed, arranged, or intended or for which land or buildings are occupied or maintained.
USE, ACCESSORY	*See* ACCESSORY USE.
USE, CONDITIONAL	*See* CONDITIONAL USE.
USE, EXISTING	*See* EXISTING USE.
USE, INHERENTLY BENEFICIAL	*See* INHERENTLY BENEFICIAL USES.
USE, INSTITUTIONAL	*See* INSTITUTIONAL USE.
USE, PERMITTED	*See* PERMITTED USE.
USE, PRINCIPAL	*See* PRINCIPAL USE.
USE, RELIGIOUS	*See* RELIGIOUS USE.
USE, TEMPORARY	*See* TEMPORARY USE.
USE, TRANSITIONAL	*See* TRANSITIONAL USE.
USE VARIANCE	*See* VARIANCE, USE.
USER CHARGES	A requirement of government under which those that benefit directly from a particular service pay all or part of the cost.

Comment: User charges are not new but the types and extent are increasing. Impact fees are similar except that they are usually paid by the developer and are included in the sale or rental cost of the project.

UTILITY, PRIVATE OR PUBLIC

(1) Any agency that, under public franchise or ownership, or under certificate of convenience and necessity, or by grant of authority by a governmental agency, provides the public with electricity, gas, heat, steam, communication, transportation, water, sewage collection, or other similar service; (2) a closely regulated enterprise with a franchise for providing a needed service. *See* PUBLIC UTILITY.

UTILITY BOX

Electric transformers, switch boxes, telephone pedestals and telephone boxes, cable television boxes, traffic control boxes, and similar devices.

UTILITY EASEMENT

The right-of-way acquired by a utility or governmental agency to locate utilities, including all types of pipelines, telephone and electric cables, and towers.

Comment: Most utility easements have restrictions on their use; however, some can be used as linear walkways and bike paths, buffer areas, and transition areas.

UTILITY SERVICES

The generation, transmission, and/or distribution of electricity, gas, steam, communications, and water; the collection and treatment of sewage and solid waste; and the provision of mass transportation.

V

VACANCY

Any unoccupied land, structure, or part thereof that is available and suitable for occupancy.

VACANCY RATE

The number of uninhabited dwelling units that are available and suitable for occupancy expressed as a ratio to the total number of dwelling units.

Comment: Vacancy rate may also apply to nonresidential use and is usually expressed as a ratio of unoccupied floor area to total floor area. *See* OCCUPANCY RATE.

VACANT LAND

(1) Land that is undeveloped and unused; (2) any nonresidential areas with significant amounts of land not covered by nonstructural impervious surfaces; (3) land suitable for redevelopment or infill at higher densities; and (4) residential areas with lot sizes in excess of two acres where environmental factors permit higher densities.

Comment: The above definitions apply specifically to vacant sites that might be appropriate for lower income housing. *See* UNDERUTILIZED LAND; UNDEVELOPED LAND; UNIMPROVED LAND.

VACATION HOME

A second home, owned or rented, usually used seasonally, and located in an area with nearby recreational opportunities or amenities.

VALLEY

(1) A stretch of lowland lying between mountains or hills; (2) the land area drained or watered by a major river system.

VAN

(1) A closed vehicle with a capacity of approximately eight to twelve passengers; (2) a self-propelled recreation vehicle containing sleeping facilities but not bathroom or cooking facilities; and (3) a large truck for carrying cargo or freight.

VAN POOLING

A share-the-expense method of commutation for approximately ten people who work in the same place and have the same work hours.

Comment: Van pools differ from car pools in that the employer or sponsoring organization usually provides the vans that are used in the program. In addition, vans used for van pooling may be registered as such with the state.

VAPOR

The gaseous phase of substances that normally are either liquids or solids at atmospheric temperature and pressure, for example, steam and phenolic compounds.

VAPOR PLUME

Stack effluent consisting of condensed flue gas or flue gas made visible by condensed water droplets or mist.

VAPORIZATION

The change of a substance from the liquid to the gaseous state.

Comment: Vaporization is one of three basic contributing factors to air pollution; the others are attrition and combustion.

VARIANCE

Permission to depart from the literal requirements of a zoning ordinance.

VARIANCE, BULK

A departure from any provision of a zoning ordinance except use. *See* VARIANCE, HARDSHIP.

VARIANCE, HARDSHIP

A departure from the provisions of a zoning ordinance relating to setbacks, side yards, frontage requirements, and lot size that, if applied to a specific lot, would significantly interfere with the use of the property.

Comment: The hardship variance is granted because strict enforcement of the zoning ordinance as it applies to a specific lot would present practical difficulties in the use of the property. Hardship relates to the physical characteristics of the property, and without the variance, the property becomes unusable.

In *Brandon* v. *Montclair* (124 N.J. 135), the New Jersey Supreme Court characterized hardship as "whether the . . . restriction, viewing the property in the setting of its environment is so unreasonable as to constitute an arbitrary and capricious interference with the basic right of private property."

Hardship may also be used to justify a use variance. For example, in cases involving obsolete uses or outdated structures, a hardship variance may be justified so that the building can be adapted or used for a different purpose. Another example of hardship as a basis for a use variance is split lot zoning, where the zone line runs through the center of the property and a part of the property is rendered useless.

VARIANCE, PLANNING

A variance granted for bulk relief that would result in an opportunity for improved zoning and planning that would benefit the community.

Comment: The planning variance is a relatively new concept that recognizes that special reasons or hardship do not always exist when relief from the bulk requirements is being sought. Granting of the variance may result in benefits to the community. Examples include protecting environmentally sensitive areas by allowing a building to be built closer to a side or front yard line than the ordinance provides, reducing the size of parking spaces to provide more parking for an existing use, and increasing setbacks on one side and encroaching on another to provide more light and air to an adjacent building.

The tests of the planning variance are:

1. The variance relates to a specific parcel of land;
2. The variance advances the purposes of the state enabling legislation;
3. The variance can be granted without substantial detriment to the public good;
4. The benefits of the deviation would substantially outweigh any detriment; and
5. The variance would not substantially impair the intent and purposes of the zone plan and zoning ordinance (Cox 1991).

VARIANCE, USE

A variance granted for a use or structure that is not permitted in the zone.

Comment: States that permit use variances impose stringent requirements. In New Jersey, the applicant must prove special reasons. Special reasons may be that the use is inherently beneficial, such as a hospital, school, or church, or generally that the use would help advance the purposes of planning as set forth in the state enabling legislation. Hardship may also constitute a special reason. In addition to special reasons, the applicant must prove that the grant will not substantially impair the intent and purpose of the zone plan and ordinance and will be without substantial detriment to the public good.

VEGETATION MAP

A pictorial depiction of the location and type of plant materials that appear in a given land area (Schultz and Kasen 1984).

VEGETATIVE PROTECTION

Stabilization of erosive or sediment-producing areas by covering the soil with permanent or short-term seeding, mulching, or sodding.

VEHICLE, MOTOR

A self-propelled device used for transportation of people or goods over land surfaces and licensed as a motor vehicle.

VEHICLE, OFF-ROAD (ORV)

Vehicles designed for use on a variety of nonimproved surfaces and including dune buggies and all-terrain vehicles, snowmobiles, trail bikes, mopeds, and motor bikes.

Comment: As recreational vehicles, the ORV can be

detrimental to the landscape and trails. Many of them are noisy and pose dangers to wildlife.

VEHICLE, PASSENGER

A motor vehicle with no more than two axles and/or four wheels, not more than 4,500 pounds in gross weight, and designed primarily for the transport of persons.

VEHICLE, RECREATIONAL

See RECREATIONAL VEHICLE.

VEHICLE SALES AREA

An open area, other than a right-of-way or public parking area, used for display, sale, or rental of new or used vehicles in operable condition and where no repair work is done.

VEHICLE TRIP

A motor vehicle moving from an origin point to a destination point. *See* TRIP.

VEST-POCKET PARK

A small land area, usually in a built-up neighborhood, developed for active or passive recreation.

Comment: Vest-pocket parks consist of one or two contiguous lots in a built-up block.

VESTED RIGHT

A right that cannot be changed or altered by changes in regulation.

Comment: A development application that has been granted approval has a vested right for a certain period of time.

VETERINARY HOSPITAL

A place where animals are given medical care and the boarding of animals is limited to short-term care incidental to the hospital use.

Comment: Some veterinary hospitals are associated with animal boarding, breeding, and/or laboratories. A zoning ordinance should distinguish between veterinary hospitals, which can be located in any nonresidential area, and animal care facilities, which may or may not include a medical treatment component. Facilities that breed and/or board animals, particularly dog kennels, need special noise-deadening construction and/or deep open-space buffering to avoid sound transmission beyond property boundaries.

VIEW PROTECTION REGULATION

Requirements to assure that development does not interfere with scenic views.

294

VILLAGE

(1) A small, compact center of predominantly residential character but with a core of mixed-use commercial, residential, and community services; (2) this term does not necessarily refer to the form of incorporation of a municipality and is often smaller than a municipality.

Comment: Villages often incorporate local scale economic and social functions that are integrated with housing. A village typically has a recognizable center, a pedestrian scale and orientation, and a hard edge separating it from adjacent farmland or open space.

VISTA

A unique view to or from a particular point.

Comment: The view may be that of great natural beauty, farmlands, settlements, such as villages, or spectacular urban scenes. Many ordinances attempt to develop vista protection provisions to ensure that unique vistas are preserved and not encroached upon by development.

VISUAL COMPATIBILITY

See HARMONIOUS RELATIONSHIP.

VISUAL OBSTRUCTION

Any structure, such as a fence or wall or natural features, that limits visibility.

Comment: Visual obstructions can be a hazard at street intersections where they interfere with traffic visibility. Many ordinances include requirements for sight easements to regulate visual obstructions.

VOCATIONAL SCHOOL

A secondary or higher education facility primarily teaching usable skills that prepare students for jobs in a trade and meeting the state requirements as a vocational facility.

VOLATILE

Evaporating readily at a relatively low temperature.

W

WADING POOL

An aboveground or inground structure containing less than eighteen inches of water.

WAIVER

Permission to depart from the requirements of an ordinance with respect to the submission of required documents. *See* EXCEPTION.

295

Comment: The terms waiver and exceptions are often used interchangeably. In fact, waiver refers to the submission of required documents while exceptions are for relief of design standards in the ordinance.

An applicant may request a waiver of the requirement to submit an environmental impact statement for a small, isolated lot and request an exception to the sidewalk requirement if there are no sidewalks on either side of the lot. The waiver would be granted by the approving agency and would be based on whether the documents for which the waiver is requested have any relevance to the application or are needed in order to make a decision on the application.

Cox (1991) notes that a request for a waiver requires the agency to make findings and conclusions in order to "permit proper judicial review."

WALK-UP

An apartment building of more than two stories that is not equipped with an elevator.

WALK-UP ESTABLISHMENT

An establishment that by design of its physical facilities, service, or packaging encourages or permits pedestrians to receive a service or obtain a product without entering the establishment.

WALL

(1) The vertical exterior surface of a building; (2) vertical interior surfaces that divide a building's space into rooms.

WAREHOUSE

A building used primarily for the storage of goods and materials.

Comment: Warehouses may be for long-term or short-term storage. Short-term storage facilities for a specific commercial establishment are called distribution centers.

WAREHOUSE OUTLET

See RETAIL WAREHOUSE OUTLET.

WAREHOUSING, PRIVATE

A building used primarily for the storage of goods and materials by the owner of the goods or operated for a specific commercial establishment or group of establishments in a particular industrial or economic field.

WAREHOUSING, PUBLIC

A building used primarily for the storage of goods and materials and available to the general public for a fee.

Comment: Public warehouses may include bulk ware-

296

houses that include tank storage, commodity warehouses that include grain elevators, refrigerated warehouses, and general merchandise warehouses. *See* SELF-SERVICE STORAGE FACILITY.

WASTE

(1) Bulky waste—items the large size of which precludes or complicates their handling by normal collection, processing, or disposal methods; (2) construction and demolition waste—building materials and rubble resulting from construction, remodeling, repair, and demolition operations; (3) hazardous waste—wastes that require special handling to avoid illness or injury to persons or damage to property; (4) special waste—those wastes that require extraordinary management; (5) wood pulp waste—wood or paper fiber residue resulting from a manufacturing process; and (6) yard waste—plant clippings, prunings, and other discarded material from yards and gardens.

WASTELAND

Land that is barren and uncultivated.

WASTEWATER

Water carrying wastes from homes, businesses, and industries that is a mixture of water and dissolved or suspended solids; excess irrigation water that is runoff to adjacent land.

WASTEWATER MANAGEMENT PLAN

A description of existing and future wastewater-related jurisdictions, wastewater service areas, and selected environmental features and domestic treatment works subject to approval by the appropriate state agency.

WATER BODIES

Any natural or artificial collection of water, whether permanent or temporary.

WATER-CARRYING CAPACITY

The ability of a pipe, channel, or floodway to transport flow as determined by its shape, cross-sectional area, bed slope, and coefficient of hydraulic friction.

WATERCOURSE

Any natural or artificial stream, river, creek, ditch, channel, canal, conduit, culvert, drain, waterway, gully, ravine, or wash in which water flows in a definite direction or course, either continuously or intermittently, and has a definite channel, bed, and banks and includes any area adjacent thereto subject to inundation by reason of overflow or floodwater.

297

WATER POLLUTION

The addition of pollutants to water in concentrations or in sufficient quantities to result in measurable degradation of water quality.

WATER QUALITY CRITERIA

The levels of pollutants that affect the suitability of water for a given use.

Comment: Generally, water use classification includes public water supply, recreation, propagation of fish and other aquatic life, agricultural use, and industrial use.

WATER QUALITY MANAGEMENT PLAN (WQMP)

The identification of strategies, policies, and procedures for managing water quality and wastewater treatment and disposal in a geographical area.

Comment: A plan for water quality management contains four major elements: (1) the use (recreation, drinking water, fish and wildlife propagation, industrial, or agricultural) to be made of water; (2) criteria to protect the water to keep it suitable for use; (3) implementation plans (for needed industrial-municipal waste treatment improvements) and enforcement plans; and (4) an anti-degradation statement to protect existing high-quality waters.

WATER RIGHTS

A property owner's right to use surface or underground water from adjacent lands.

Comment: The western and eastern United States have different water rights laws. Riparian rights are applicable mainly to eastern areas. Western law generally provides that the first to claim the water has the use of it.

WATER SUPPLY SYSTEM

The system for the collection, treatment, storage, and distribution of potable water from the source of supply to the consumer.

WATER TABLE

The upper surface of groundwater or the level below which the soil is seasonally saturated with water.

WATER TOWER

A water storage facility, usually above ground and often round or cylindrical in shape.

WATER TRANSPORTATION

Establishments engaged in freight and passenger transportation in the open seas or inland waters and the furnishing of incidental services, such as lightering, towing, and canal operation.

Comment: This major group includes excursion boats, sight-seeing boats and water taxis, as well as cargo and hauling operations.

WATERFRONT PROPERTY   A property that has frontage on a water body.

WATERSHED   The drainage basin, catchment, or other area of land that drains water, sediment, and dissolved materials to a common outlet at some point along a stream channel. *See* BASIN; RIVER BASIN.

WEAVING   The crossing of two or more traffic streams traveling in the same general direction along a significant length of highway without the aid of traffic control devices.

WETLANDS, FRESHWATER   An area that is inundated or saturated by surface water or groundwater at a frequency and duration sufficient to support, and that under normal circumstances does support, a prevalence of vegetation typically adapted for life in saturated soil conditions.

Comment: Wetlands are characterized by one of three parameters: certain soil types, aquatic plants, and hydrology. Recent federal and state legislation make the filling or dredging of wetlands extremely difficult. Many states also require buffer or transition areas to provide additional protection to wetlands.

WHARF   A structure used to load and unload ships and usually built parallel to the shore.

WHEEL STOP   *See* BUMPERS.

WHOLESALE TRADE   Establishments or places of business primarily engaged in selling merchandise to retailers; to industrial, commercial, institutional, or professional business users; to other wholesalers; or acting as agents or brokers and buying merchandise for, or selling merchandise to, such individuals or companies.

Comment: Lumber, plywood, and mill work yards, such as building materials establishments, are generally classified as wholesale unless the primary operation is directly to the general public as opposed to builders. In such case, they are classified as retail operations.

WILDLIFE HABITAT   Land set aside for animal habitat.

WINDBREAK

Berms, vegetation, landscaping, fences, or a combination of all four to provide a barrier against wind, snow, dust, or other natural elements.

WINDROWING

Composting employing large rows of shredded waste, turned from time to time to encourage aeration.

WORKING DRAWINGS

Detailed, precise drawings by an engineer or architect from which construction may be undertaken.

Comment: Working drawings for buildings are required for issuance of a building permit. For roads and other structures, working drawings are usually required as part of the final approval process.

Y

YARD

An open space that lies between the principal building or buildings and the nearest lot line. The minimum required yard as set forth in the ordinance is unoccupied and unobstructed from the ground upward except as may be specifically provided in the zoning ordinance. *See* BUILDABLE AREA; LOT LINE; YARD DEPTH; YARD LINE. *See Figures 11 and 74.*

Comment: Uses and structures that are typically permitted in required yards include accessory buildings and swimming pools (rear or side yards only), patios and open porches, bay windows, open steps, driveways, fences, and permitted signs and lighting.

YARD, FRONT

A space extending the full width of the lot between any building and the front lot line and measured perpendicular to the building at the closest point to the front lot line.

Comment: Note that this term defines a space and not a required setback. The definition specifies that the line of measurement is perpendicular to the building and extends to the lot line. If the line of measurement was perpendicular to the lot line, there would be problems with pie-shaped and irregular lots.

Typically, while many ordinances require that the minimum required yard remain open and unoccupied, some ordinances, for example, will not permit parking to

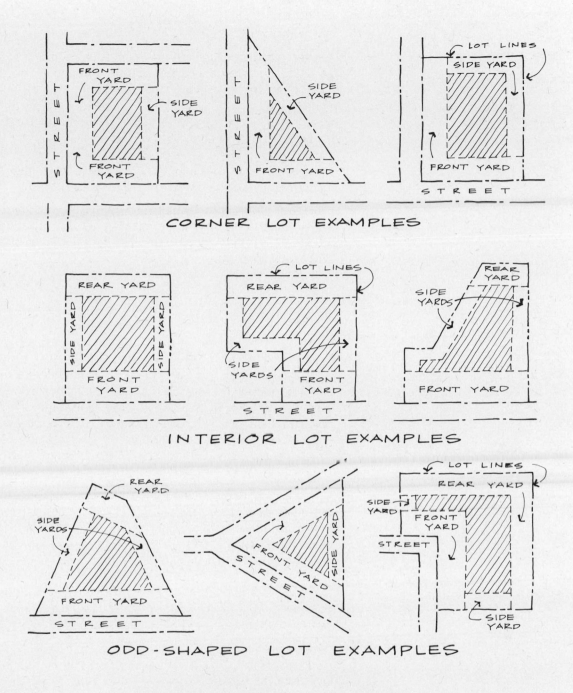

CORNER LOT EXAMPLES

INTERIOR LOT EXAMPLES

ODD-SHAPED LOT EXAMPLES

REQUIRED YARDS

BUILDING (ZONING) ENVELOPE
(TWO DIMENSIONAL)

Figure 74

301

be located in the front yard of multifamily or commercial uses regardless of whether the principal structure is set farther back than required. This is done for aesthetic purposes.

YARD, REAR
A space extending across the full width of the lot between the principal building and the rear lot line and measured perpendicular to the building to the closest point of the rear lot line. *See* comment under YARD, FRONT.

YARD, REQUIRED
The open space between a lot line and the yard line within which no structure shall be located except as provided in the zoning ordinance. *See Figure 74*.

YARD, SIDE
A space extending from the front yard to the rear yard between the principal building and the side lot line and measured perpendicular from the side lot line to the closest point of the principal building.

YARD DEPTH
The shortest distance between a lot line and a yard line.

YARD LINE
A line drawn parallel to a lot line at a distance therefrom equal to the depth of the required yard. *See Figure 11*.

YOUTH CAMP
Any parcel or parcels of land having the general characteristics of a camp as the term is generally understood, used wholly or in part for recreational or educational purposes and accommodating five or more children under eighteen years of age for a period of, or portions of, two days or more and including a site that is operated as a day camp or as a resident camp.

Z

ZERO LOT LINE
The location of a building on a lot in such a manner that one or more of the building's sides rest directly on a lot line.

ZONE
A specifically delineated area or district in a municipality within which uniform regulations and requirements govern the use, placement, spacing, and size of land and buildings. *See* FLOATING ZONE; TRANSITION ZONE.

ZONING

The delineation of districts and the establishment of regulations governing the use, placement, spacing, and size of land and buildings.

ZONING BOARD

See BOARD OF ADJUSTMENT.

ZONING DISTRICT

See ZONE.

ZONING ENVELOPE

The three-dimensional space within which a structure is permitted to be built on a lot and that is defined by maximum height regulations, minimum yard setbacks, and sky exposure plane regulations when applicable. *See Figure 75.*

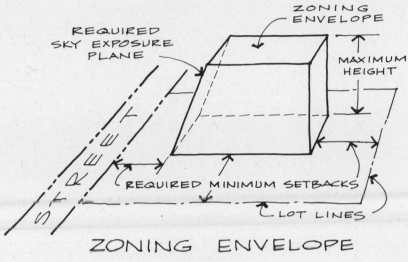

ZONING ENVELOPE

Figure 75

ZONING MAP

The map or maps that are a part of the zoning ordinance and delineate the boundaries of zone districts.

ZONING OFFICER

The administrative officer designated to administer the zoning ordinance and issue zoning permits.

Comment: In many smaller communities, the building inspector is also the zoning officer.

ZONING PERMIT

A document signed by a zoning officer, as required in the zoning ordinance, as a condition precedent to the commencement of a use, or the erection, construction, reconstruction, restoration, alteration, conversion, or installa-

303

tion of a structure or building, that acknowledges that such use, structure, or building complies with the provisions of the municipal zoning ordinance or authorized variance therefrom.

Comment: Where a building permit is required, the building permit often includes a zoning permit.

ZOO

A place where animals are kept, often in combination of indoor and outdoor spaces, and are viewed by the public.

References

Babcock, R. F., and Bosselman, F. P. 1973. *Exclusionary zoning, land use regulations, and housing in the 1970's*. New York: Praeger.

Building Officials and Code Administrators. *BOCA Basic/National Building Code*. Country Club Hills, IL: author.

Burchell, R. W., and Listokin, D. 1980. *Practitioner's guide to fiscal impact analysis*. New Brunswick, NJ: Center for Urban Policy Research, Rutgers University.

Business and industrial development handbook. 1988. Community Builders Handbook Series. Washington, DC: Urban Land Institute.

Cox, W. M. 1991. *New Jersey zoning and land use administration*. Newark, NJ: Gann Law Books.

DeChiara, J., and Koppelman, Lee E. 1982. *Urban planning and design criteria*. New York: Van Nostrand Reinhold.

Frizell, D. J., and Pozycki, H. S., Jr. 1989. *New Jersey practice*. Vol. 36, *Land use law*. St. Paul, MN: West Publishing.

Hagman, D. G. 1975. *Urban planning and land development control law*. St. Paul, MN: West Publishing.

Highway capacity manual. 1985. Special Report No. 209. Washington, DC: Transportation Research Board, National Research Council.

IES lighting handbook—application volume. 1987. New York: Illuminating Engineering Society of North America.

Listokin, D. 1976. *Fair share housing allocation*. New Brunswick, NJ: Center for Urban Policy Research, Rutgers University.

Listokin, D., and Walker, C. 1989. *The subdivision and site plan handbook*. New Brunswick, NJ: Center for Urban Policy Research, Rutgers University.

Little, C. E. 1990. *Greenways for America*. Baltimore and London: Johns Hopkins University Press.

Mallach, A. 1984. *Inclusionary housing programs: policies and practices*. New Brunswick, NJ: Center for Urban Policy Research, Rutgers University.

Mandelker, D. R., and Ewald, W. R. 1988. *Street graphics and the law*. Chicago: Planners Press, American Planning Association.

Mixed-use development handbook. 1987. Washington, DC: Urban Land Institute.

Morgan, G. 1989. *Electric and magnetic fields from 60 hertz electric power: what do we know about possible health risks?* Pittsburgh: Department of Engineering and Public Policy, Carnegie-Mellon University.

National League of Cities, Education, and Information Resources. *Local officials guide: complying with the Americans with Disabilities Act of 1990*. Washington, D.C.: author.

National Recreation and Park Association. 1983. *Recreation, Park, and Open Space Standards and Guidelines*. Alexandria, VA: author.

The new Lexicon Webster dictionary of the English language. 1989. New York: Lexicon Publications.

Not in my back yard: removing barriers to affordable housing. 1991. Rockville, MD: President's Advisory Committee on Regulatory Barriers to Affordable Housing, U.S. Department of Housing and Urban Development.

Planning Advisory Service Report No. 72. 1955. *Planning definitions*. Chicago: American Society of Planning Officials.

Planning Advisory Service Report No. 322. 1976. *The language of zoning, a glossary of words and phrases*. Chicago: American Society of Planning Officials.

Planning Advisory Service Report No. 379. 1983. Grassford, P. *Appearance codes for small municipalities*. Chicago: American Society of Planning Officials.

Planning Advisory Service Report No. 396. 1986. DeGroh, T. and German, R. *Standard for self-service storage facilities*. Chicago: American Planning Association.

Planning Advisory Service Report No. 419. 1989. Kelly, E. D. and Raso, G. J. *Sign regulation for small and mid-size communities*. Chicago: American Planning Association.

Planning Advisory Service Report No. 421. 1989. Burrows, T., ed. *A survey of zoning definitions*. Chicago: American Planning Association.

Planning Advisory Service Report No. 431. 1990. Marks, W. A., with Morris, M. *Preparing a landscape ordinance*. Chicago: American Society of Planning Officials.

Rose, J. G., and Rothman, R. E. 1977. *After Mount Laurel: The new suburban zoning*. New Brunswick, NJ: Center for Urban Policy Research, Rutgers University.

Sawicki, D. Summer 1989. The festival marketplace as public policy. *Journal of the American Planning Association* 55, 3: 347.

Schultz, M. S., and Kasen, V. L. 1984. *Encyclopedia of community planning and environmental management*. New York: Facts on File Publications.

Standard industrial classification manual. 1987. Executive Office of the President, Office of Management and Budget. Springfield, VA: National Technical Information Service.

Toenjes, L. P. 1989. *Building trades dictionary*. Homewood, IL: American Technical Publishers.

Trip generation. 1991. 5th ed. Washington, DC: Institute of Transportation Engineers.

Webster's third new international dictionary of the English language. 1976. Springfield, MA: G. & C. Merriam.

Williams, Norman Jr. 1977. "On 'from *Mount Laurel:* Guidelines on the regional general welfare,' " in Rose, J. G., and Rothman, R. E., *After Mount Laurel: The new suburban zoning*. New Brunswick, NJ: Center for Urban Policy Research, Rutgers University. 79–103.

Ziegler, E. H., Jr. 1991. *Rathkopf's the law of zoning and planning*. New York: Clark Boardman.

Zoning news. February 1990. Chicago: American Planning Association.

Zoning news. February 1992. Chicago: American Planning Association.